THE MILD VOICE OF REASON

AMERICAN POLITICS AND POLITICAL ECONOMY SERIES
Edited by Benjamin I. Page

☆ THE MILD VOICE OF REASON ☆ ☆ ☆

Deliberative Democracy and American National Government

Joseph M. Bessette

The University of Chicago Press
Chicago and London

The University of Chicago Press, Chicago 60637
The University of Chicago Press, Ltd., London
© 1994 by The University of Chicago
All rights reserved. Published 1994
Paperback edition 1997
Printed in the United States of America
02 01 00 99 98 97   2 3 4 5
ISBN: 0-226-04423-8 (cloth)
ISBN: 0-226-04424-6 (paperback)

Library of Congress Cataloging-in-Publication Data
Bessette, Joseph M.
    The mild voice of reason : deliberative democracy and American
national government / Joseph M. Bessette.
        p.   cm. — (American politics and political economy series)
    Includes bibliographical references and index.
    1. United States. Congress.   2. Legislation—United States.
3. Democracy—United States.   I. Title.   II. Series: American
politics and political economy.
    JK1001.B47   1994
    328.73′077—dc20   93-30669
                                                                CIP

To my parents
Ann Bessette
and
Joseph A. Bessette
for all they have done

[T]he mild voice of reason, pleading the cause of an enlarged and permanent interest, is but too often drowned, before public bodies as well as individuals, by the clamors of an impatient avidity for immediate and immoderate gain.

James Madison, *Federalist* no. 42

CONTENTS

PREFACE

This book grows out of an interest in deliberation kindled during my years as a graduate student at the University of Chicago in the 1970s. At the time I completed my dissertation in 1978 on "Deliberation in Congress," the concept of deliberation, which I defined simply as "reasoning on the merits of public policy," had fallen out of use within the political science discipline. Even the literature on the American Congress, an institution designed to be preeminently deliberative, had virtually nothing to say about deliberation. As I wrote then, "One searches in vain among the hundreds of studies to find one of deliberation in Congress. Indeed, the word 'deliberation' or synonyms rarely appear in the congressional literature."[1]

During the intervening decade and a half the concept of deliberation has enjoyed a resurgence befitting its importance. One thinks of such books as those by Michael Malbin, Arthur Maass, Randall Strahan, Steven S. Smith, James Payne, and David Vogler and Sidney Waldman on Congress;[2] by William Muir on the California state legislature;[3] by Steven Kelman and Giandomenico Majone on policymaking;[4] by Martha Derthick and Paul Quirk on deregulation;[5] by Robert Reich and his colleagues on the importance of ideas;[6] by James S. Fishkin and by Benjamin I. Page and Robert Y. Shapiro on public opinion;[7] by Jeffrey Tulis on the presidency;[8] by Steven Rhoads on economics and economists;[9] and by Jane Mansbridge on democracy, on the Equal Rights Amendment, and on the limits of the self-interest model.[10] Yet as welcome as these contributions are, it must be acknowledged that even as deliberation has attracted renewed attention in recent years, scholars of American government and politics seem increasingly drawn to an analytical framework that sees lawmaking and policymaking as the aggregation of individual interests and preferences—the rational actor, or self-interest, model—and not the result of argument, reasoning, and persuasion about common ends or goals. As James Q. Wilson has noted, this is "the stronger wind" that pushes the research of "many younger scholars."[11] Decades before modern social science formulated the rational actor approach, Woodrow Wilson aptly distinguished the traditional concept of deliberation, which he called "common counsel," from the mere aggregation of preferences: "Common counsel is not aggregate counsel. It is not a sum in addition, counting heads. It is compounded out of many views in actual contact; is a living thing made out of the vital substance of many minds, many personalities, many experiences; and it can be made up only by the vital contacts of actual conference, only in face to face debate, only by word of mouth and the direct clash of mind with mind."[12]

Although some of my fellow graduate students and early academic colleagues used to refer to my approach playfully (I assumed not derisively) as the "Boy Scout theory of American government," there is nothing in the attention to deliberation, as I fully acknowledged then and do so again throughout this volume, that precludes a role for such non-deliberative influences as private interests, political ambition, bargaining, and what has been called "the play of power."[13] I think it is fair to say, however, that the converse cannot be said for rational actor theories of American government and policymaking. That is, the proponents of such theories do not, as a rule, acknowledge the importance of deliberation about common goals to the functioning of American institutions or to the fashioning of public policy.

After only a few years at the academy, I left to enter "public service" (the very term reflects the popular view that more than self-interest is involved in such work) for what became a nine-year hiatus from full-time teaching and research: three and a half years with the Cook County, Illinois, State's Attorney's Office, some months as issues coordinator for Richard M. Daley's unsuccessful 1983 mayoral campaign, and five and a half years in the Bureau of Justice Statistics (BJS) in the U.S. Department of Justice, first as Deputy Director for Data Analysis and then as Acting Director.

This near decade of absence from academia had several consequences for the work at hand. First, and most obviously, it delayed it. Second, it gave more time for my ideas to mature. And, third, it gave me an opportunity to test my ideas against "real world" experience. One does not, for example, come away from three and a half years of work in Cook County and Chicago government and politics with a naive view that disinterested analysis of the public interest is the decisive and controlling force in public affairs. But neither did I come away from that experience as a disheartened cynic, persuaded by the harsh realities of public life that private ambition and power politics constitute the essential core of government and politics. On the contrary, I came to appreciate more fully and more viscerally than any purely academic research could have taught me that the real world of government and politics is a complex mix of public-spiritedness and private interest, of reasoned persuasion and hard political bargaining, of, if you will, the high and the low.

Nothing in my subsequent years in the Department of Justice disabused me of this belief. Admittedly, the move to BJS placed me in a more purely deliberative environment; for the very existence of the agency, which collects, analyzes, and disseminates statistics on crime and justice, presumes that policymakers deciding on criminal justice matters can be influenced by credible data on the subject. If there is no serious deliberation in American public life, there is no reason to spend $20 million per year on BJS—or similar and greater amounts on its sister statistical agencies in other departments of the federal government. Even in this deliberative environment, however, I was exposed to numerous examples of nondeliberative behavior, including private ambition severed from, or only tenuously related to, public ends, and congressional behavior designed to promote narrow partisan advantage at the expense of a serious analysis of public issues. Although this volume is not derived in a direct way from my work in government, a few reflections on my experiences will help to set the stage for what follows.

Most observers of Chicago politics assumed when Richard M. Daley was elected State's Attorney of Cook County in November of 1980 that he had, even at that time, an ambition to become mayor of Chicago. Not only did it not surprise me when he ran for mayor in 1982–83, I had positively counted on it when I accepted a job in his office in June of 1981. At the time, I, a nonlawyer, had little interest in spending an indefinite number of years in the prosecutor's office in Cook County. But a few years surrounded by lawyers to be followed by work on a mayoral campaign and then, if all went well, some number of years dealing with the range of policy issues that confront a city like Chicago—well, that was another matter.

Posit, then, as I did at the time, State's Attorney Richard Daley's ambition to become, like his father, mayor of the city of Chicago. What consequences followed for his behavior as a public official? First, the new state's attorney had a strong desire to establish a record of accomplishment in office. He knew full well that many, especially in the media, doubted his capacities and his motivations, and he wanted to prove them wrong. He wanted more prosecutions, more convictions, and more prison sentences than his predecessor. He wanted more effective efforts against white collar crime and consumer fraud. He wanted to force absent fathers to meet their child support obligations. He wanted to reform the juvenile justice system so that older juveniles who committed particularly heinous crimes like murder and rape would be tried in adult court where punishments could extend beyond the twenty-first birthday.

In a word, Daley had an ambition to foster the perception that he was doing a good job and, by implication, that he could be an effective mayor. But he also understood that mere public relations would not be enough to accomplish this end. Press conferences and newsletters alone would not persuade the media, the politicians, and the good-government types that the state's attorney had measured up to the challenges of his office. The most effective way to convince the citizenry of Chicago that he was doing a good job was, most simply, by actually doing a good job.

I was convinced at the time, and remain so today, that Daley's political ambitions were fostering genuine efforts at public service (in a way not accounted for by the reigning models in political science). How and under what conditions political ambition can be directed to serve the common good is an old question—evidenced, for example, by Alexander Hamilton's essays on the presidency in the *Federalist Papers*—but one about which little is now written. By contrast, much is written about the disjunction between private interest and the common good.

Is this, then, the full explanation for Daley's behavior? I think not; for none of us who worked with him during those early years in the State's Attorney's Office doubted his genuine commitment to the effective administration of his office and to the legal reforms he so vigorously sought. Daley wanted, for example, more prosecutions, more convictions, and more sentences to prison than his predecessor not only because he thought that this would "play well" with the voters but also because he genuinely believed that too many criminals in Chicago were slipping through the cracks of the criminal justice system and too many innocent people were paying the price. To put it most simply, Daley was committed to making Chicago a safer place to live and thus to using the influence of his office to that end. While it is undoubtedly true that he had an ambition to be perceived as an effective state's attorney, my three-plus years of fairly close observation also told me that he had an independent desire to serve faithfully the public purposes of his office. If I had had any doubts on the matter upon joining the office, they were removed within days after the state's attorney made quite clear to me in a private meeting that the attorney training programs of the office were one of his highest priorities—part of my portfolio, but an activity that could bring him few, if any, direct political benefits.

What ought we to call this desire to do a good job, and what accounts for it? To ascribe it to altruism—the motive often contrasted with self-interest—hardly seems right; for we would not normally describe as altruistic the behavior of an officeholder who faithfully carries out the responsibilities of his or her position. Rather, phrases like "devotion to duty," "sense of personal responsibility," or even "public-spiritedness" seem to come closer to the mark.[14]

I dwell on this example for the simple reason that Richard M. Daley is the only elected politician for whom I have directly worked and therefore the only one I have been able to observe personally for an extended period. I suspect that thousands of others who have worked for elected or appointed officials at various levels of government would join me in holding both that private ambition often serves the public good (at least the public good as perceived by the official) and that ultimately private ambition cannot account for much that public officials do to promote the public good as they see it. It is my hope in this respect that this work—with its attention to both private interest and public good, to both the play of power and collective reasoning about shared goals—will ring true both to those who have participated closely in the workings of American government and to those who have studied it in a more formal and scholarly way.

As the roots of this project extend back to graduate school, I owe a great debt to those who guided my initial forays into the subject of deliberation in Congress at the University of Chicago: Benjamin Page, Herbert Storing, and Kenneth Prewitt. As the footnotes to this volume attest, I have continued to learn much about American government and politics from Ben Page's insightful writings. I greatly appreciate his detailed reading of the entire manuscript and his quite helpful comments.

Some years ago, during the break in my academic career, Jane Mansbridge came across my earlier work on deliberation and strongly encouraged me to move ahead with the book-length project. Had it not been for her encouragement then, it is doubtful that this work would now be at its present stage. There is no one currently writing on deliberation from whom I have learned more. This book has also benefited much from her extensive and detailed comments on the first draft.

Others who read the entire manuscript and provided extensive and helpful comments were James Ceaser and Gary Schmitt, both of whom have heard portions of my argument off and on for some years now. Whatever the merits of this book, it would have been a lesser product without their sympathetic ear and thoughtful advice. I am also grateful to the following individuals who read and commented on parts or all of the earlier draft: Martha Derthick, Ward Elliott, Charles Kesler, James Nichols, Paul Quirk, Robert Scigliano, and Thomas West.

Others whose research and writings have proven quite helpful include Richard Fenno, William K. Muir, Jeffrey Tulis, and the many other authors cited in the text and footnotes.

Claremont McKenna College and its Henry Salvatori Center provided summer research support and a congenial atmosphere for completing this work. My wife, Anne Nutter Bessette, has been extraordinarily patient and supportive throughout, for which I am immensely grateful.

My greatest intellectual debt is owed to Professor Herbert J. Storing, my mentor at the University of Chicago, who died in 1979 at the age of forty-nine. What I learned about the principles of American democracy through Storing's courses on the American founding, American political thought, constitutional law, and the American presidency provided me with the essential intellectual foundation for the current project. It is my hope that this volume measures up to his high standards.

☆ CHAPTER ONE

Introduction

> What is meant by "republic" in the United States is the slow and quiet action of society upon itself. It is an orderly state really founded on the enlightened will of the people. It is a conciliatory government under which resolutions have time to ripen, being discussed with deliberation and executed only when mature.
>
> Alexis de Tocqueville [1]

The architects of the American constitutional order sought to infuse their fledgling democracy with two essential qualities: deliberation and energy. They wanted both a *deliberative democracy*, one which would foster rule by the informed and reasoned judgments of the citizenry, and an *energetic democracy*, one in which the nation's security and vital interests would be defended against external threats and in which national laws and policies would be effectively enforced throughout a territory unprecedented in size for a republican government. Neither deliberative democracy nor energetic democracy had been achieved in the new nation or states during the critical years between independence (1776) and the meeting of the Constitutional Convention (1787). The Constitution of 1787 sought to remedy both defects. [2]

Reflecting a view widely shared by the leading liberal statesmen and theorists of the eighteenth and nineteenth centuries, the framers believed that if democracy was to be successful, lawmaking must reflect what Publius called "the cool and deliberate sense of the community." [3] Procedures and institutions must have the capacity to check or moderate unreflective popular sentiments and to promote the rule of deliberative majorities. In the particular type of deliberative democracy fashioned by the American framers, the citizenry would reason, or deliberate, through their representatives; on most issues the deliberative sense of the community would emerge not so much through debate and persuasion among the citizens themselves as through the functioning of their governing institutions. There are two general reasons why representatives could be expected to do a better job of deliberating about public policy than their constituents. First, they are typically more knowledgeable and experienced in public affairs. Second, they function in an institutional setting that fosters collective reasoning about common concerns, while their constituents usually lack the time, inclination, or environment to engage in a similar enterprise.

Deliberative democracy also demands, however, that the representatives of the people share the basic values and goals of their constituents; their own deliberations about public policy must be firmly rooted in popular interests and inclinations. The electoral connection is the chief mechanism for ensuring such a linkage between the values and goals of representatives and represented. If that linkage is sufficiently strong, then the policies fashioned by political leaders will effectively be those that the people themselves would have chosen had they possessed the same knowledge and experience as their representatives and devoted the same amount of time considering the information and arguments presented in the national councils.

Thus, the deliberative democracy fashioned by the architects of the American constitutional order is distinct both from direct democracy, where the people themselves make the key political decisions, and from the kind of democracy proposed by Edmund Burke, or at least some of his interpreters, in which the wise and virtuous, freely chosen by the community, rule through the exercise of their independent and superior political judgment, disconnected from popular sentiments. The deliberative democracy of the framers, it can be said, is less democratic than direct democracy but more democratic than this version of the Burkean prescription.

It is the framers' intention to fashion a deliberative democracy that explains the apparently contradictory elements of their governmental design. It is well known, for example, that the framers created institutions and powers—such as a bicameral legislature, a Supreme Court with lifetime tenure, and an independent presidency with a qualified power to veto legislative acts—that would make it possible for the national government to oppose unwise or unjust popular inclinations. Indeed, those who wrote the Constitution of 1787 could hardly have been more explicit in making the case for moderating, restraining, or even blocking, at least for a time, some public demands on government. The people "know from experience that they sometimes err," Publius forthrightly maintained in newspaper essays addressed to the citizens of New York during the ratification struggle. On such occasions "it is the duty of the persons whom they have appointed to be the guardians of [their] interests to withstand the temporary delusion in order to give them time and opportunity for more cool and sedate reflection." Thus will the institutions of government "suspend the blow meditated by the people against themselves."[4]

As anyone who has taught the *Federalist Papers* to college students can attest, the rhetoric of the framers is quite jarring to the modern ear; few students have *ever* heard a politician or governmental official speak so directly about the need, at times, for representatives of the people to resist public desires. Indeed, there may be a tendency to conclude, as did the Progressive historians, that the framers simply did not believe in majority rule. Yet those who wrote the Constitution of 1787 consistently maintained that the system they set up was "strictly republican" and that "the sense of the majority [would] prevail" in the new government.[5] As will be elaborated in the next chapter, the key to the reconciliation of these apparently contradictory intentions—to restrain popular majorities but also to effectuate majority rule—lies in the framers' broad purpose to empower deliberative majorities at the expense of uninformed, immoderate, or passionate majorities.

It is one thing, however, to articulate the framers' design and quite another to show its continuing relevance to contemporary American institutions. Is modern American democracy a deliberative democracy in any important respect? Do the institutions of American national government, particularly the Congress, "refine and enlarge the public views"[6] so that what emerges as national policy approximates "the cool and deliberate sense of the community"? If the leading interpretations of Congress are to be believed, the answer to both questions must be "no"; for the Congress depicted in these accounts is not one in which serious and responsible lawmakers reason together about common goals, but rather one in which self-interested officeholders, with little regard for their public responsibilities or for national needs and interests, aggregate their individual preferences through various bargaining devices, such as log-rolling. Such a view could hardly be further from the framers' desire for laws to be made by "the mild voice of reason, pleading the cause of an enlarged and permanent interest."[7]

Because Congress was designed to be the principal locus of deliberation in American national government, much of the analysis here is a detailed examination of evidence for and against the case that the modern Congress (defined broadly to cover the past half-century or so) remains in important respects a deliberative institution. Here I draw on both original research and the work of others, particularly case studies of policymaking in Congress and portraits of American lawmakers. These are a rich, though too rarely tapped, source of data on Congress, demonstrating both the limitations of nondeliberative explanations for how our laws are made and the continued vitality of genuine reasoning on the merits of public policy.

It should be noted that the disproportionate attention to Congress in this volume (chapters 4, 5, and 6, and part of chapters 3 and 8) is a reflection of the topic at hand and not an indication of congressional dominance in either the framers' design or in the actual workings of modern American government. Congress is the focus of this book in the same way that the presidency would of necessity be the focus of a parallel book on "energetic democracy." Nonetheless, as will be elaborated in chapter 7, presidents and their subordinates have made and continue to make a substantial, if normally subordinate, contribution to policy deliberation in American national government.

Perhaps the deepest issue raised by a theory of American government as a deliberative democracy is the relationship of policymaking to public opinion and the concomitant responsibilities of public officials. Indeed, few issues have more actively engaged the attention of scholars of American government and politics over the years than the relationship of the people's interests and desires to the functioning of their governing institutions. The debate over whether the governmental arrangements established in 1787 were sufficiently democratic began literally before the ink was dry on the document creating them.[8] The themes articulated in the original contest of opinion between Federalists and Anti-Federalists have echoed throughout American history in the great public debates surrounding the Jeffersonian "revolution" of 1800, Jacksonian democracy, the Progressive movement, the New Deal of Franklin Roosevelt, the "New Left" movement of the 1960s, and the "Reagan Revolution" of the 1980s. And in recent years we have heard new calls for a kind of "electronic democracy" in which two-way televisions, personal computers, or other electronic devices would provide the means for the citizenry to communicate their views to their leaders virtually daily on the great issues facing the nation. An underlying theme throughout this book, the relationship of public opinion to public policy is addressed formally and at some length in chapter 8. As I will try to show there, an understanding of American government as deliberative democracy illuminates the particular character of democratic statesmanship.

The argument advanced here rests on two principles: (1) that our governing institutions must have the capacity to deliberate well, to make informed and wise judgments about public policy; and (2) that those deliberations must be firmly grounded in the interests and desires of the American citizenry. One can imagine both undemocratic governments capable of quite sound political deliberation and democratic ones incapable of reasoned decisionmaking. The genius and the peculiar challenge of the American system, I maintain, is the conjunction of deliberation and democracy. Just as deliberation insulated from the public—by, for example, kings and their courts, dictators, religious or political sects, bureaucracies, or ideological elites who claim to represent the masses—may threaten the interests of the majority, so too a government that empowers the majority but does not provide for appropriate institutional capacities may make sound deliberation, and therefore sound governing, impossible.

Thus, the approach here is both descriptive, or empirical, and normative. Analyzing U.S. national government as a deliberative democracy both enhances our understanding of the real workings of American democracy and provides us with a set of norms or standards for assessing how our governing institutions *ought* to work.

Building upon a critique of the reigning paradigms, I seek here to contribute to the rehabilitation of the concept of deliberation (whose lineage is as old as the study of politics),[9] to demonstrate its continued vitality in American national government, to articulate the demands deliberation places on our public officials, and to clarify the forces that promote or inhibit the collective reasoning about common goals so necessary to the continued success of American democracy.

☆ CHAPTER TWO

The Creation of Deliberative Democracy in

the United States

> In the state governments generally [during the 1780s],
> no principle had been introduced which could resist the
> wild projects of the moment, give the people an oppor-
> tunity to reflect, and allow the good sense of the nation
> time for exertion.
>
> Chief Justice John Marshall[1]

Deliberative democracy was the conscious creation of the delegates to the Constitutional Convention of 1787, ratified by the "reflection and choice" of the people of the United States acting through representative state conventions.[2] However deep the historical roots of the American concepts of rights, representation, and separation of powers, deliberative democracy as both a set of specific institutional prescriptions and as a broader theory of popular government owes its creation in the new nation particularly to the rapid flux of events that occurred in the decade immediately after independence was declared in 1776. These events forced political leaders to think through more fully and more deeply than they previously had the principles, problems, and institutional basis of effective self-government. Although much has changed in the American political and governmental system since 1787–89, many features of the original institutional design continue to shape deliberative democracy in the United States.

Deliberation Imperiled: The Critical Period

The Constitution of 1787 was written to meet the political and governmental crisis that gripped the new nation in the years after success on the battlefield effectively ended the Revolutionary War in 1781. Although American historians have disagreed about the nature and seriousness of that crisis, what seems indisputable is that those who fashioned the new national government shared the sentiment expressed by John

Quincy Adams in the commencement address he delivered at Harvard College in July of 1787 (at the very time the delegates to the Constitutional Convention were meeting behind closed doors in Philadelphia). The new nation, he told the graduates, was in the midst of a "critical period[,] . . . [and was] groaning under the intolerable burden of . . . accumulated evils."[3] Indeed, it was a view widely shared throughout the country. According to the historian Gordon Wood, "The evidence is overwhelming from every source—newspapers, sermons, and correspondence—that in the minds of many Americans the course of the Revolution had arrived at a crucial juncture."[4] Even those who opposed the Constitution of 1787 recognized the seriousness of the situation. "Few Anti-Federalists," the late Herbert J. Storing has noted, "would . . . have objected to the designation of 1787 as the 'critical period,' and many used that or synonymous phrases."[5] The crisis took several forms, including the near bankruptcy of the central government, the inability of the national Congress to conduct an effective foreign policy, commercial strife among the thirteen states, and economic and social distress throughout the nation.

The majority of those who served at the Constitutional Convention believed that the nation's troubles were at least in part the result of radical deficiencies in the structure and powers of the governing arrangements established by the Articles of Confederation. Among these deficiencies were the lack of an independent power to tax and to regulate commerce, the equal representation of the states in the national Congress regardless of population, the inability of the federal government to exercise authority directly on individuals, and the absence of a constitutionally independent executive and judiciary. All these deficiencies were remedied by the new structure of government created at Philadelphia.

Yet, as vital as the new structural changes were to the framers' design, many of the leading figures at the Convention believed that the deepest problems facing the nation stemmed not simply from the impotence of the central power but rather from the actions and inadequacies of the states. For example, James Madison's "Vices of the Political System of the United States"—the most systematic and detailed analysis of the problems facing the nation in the mid-1780s—identified eleven distinct problems, fully seven of which were failures of state government.[6] The states, for example, had failed to provide stipulated revenues to the national government, had encroached on the national authority through unauthorized interstate compacts dealing with commercial and military matters, had violated federal treaties, and had imposed tariffs and duties on the goods of their neighbors just as if they were foreign nations.

Even more serious, however, than these conflicts among the states and between the states and the central government was the inability of the state governments to provide stable, effective, and just governance within their own borders. Madison specifically faulted the states for the "multiplicity," "mutability," and "injustice" of their laws. The sheer number of new laws and the rapidity with which they were "repealed or superseded" was "a nuisance of the most pestilent kind" that caused confusion and instability within the states.[7] But an even "greater evil" was the "injustice" of state laws, because this "brings more into question the fundamental principle of republican Government, that the majority who rule in such governments are the safest Guardians both of public Good and private rights."[8] As Madison wrote to his friend, Thomas Jefferson, a month after the Convention ended:

> The mutability of the laws of the States is found to be a serious evil. The injustice of them has been so frequent and so flagrant as to alarm the most stedfast friends of Republicanism. I am persuaded I do not err in saying that the evils issuing from these sources contributed more to that uneasiness which produced the Convention, and prepared the public mind for a general reform, than those which accrued to our national character and interest from the inadequacy of the Confederation to its immediate objects.[9]

Not the least of Madison's concerns was the cavalier way in which virtually omnipotent legislatures in the states encroached upon the express constitutional spheres of the executive and judicial branches of government. Pennsylvania's unicameral legislature was one of the worst offenders. It arrogated executive authority by appointing various state and local officials, pardoning criminals, and drawing money from the treasury; and it assumed judicial power by deciding specific legal disputes and even dissolving marriages.[10] Similarly, the North Carolina legislature, lacking confidence in Governor Nash's ability to deal with a deteriorating military situation in 1780, created a Board of War and vested it with complete authority over military affairs. "[B]y your acts," the governor protested to the legislature, "you have effectually transferred the powers vested by the Constitution in the Governor into the hands of commissioners."[11] Even in Virginia, which was better governed than most states, "[a]ll the powers of government," Jefferson maintained, "result to the legislative body." Writing just after serving as governor (1779–81), Jefferson accused the legislature of "decid[ing] rights which should have been left to judiciary controversy" and of imposing a "habitual and familiar" direction of the executive "during the whole time of their session." [12]

Unchecked by counterbalancing institutions, legislatures too often passed foolish and short-sighted measures. Pennsylvania, for example, repealed the charters of both the College of Pennsylvania and of the Bank of North America, an institution vital to a stable currency and commerce. [13] North Carolina, in a misguided attempt to combat scarcity of provisions, prohibited the export of beef, pork, and maize, thereby destroying an active commerce between its farmers and the merchants of South Carolina: "Hundreds of wagons had yearly creaked over the rough roads to Charleston, and the State now badly needed the money and manufactures obtainable in return." [14] But the laws that most alarmed responsible leaders were those that resulted from what Madison called "the general rage for paper money" that spread throughout the states in 1785 and 1786.

The historian Andrew C. McLaughlin, writing at the beginning of this century, described the situation this way:

> Amid all the genuine distress caused by the war, by heavy taxes, and by the need of a sound and reliable circulating medium, came still greater trouble caused by the restlessness of the people, by the honest-minded but uneasy poor, and by the debtors who sought an avenue of escape. The times were indeed hard for a man that was once down; imprisonment for debt was common; the jails were dreadful and filthy; the processes of the courts were expensive and summary. Some quick method of paying old debts, some way of getting rid of the truly formidable consequences of either idleness or misfortune, was naturally sought after, and, following the precedents of earlier days, there was a demand for paper money, tender-laws, and other measures of relief. [15]

In state after state in 1785 and 1786 the voters swept into office men committed to using the printing press to solve economic distress, to ease the tax burden, and to provide relief to debtors.

In New Jersey the legislature passed a bill for issuing half a million paper dollars, which would be legal tender in all business transactions and for all private and public debts. The bill was vetoed by Governor William Livingston and his executive council. John Fiske describes what happened next:

> The aged Governor Livingston was greatly respected by the people; and so the mob at Elizabethtown, which had duly planted a stake and dragged his effigy up to it, refrained from inflicting the last indignities upon the image, and burned that of one of the members of the council instead. At the next session the governor yielded, and the rag money was issued.[16]

Whatever the reach of its formal lawmaking authority, however, the legislature of New Jersey was unable to turn paper into silver or gold. Merchants, especially in New York City and Philadelphia, refused to accept the money and it quickly depreciated in value. This further drove silver and gold coin out of circulation since lenders feared loaning anyone hard money when they might be forced to accept virtually worthless paper in repayment.

The North Carolina legislature, frustrated that its paper money was too slow in getting into circulation, used the new currency to make large purchases of tobacco from the state's farmers at twice the tobacco's value in gold or silver. This guaranteed an immediate depreciation of the paper. One angry citizen wrote in a local paper, "the wretched creditor is obliged to receive this paper trash for sterling debts, nay, frequently happy to receive it as the only liquidation he can get of accounts that have been standing for years."[17]

The Georgia legislature tried a more direct approach to force the acceptance of its depreciating paper by prohibiting any planter or merchant from exporting any produce from the state without taking an oath that he had never refused to receive the paper money at its full face value. As in other states, however, the more the legislature forced the use of the paper at full value, the faster it depreciated.[18]

In Virginia, by contrast, responsible leaders in the legislature were able to resist and moderate popular calls for paper money by passing a less injurious measure to allow certain state taxes to be paid in tobacco. Madison, who was then serving in the state legislature, explained to Jefferson that "[t]his indulgence to the people, as it is called and considered, was so warmly wished for out of doors, and so strenuously pressed within, that it could not be rejected without danger of exciting some worse project of a popular cast."[19] His acquiescence in the tobacco measure, he wrote to George Washington, was "a prudential compliance with

the clamours within doors and without, and as a probable means of ob-
viating more hurtful experiments."[20]

Maryland also successfully resisted popular agitation for paper money
in 1785 and 1786 because, in the words of one historian, "the old Senate,
its five-year term almost ended, stood like a stone wall against the paper
emission which . . . the House of Delegates [was] demanding."[21] A
new Senate was indirectly elected by the people in September of 1786
through the electoral college mechanism prescribed in the state constitution. It continued to oppose paper money.

In no state did the paper money forces gain a firmer grip on state
government and with more disastrous results than in Rhode Island.[22]
In the February 1786 session of the state legislature, members from
six towns brought instructions calling on the legislature to issue paper
money. At this time, however, paper money advocates constituted only a
small minority of the legislature, and the issue lost in March by a decisive
margin of 43 to 18. Elections one month later (state legislators served
six-month terms) resulted in wholesale turnover in state government and
the complete ascendancy of the proponents of paper money in both the
legislative and executive branches. Within a few weeks the legislature
issued paper money with a nominal value of 100,000 pounds. Property
owners were able to borrow the paper for up to half the value of their
land, with payments on the principal to begin in seven years. The paper
was made full legal tender in all commercial transactions and in payment
for all debts, past, present, or future. Realizing that creditors who had
previously loaned out gold or silver would not freely accept the new paper in repayment, the legislature stipulated that anyone could discharge
a debt by depositing an appropriate amount of paper money at a court.

The resulting huge infusion in the money supply led to a rapid depreciation of the paper. Within three short months it was worth only one-
fourth of its face value. Because merchants simply refused to accept the
currency at anything like its nominal value, the legislature, meeting in
special session, made it a criminal offense to refuse the paper. Trial
would be within three days of the offense, without jury, before a panel
of three judges. No delay would be permitted. The judgment of a majority of the panel was final and without appeal.

The issuance of the paper money and the subsequent measures to
force its acceptance were ruinous for the economy of Rhode Island:

> A period of absolute stagnation in business began. Rather
> than sell their goods and receive in return paper bills, mer-

chants closed their stores. It was only with the greatest difficulty that provisions could be obtained. Many people removed
to the neighboring states. The farmers who had mortgaged
their farms to secure paper, being unable to purchase goods
without it, sought to compel the townspeople to accept it by
withholding produce from the market. Few farmers from
neighboring states could be induced to bring their produce
into Rhode Island, where they might be obliged to accept
worthless paper for it. . . . Debtors were everywhere eager to
pay their debts. Creditors scarce dared show themselves on
the street for fear of meeting a debtor with the paper money
in his hand.[23]

Yet even in the face of these results the legislature refused to alter its
policies: "the majority [of legislators] was not checked in the least by the
arguments of the shippers, traders, and propertied men generally." Indeed, at its October 1786 session "the assembly lost the appearance of a
deliberative body . . . , for secret conclaves decided upon most measures
and hurried them through without real debate."[24]

A crisis of sorts had come in September of 1786 when the Superior
Court of Rhode Island heard the case against John Weeden, a Newport
butcher, who had refused to accept the state paper at its face value from
John Trevett. The court sided with Weeden, maintaining that the denial
of a jury trial violated Rhode Island's constitution (actually a continua-
tion of its charter government from the colonial period) and that the
court had the authority to declare as void legislative acts contrary to the
constitution. Rhode Island's legislators, outraged by the court's decision,
demanded that the judges attend the assembly to account for their actions. Although the judges were not impeached by the legislature, all but
one of them were subsequently defeated for reelection. In the face of
judicial opposition and continued economic distress, the acts forcing acceptance of the paper were soon repealed and by 1789 so was the requirement that the much depreciated paper be treated as legal tender.[25]
As the historian Merrill Jensen notes, this entire unfortunate episode
had been closely followed throughout the country: "Virtually every
newspaper in the United States carried accounts of the events in Rhode
Island."[26]

The first decade of American independence was a time of great democratic experimentation. Although the new state constitutions differed in

many details, nearly all concentrated decisive governmental authority within the legislative branch. The results, in both form and process, were highly democratic, but in substance and effect nearly disastrous for the fledgling democracies. In most states the legislatures had simply proven incapable of deliberating and legislating effectively, raising the question whether sound political deliberation was compatible with democratic forms.

The Framers' Design for Deliberative Democracy

The task that confronted the framers was to design a governmental system that would promote informed, reasoned, and responsible policy-making while also "preserv[ing] the spirit and the form of popular government," a system, that is, that would combine deliberation and democracy.[27] The failures of republican government during the "critical period" had raised serious questions about whether this was even possible. The governmental experience of the 1780s taught the framers that their new plan of government would have to solve four problems if deliberative democracy was to be achieved: (1) it had to defuse the problem of majority faction, (2) it had to restrict the legislative authority to properly legislative matters, (3) it had to promote the election of more responsible and knowledgeable political leaders, and (4) it had to fashion an institutional environment th t would foster genuine deliberation

Defusing Majority F :tion

When Madison and others cc mplained about the injustice of state laws during the "critical period" they especially had in mind the short-sighted, if well-intentioned, efforts of the states' legislatures to solve economic distress through irresponsible and simplistic measures. The extremes reached in Rhode Island cast the issue in its sharpest relief. With the possible exception of the denial of jury trials, everything done by Rhode Island's government during the paper money episode—no matter how foolish or unwise, no matter how injurious to private rights or to the broader public good—was duly enacted by the representatives of the people following prescribed constitutional procedures. The majority in the state, in complete control of the governing institutions, pushed through a series of disastrous policies that violated the rights of creditors and merchants and that seriously impaired commerce, industry, and economic enterprise within the state.

This is the "majority faction" about which Madison wrote so eloquently in the famous Tenth Federalist essay: "united and actuated by some common impulse of passion, or of interest, adverse to the rights of other citizens, or to the permanent and aggregate interests of the community."[28] Madison's was not a merely theoretical concern. Reading his masterpiece of political disquisition two hundred years later, we are likely to forget that majority faction was not a problem Madison "discovered" through theoretical reasoning but was instead, to him and his colleagues at Philadelphia, a very real and immediate threat to the success of self-government in the new nation.

In Rhode Island's neighbor, Massachusetts, the paper money movement had taken a different turn. Not able to gain control over the government, the paper money forces took to arms under the leadership of Daniel Shays. At the height of the rebellion (the fall of 1786 and the winter of 1787) an armed force of up to two thousand men, in open defiance of lawful authority, camped for two months in Worcester, a mere forty miles from Boston, and then attacked the arsenal at Springfield.[29] Writing to Jefferson just a few months after Shays's rebellion was suppressed, Madison applauded the "vigorous measures finally pursued by the Governor of Massachusetts against the insurgents," but he feared their next step: "It would seem that they mean to try their strength in another way; that is, by endeavoring to give the elections such a turn as may promote their views under the auspices of Constitutional forms."[30]

As a violent and lawless challenge to legitimate constituted authority, Shays's rebellion—and others it might spawn—posed a direct threat to the success of republican government in the United States. Indeed, it is impossible to overstate the seriousness with which the delegates to the Constitutional Convention, meeting only four months after the rebellion was suppressed, viewed that threat. Nonetheless, even armed rebellion was not as great a danger to the prospects of self-government in the United States as a determined majority, in control of the governing institutions, intent on using the laws to promote unwise or unjust ends. If, as in Massachusetts, a faction is less than a majority, "it may clog the administration, it may convulse the society; but it will be unable to execute and mask its violence under the forms of the Constitution." But if, as in Rhode Island, "a majority is included in a faction, the form of popular government . . . enables it to sacrifice to its ruling passion or interest both the public good and the rights of other citizens."[31]

If deliberative institutions were to have any prospect of success in the new nation, then this fundamental problem of majority faction would have to be solved; for if a majority of the citizens, in control of the governing institutions, pursue policies adverse to private rights or to the broader public good, they will not be inclined to judiciously hear all points of view or to calmly think through the long-term consequences of their actions. "[I]ndirect and remote considerations," Madison wrote, "will rarely prevail over the immediate interest which one party may find in disregarding the rights of another or the good of the whole."[32] Prior to the excesses of the "critical period" the received wisdom had accepted Montesquieu's argument (specifically discussed by Hamilton in *Federalist* no. 9) that successful republics must be limited to relatively small territories and populations. Madison maintained, on the contrary, that small republics can offer no cure for the disease of majority faction short of suppressing liberty itself. No set of democratic governing institutions, no matter how well designed, can prevent the "instability, injustice, and confusion" caused by majority faction in small republics: "for it cannot be believed that any form of representative government could have succeeded within the narrow limits occupied by the democracies of Greece."[33] In Madison's well-known formulation, the solution to the problem of majority faction was to combine representative institutions with an extended territory encompassing such a multiplicity and variety of interests as to render majority factions unlikely to form or, if formed, unlikely to control the government.

Reflecting their lack of confidence in the ability of the relatively small democracies of the states to withstand the demands of unjust majorities, the framers wrote into the new national Constitution major prohibitions on state power. Most important, the Constitution prohibits states from coining money, emitting bills of credit, making anything but gold or silver a tender in payment of debts, or passing any laws impairing the obligation of contracts. These are sweeping prohibitions on the whole range of irresponsible state actions that had culminated in the paper money "rage" of 1785–86. None of these prohibitions, however, is also placed against the new national government, although other restrictions—like no bills of attainder and no ex post facto laws—are applied to both states and nation. Indeed, the Constitution specifically vests the Congress with authority to borrow money on the credit of the government, to coin money, and to pass bankruptcy laws.

Thus, through express prohibitions on the states and explicit grants to Congress, the framers raised to the national level the decisive authority over currency and contracts. Just as large states like Massachusetts were less likely to be controlled by unjust majorities than small states like Rhode Island, so too the national government, embracing, by historical standards for republics, a huge territory with a diverse and rapidly expanding population, would be even less subject to the demands of unjust majorities than the largest states. For this reason such delicate and potentially dangerous powers as the authority over the money supply, the currency, the payment of debts, and the obligation of contracts could be more safely entrusted to the national government.

Defusing majority faction was the first step in establishing representative institutions capable of sound political deliberation. If the well-being and long-range interests of the parts and the whole were to be reasonably and fairly determined, then policymaking would have to be insulated, to some degree, from the bitter and passionate disputes that arise from deep-seated economic, religious, or political cleavages within the community.

SEPARATING THE POWERS OF GOVERNMENT

The state experience during the "critical period" taught the framers that in republican government there was a natural tendency for the legislative branch "to exert an imperious control over the other departments," threatening "the balance of the Constitution."[34] This tendency was aggravated by provisions in the state constitutions designed to keep governors weak. These included election by the legislature, short terms of office, strict limits on reeligibility, and the sharing of power with executive councils. In most states the legislatures held formal authority over the reach of both the executive and judicial powers and generally controlled the salaries of all state officials. The result was legislative domination, and at times legislative tyranny, over state government.

Not only did legislative supremacy in most of the state constitutions make it easier for lawmaking branches to pursue unwise and unjust measures, it also allowed them to interfere in administrative and judicial matters for which they were not well suited. The national Congress, established by the Articles of Confederation as the sole organ of central authority, demonstrated a similar propensity; for even after it had set up an administrative apparatus to carry out the national government's daily business, it often devoted long and tedious hours to the details of administration, thereby deflecting time and energy from broad policy issues. Jefferson, who after his term as governor of Virginia served six months in the national Congress, forcefully proposed a separation of the executive and legislative powers: "Nothing is so embarrassing nor so mischievous, in a great assembly, as the details of execution. The smallest trifle of that kind occupies as long as the most important act of legislation, and takes place of everything else. . . . I have ever viewed the executive details as the greatest cause of evil to us, because they in fact place us as if we had no federal head, by diverting the attention of that head from great to small subjects."[35] In this Jefferson shared a sentiment voiced by Alexander Hamilton a few years before: "Congress have kept the power too much into their own hands and have meddled too much with details of every sort. Congress is properly a deliberative corps and it forgets itself when it attempts to play the executive."[36]

Legislative usurpation of executive or judicial authority presented the framers with a serious structural problem. How could an institutional framework based on a functional separation of powers be designed that would keep the legislative body, the branch of government closest to the people, whose members "seem sometimes to fancy that they are the people themselves,"[37] within the bounds marked out in the formal, written constitution? For this structural problem the framers proposed a structural solution. First, they divided the legislative power into two branches, one less closely tied to the people. Second, they fortified the executive power by (1) vesting it in a single hand unconstrained by a council, (2) providing a mode of election independent of Congress, (3) giving it a four-year term (longer than any governor) with indefinite reeligibility, (4) insulating its salary from legislative will during any one term, and (5) providing it a qualified veto over legislative acts. Finally, they strengthened the judicial power by placing it in judges with life tenure whose salary could not be diminished while they served.

The framers hoped that their new design would give the members of the nonlegislative branches both the incentive and the means to resist encroachments. In terms of legislative-executive relations, this would help to accomplish two important ends. First, by inhibiting legislative intrusions into executive matters, it would make for a more consistent and energetic administration of the laws. Second, by concentrating legislative attention on properly legislative matters, it would improve policy deliberation within the new House of Representatives and Senate.

IMPROVING THE CHARACTER OF POLITICAL LEADERS

Throughout the 1780s responsible leaders blamed much of the inadequacy of the state legislatures on the character of the men who filled those bodies. A writer to a Rhode Island newspaper in 1787 complained that he "never saw so great a proportion of ignorant men in a public body. . . . There are but four or five that appear to understand the nature of money and the operation of the law . . . . You never heard language and common sense so tortured and murdered as in this House."[38]

Samuel Johnston, a prominent conservative leader in North Carolina, wrote a friend that many legislators were "fools and knaves, who by their low arts have worked themselves into the good graces of the populace."[39] Reflecting on his service in the North Carolina legislature, James Hogg wrote to James Iredell (who later served on the U.S. Supreme Court) that "[a] set of unprincipled men, who sacrifice everything to their popularity and private views, seem to have acquired too much influence in all our assemblies."[40]

In somewhat less colorful language Madison, Hamilton, James Wilson, and other leading framers concurred that the low quality of political leadership was a serious problem in the state governments. They believed that the fault lay with the relatively small legislative districts in the states, which enabled men with "talents for low intrigue, and the little arts of popularity" to achieve public office.[41] Within the narrow compass of one or a few towns or villages, ambitious but irresponsible men could inflame popular resentment over taxes and debts, incite envy of the commercial or propertied classes, and promise the simplistic solution of paper money, tender laws, or the abolition of debts. These "little arts of little politicians"[42] were often successful, raising to positions of authority within the states "men of factious tempers, of local prejudices, or of sinister designs."[43]

In the debate on the House of Representatives at the Constitutional Convention, Madison argued that there was a straightforward solution to this problem: "if the election is made by the people in large districts there will be no danger of demagogues."[44] James Wilson concurred: "There is no danger of improper elections if made by *large* districts. Bad elections proceed from the smallness of the districts which give an opportunity to bad men to intrigue themselves into office."[45] The large electoral districts that a large republic makes possible would diminish the influence of those who have little to commend themselves but the rhetoric of democratic envy. In an era without mass communication and with only primitive transportation, electoral districts of the size of those originally established for the House of Representatives (e.g., only three representatives for all of Georgia, four for New Jersey, five each for North and South Carolina and Connecticut, six for New York, etc.) would render demagogic rhetoric alone of little utility in seeking office. Instead, "the suffrages of the people . . . will be more likely to center on men who possess the most attractive merit and the most diffusive and established characters."[46] Prospective representatives would become known to the voters less by rhetorical appeals—what Madison later called "personal solicitations practicable on a contracted theatre"[47]—than through a reputation for merit and accomplishment often derived from previous public service. Those chosen would likely be more knowledgeable about broad statewide and national issues and less tied to narrow local concerns than those elected from small districts.

The delegates to the Constitutional Convention were not, however, sufficiently confident in the beneficial effects of direct popular election in large districts to extend this mode of selection to the Senate and presidency. Reflecting "the policy of refining the popular appointments by successive filtrations,"[48] the framers vested the election of the Senate in the state legislatures and that of the president in a temporary body (electoral college) chosen as the state legislatures saw fit. John Jay said of these intermediary electoral bodies that "there is reason to presume that their attention and their votes will be directed to those men only who have become the most distinguished by their abilities and virtue, and in whom the people perceive just groun s for confidence."[49] These "assemb [ies] of select electors [will] possess . the means of extensive and accurate information relative to men a d characters" with the result that "the President and the senators so chosen will always be of the number of those who best understand our national interests, . . . who are best able to promote those interests, and whose reputation for integrity inspires and merits confidence."[50]

Thus, the combination of large electoral districts for the House and indirect modes of popular election for the Senate and presidency would foster the selection of political leaders with the following kinds of characteristics: (1) an acquaintance with "the general genius, habits, and modes of thinking of the people at large and with the resources of the country";[51] (2) experience in public affairs with a resulting knowledge of financial, economic, or commercial matters affecting the states and nation; (3) freedom from excessive attachment to local issues or interests and a corresponding breadth of outlook and approach; (4) a personal temperament conducive to reasoned argument and persuasion; (5) sound judgment; and (6) a public-spiritedness that while not inconsistent with high ambition would discourage the pursuit of narrow political advantage through dangerous demagogic appeals or the gratification of immediate public desires. Possessed of these qualities, political leaders would have both the inclination and the capacity to deliberate well for the new national government.

One of the *Federalist Papers'* most famous statements—"Enlightened statesmen will not always be at the helm"[52]—reminds us that the framers did not expect their new selection mechanisms to guarantee success. Nonetheless, these were considerably more likely to vest governing authority in wise and responsible leaders than the systems in place in the states. As Hamilton wrote of the electoral college system for selecting presidents, "there will be a constant probability of seeing the station filled by characters pre-eminent for ability and virtue."[53] If the new electoral mechanisms did not guarantee wise choices, they at least created a "constant probability" of this result.

Although the framers did not rest the success of their design on "enlightened statesmen" and although they sought to create "inventions of prudence" that would supply "by opposite and rival interests, the defect of better motives" in political leaders,[54] it is also abundantly clear from both the Convention debates and the *Federalist Papers* that they attributed the failure of democratic governance during the "critical period" at least in part to the deficiencies of those who served in state government and that among their highest priorities was designing a system that would raise to governing authority men of broad experience, proven ability, and national outlook. Indeed, there is at least as much discussion in the *Federalist* of the character and necessary virtues of political leaders as there is of the need to compensate for deficiencies in wisdom and virtue. "The aim of every political constitution," Madison wrote in *Federalist* no. 57, "is, or ought to be, . . . to obtain for rulers men who possess most wisdom to discern, and most virtue to pursue, the common good of the society."[55]

Designing the Institution

How Small Size Promotes Reason. Vesting governmental authority in the hands of those with the inclination and capacity to deliberate well, though essential to the framers' design, was not sufficient to ensure the success of deliberative democracy. Madison argued that large democratic assemblies, even if filled with wise and virtuous leaders, were invariably subject to "the confusion and intemperance of a multitude. In all very numerous assemblies, of whatever characters composed, passion never fails to wrest the scepter from reason. Had every Athenian citizen been a Socrates, every Athenian assembly would still have been a mob."[56] Moreover, the larger the assembly,

> the greater will be the proportion of members of limited information and of weak capacities. Now, it is precisely on char-

acters of this description that the eloquence and address of the few are known to act with all their force. In the ancient republics, where the whole body of the people assembled in person, a single orator, or an artful statesman, was generally seen to rule with as complete a sway as if a scepter had been placed in his single hand. On the same principle, the more multitudinous a representative assembly may be rendered, the more it will partake of the infirmities incident to collective meetings of the people. Ignorance will be the dupe of cunning, and passion the slave of sophistry and declamation.[57]

Democracies and republics had traditionally been governed by mass assemblies of the citizenry or by relatively large representative institutions. Yet such bodies, too easily swayed by demagogues and sophists and too often characterized by passion, confusion, and intemperance, are ill-suited for calm and regular deliberation on the merits of public measures.

Thus, the more closely the governing body in a republic or democracy resembles the people themselves in number and types, the less it will be suited for the business of sound political deliberation. This is the crux of the tension between democracy and deliberation. Deliberation puts a premium on reason, order, information, commonality of interests, and farsightedness; yet these qualities do not in general characterize decisionmaking through the most apparently democratic forms: that is, by mass assemblies of the people or by very large representative bodies. Electoral mechanisms that would promote the selection of wise and virtuous leaders would mitigate but not solve this fundamental problem. What was also necessary was a set of institutional features that would foster the kinds of qualities essential to deliberation.

The most important of these institutional features was size. All else being equal, small bodies, the framers believed, were less subject to confusion, intemperance, and passion than large ones; conversely, they are more suited to reason, order, and regularity. It is for this reason that the House of Representatives was originally to have only sixty-five members and the Senate but twenty-six. By contrast, the legislature of Massachusetts, one of the largest in the states, had over three hundred members.

The small size of the House in particular was a matter of great controversy during the ratification debate. Leading Anti-Federalist essayists such as "Cato," "Brutus," and "The Federal Farmer" all attacked the small size of the House as inconsistent with the democratic principles that ought especially to characterize that body. So small a body would make a "full and equal representation of the people in the legislature" impossible since it would not "allow professional men, merchants, traders, farmers, mechanics, etc. to bring a just proportion of their best informed men respectively into the legislature."[58] Moreover, "a small representation can never be well informed as to the circumstances of the people, the members of it must be too far removed from the people, in general, to sympathize with them: . . . the constituents in turn cannot, with tolerable convenience, make known their wants, circumstances, and opinions, to their representatives."[59] In *Federalist* no. 55, Madison noted regarding the size of the House that "[s]carce any article, indeed, in the whole Constitution seems to be rendered more worthy of attention by the weight of character and the apparent force of argument with which it has been assailed."[60] He proceeded to devote four essays directly or indirectly to this issue.

The Constitution, of course, provides that the size of the House may be increased based on a periodic census of the population, as long as the number of representatives does not exceed one for every thirty thousand persons.[61] Madison estimated that based on this ratio and the rate of population growth in the United States the House could grow to at least one hundred members after the first census in three years, to two hundred members after twenty-five years, and to four hundred members after fifty years.[62] Thus, while not opposed to a gradual and significant increase in the size of the House, the framers were intent on beginning relatively small and, barring constitutional amendment, limiting growth to what would be allowed under the one-to-thirty-thousand ratio. Indeed, until the very last day of the Constitutional Convention, the ratio had been an even more stringent one to forty thousand. After a motion was made to change this to thirty thousand, George Washington, presiding officer at the Convention, who apparently had not once before entered into substantive debate on the Constitution, rose to support the more liberal provision. As late as it was for making amendments, he "desired that the objections to the plan recommended might be made as few as possible" since "[t]he smallness of the proportion of Representation had been considered by many members of the Convention, an insufficient security for the rights & interests of the people."[63] No opposition was raised and the motion passed unanimously.[64]

The controversy over the original size of the House of Representatives and the ceiling placed on representation by the ratio established in the Constitution highlight the importance with which the framers viewed the matter of the size of the House and its significance to their plan for deliberative democracy. They could easily have created a House with an initial membership of two to three hundred, making it appear much more like the state legislatures and thereby reducing anticipated objections to their plan. Yet they feared that such an institution would be subject to the kind of tumult, disorder, and passion that had often characterized the state bodies and had frequently made sound deliberation impossible.

The framers carried the size principle a step further with the new Senate. If sixty-five or a few hundred was better than a mass assembly or a very large body, then twenty-six was better still. Governor Edmund Randolph, who introduced the Virginia plan at the Convention, maintained that the Senate ought to be "so small as to be exempt from the passionate proceedings to which numerous assemblies are liable." [65] Similarly, in the first weeks of debate Madison argued that a small Senate was essential: "The use of the Senate is to consist in its proceeding with more coolness, with more system, and with more wisdom, than the popular branch. Enlarge their number and you communicate to them the vices which they are meant to correct." [66] It is clear that the framers were not fully confident that their new House of Representatives would be entirely free from the defects of large legislative bodies. [67]

How Lengthy Terms Promote Knowledge. Next to size, the most important structural provision for Congress was term of office: two years for the House and six years for the Senate. The House term was twice the one-year norm for state legislatures and thus violated the popular axiom that "where annual elections end, tyranny begins." Madison argued, however, that the longer term was necessary to give the legislator time to acquire "knowledge of the subjects on which he is to legislate." Some of this knowledge may be acquired "in a man's closet"; but another part "can only be derived from public sources of information" and through "actual experience in the station which requires the use of it." [68]

The need to acquire knowledge through actual legislative service is made even more necessary by the extent and diversity of the nation. Foreign and interstate trade, taxes, and regulations for the militia—"the principal objects of federal legislation"—all require "extensive information" of "the affairs, and even of the laws, of all the States." [69] Representatives from throughout the nation will bring to Congress and share with their colleagues detailed knowledge about their own states on matters of common concern. Two-year terms will provide opportunity for assimilating and acting on such information. Moreover, to the extent that the House legislates in the area of foreign policy, its members will also need time to become acquainted with "treaties between the United States and other nations," "the commercial policy and laws of other nations," and "the law of nations."[70]

Based on experience in the states, the framers expected rapid turnover in the membership of the House. And since members would be drawn from "pursuits of a private nature" and would likely spend only a few months each year in session, even a two-year term placed substantial limits on what such representatives could learn about "the laws, the affairs, and the comprehensive interests of their country."[71] Hence, the need for the much longer six-year term for the Senate. As John Jay put it, only a body like the Senate with a lengthy term of office would be capable of achieving those "great objects" that require "not only talents, but also exact information, and often much time . . . to concert and to execute." It was particularly wise to vest the treaty power in a body of "able and honest men" who would "continue in place a sufficient time to become perfectly acquainted with our national concerns, and to form and introduce a system for the management of them." The six-year term would give them "an opportunity of greatly extending their political informations, and of rendering their accumulating experience more and more beneficial to their country." Moreover, by staggering Senate elections every two years, "a considerable residue of the old ones [would remain] in place, [and] uniformity and order, as well as a constant succession of official information, will be preserved."[72]

Sound deliberation requires informed decisionmaking by knowledgeable leaders. Some part of the information and knowledge necessary for deliberation would be brought into the national government by those selected through the framers' electoral mechanisms; but another part would result from the legislative process itself as those in the House and Senate shared their knowledge with fellow legislators, investigated public issues, gained experience in national affairs, and framed policies to promote the well-being of the nation.

How Lengthy Terms Promote Farsightedness. In addition to promoting knowledgeable decisionmaking, relatively lengthy terms of office would allow and encourage legislators to consider the long-term consequences of their actions. The framers were keenly aware that abrupt shifts in public attitudes and desires, such as those that rocked Rhode Island and other states in 1785 and 1786, can overwhelm a governmental system in which all legislators serve short terms. This can happen either through the wholesale replacement of incumbents by those committed to new and hastily conceived policies (as happened in Rhode Island) or by the intimidation of those in office looking forward to future reelection. Lengthy terms can help to mitigate both problems. First, the longer the term, the less frequently a wholesale turnover in membership can occur. The national House of Representatives, for example, was guaranteed a stable membership for a period four times as long as the popular branches in Rhode Island and Connecticut and twice as long as the popular branches in every other state but South Carolina.[73] The national Senate, with its staggered elections, was assured that two-thirds of its membership would be unchanged over any four-year period between elections. Second, individual legislators interested in reelection are less likely to succumb to sudden changes in public opinion if they have the protection of a lengthy term. This principle, of course, was expected to apply especially to the Senate. Though selected by the very democratic state legislatures, and thus presumably in step with the dominant interests and attitudes of the citizens of their state, senators were insulated to some degree from the need to court public opinion. Since senators would not be recallable between elections—unlike the delegates to the Congress under the Articles of Confederation[74]—they were assured of at least six full years in office no matter how they voted. Moreover, even if they actively sought reelection, the rapid turnover in state legislatures would make it quite difficult for even the most calculating and self-serving senator to predict how voting behavior in his first three or four years in office would promote reappointment.[75]

Thus, lengthy terms of office would foster and secure the independent judgment of legislators that was indispensable to sound deliberation. It was in the legislative branch and through the lawmaking process that a wealth of information on the resources of the country and the economic and commercial activities of its citizens would be accumulated, that arguments and proposals would be advanced for promoting the welfare and prosperity of the nation, and that sound policies would be formulated. This deliberative process, in its full manifestation, would occur only within the national councils. Legislators, accordingly, must be free to exercise their independent judgment on the merits of proposed policies, for to simply defer to public attitudes would be to devolve the decisionmaking authority upon those who had not been educated by the information and arguments presented during congressional deliberations.

Deliberation and the Common Interest

By defusing the fundamental problem of majority faction, by restricting the reach of the legislative power through an effective separation of powers system, by establishing selection mechanisms that would draw into the national government responsible and knowledgeable political leaders, and by fashioning representative bodies that would promote informed and reasoned decisionmaking, the framers hoped to institutionalize in the new government the qualities essential to sound political deliberation. Foremost among these qualities was an attention to national issues and the national interest.

If majority faction was the most deep-seated problem that confronted popular governments, it was not the only way in which the "spirit of faction" or "party animosities" threatened sound deliberation. Experience taught the framers that an excessive attachment to local or partial interests "is apt to mingle its poison in the deliberations of all bodies of men"[76] and that "the pestilential influence of party animosities [is] the disease most incident to deliberative bodies and most apt to contaminate their proceedings."[77] In the first decade of American independence a "local spirit" infected both the state legislatures and the national Congress. Within the states, Madison maintained, legislators "sacrifice the comprehensive and permanent interest of the State to the particular and separate views of the counties or districts in which they reside."[78] Similarly, the delegates to the national Congress "too frequently displayed the character rather of partisans of their respective States than of impartial guardians of a common interest." As a result, "the great interests of the nation have suffered on a hundred [occasions] from an undue attention to the local prejudices, interests, and views of the particular States."[79]

At first glance, it might appear that the solution to the problem of majority faction—extending the sphere of government to encompass a multiplicity of diverse and often competing interests and sects—would actually aggravate the more general problem of the factious spirit or party animosities; for the legislature of a large and diverse republic would face many more controversial issues affecting the material interests of discrete groups than would the legislature of a smaller and more homogenous country. As Madison noted in *Federalist* no. 10, "what are the different classes of legislators but advocates and parties to the causes which they determine?"[80] Such legislators are likely to decide matters according to the interest of the group they represent rather than "with a sole regard to justice and the public good."[81]

Yet, as Madison indicated in *Federalist* no. 51, if the number and variety of groups is sufficiently great, then "a coalition of a majority of the whole society could seldom take place on any other principles than those of justice and the general good."[82] If each group is but a small fraction of the whole, then it will be required to make its appeals to other groups on some basis other than its own self-interest. It will be led to present its programs or policies as beneficial to other groups, as good for the entire nation, or as dictated by some overarching principle such as justice or equity. While it is not clear that Madison here is talking about behavior within legislative bodies, as opposed to broader movements within society, his argument has an obvious legislative analogy. It suggests coalition building through reasoned appeals, as those who represent separate groups in society seek to find or fashion a common interest or principle around which a majority can form.

Despite the possibility of a kind of deliberative coalition building within Congress, it is abundantly clear from the founding records that the framers very much sought to create legislative institutions that would not be mere collections of advocates of narrow interests. An excessive "local spirit" had undermined sound policymaking within the states and had been nearly fatal in the Congress of the Confederation. In light of this experience it was the framers' hope and expectation (1) that their electoral mechanisms would bring into government men of broad experience and outlook who were not unduly tied to local or partial interests and (2) that their institutional design would foster a growing knowledge of and attachment to national concerns. As legislators in the new government studied and debated how to promote commercial prosperity, a sound national defense, and productive relations with other nations, their deliberations would focus less on the specific interests of their district or state and more on "the permanent and aggregate interests of the community"[83]—also described in the *Federalist Papers* as "the public good,"[84] "the good of the whole,"[85] "the public weal,"[86] "great and national objects,"[87] "the great and aggregate interests,"[88] "the national prosperity and happiness,"[89] "the great interests of the nation,"[90] the "common interest,"[91] "the common good of the society,"[92] and "the comprehensive interests of [the] country."[93]

This is not to argue, however, that the common interest is disembodied from the interests or well-being of the parts. A thriving commerce and economy will benefit the parts as well as the whole, and a sound national defense will protect the states as well as the union. As John Jay wrote in the *Federalist*, "the good of the whole can only be promoted by advancing the good of each of the parts or members which compose the whole."[94] In its formal written response to President Washington's First Inaugural Address, the U.S. Senate expressed a similar view: "We are conscious that the prosperity of each State is inseparably connected with the welfare of all, and that in promoting the latter we shall effectually advance the former."[95] On the other hand, the common interest of the American union is more than the aggregation of the perceived interests of the parts. During the Confederation period, for example, states with good harbors, like New York and Virginia, believed it was in their interest to impose duties on goods transported through their territory to or from neighboring states. But those who wrote the Constitution of 1787 believed, on the contrary, that commerce and economic activity would only flourish throughout the nation if states were prohibited from such activity and if the regulation of commerce among the states and with foreign nations was left to the central authority. The experience under the Articles of Confederation had demonstrated that if the parts of the union retained the decisive authority over commerce, taxes, and national defense, they would too often pursue a short-sighted and narrow view of their interests in a way that would ultimately harm the whole as well as the parts. Thus, as the nation's new senators wrote to Washington, "it shall be our invariable aim to divest ourselves of local prejudices and attachments."[96]

Indeed, the entire case for replacing the Articles of Confederation with the Constitution of 1787 was a massive argument that there *is* a common interest that binds the parts of the union, that a new government—a "more perfect Union"—is necessary to achieve that common interest, and that such a government would better ensure the security and prosperity of the parts than existing arrangements. Although it was not the framers' plan or expectation that deliberations in the new government would ignore the interests of the parts, their intention and hope was that service in the national House of Representatives and Senate would broaden the perspective of legislators by showing them how the well-being of their district or state was inextricably bound to the well-being of the nation.[97]

Deliberation and Energy: Congress versus the Executive

As we have seen, the framers' efforts to design governing institutions that would combine deliberation and democracy focused primarily on legislative institutions. It had been the failures of the state legislatures during the "critical period" that had caused the greatest alarm to responsible leaders, and it was primarily in the design of the new Congress that the framers rested their hopes that democratic forms could be made compatible with the requisites of sound deliberative policymaking. Nonetheless, the new independent executive branch (the national government under the Articles of Confederation had no constitutionally independent executive) was to make an important, if subordinate, contribution to sound deliberation.

First, as noted earlier, a strong and independent executive would serve as a political and institutional check on the natural tendency of the legislative branch in a republican government to encroach on the constitutional authority of the executive and the judiciary. Both the national and state legislatures had regularly interfered in strictly administrative matters, deflecting legislative time and energy from broad policy issues. The new separation of powers scheme for the national government would improve policy deliberation by concentrating legislative attention on properly legislative matters.

Second, the president was given a constitutional role in the legislative process both in his qualified veto over acts of Congress and in his obligation to give Congress "Information of the State of the Union" and to recommend for their consideration "such Measures as he shall judge necessary and expedient." [98] The president is thus obligated to contribute to congressional deliberations on important matters facing the nation. Indeed, if he vetoes an act of Congress, he must, according to the Constitution, formally give his reasons, which in turn must be entered in the journal of the branch that originated the bill and then again submitted to the second branch if the first votes to override the veto. In this way the Constitution seeks to raise a veto conflict above a mere battle of wills to a contest of reason, argument, and persuasion. In this light Hamilton described the veto as "the mere suggestion of argumentative objections to be approved or disapproved by those to whom they are addressed." [99] An absolute veto, by contrast, would place the president under no obligation to convince others of the wisdom of his actions and thus would be little more than an act of will.

Finally, the president's constitutional role in foreign policy—derived from the Commander-in-Chief clause, his duty to appoint (with Senate confirmation) and to receive ambassadors, his power to make treaties (with Senate ratification), and perhaps from the general vesting of "executive Power"—gave him an essential deliberative function in this area.

In conducting American foreign policy presidents would be required to think through in a serious and sustained way the dictates of national security and prosperity; and when foreign policy decisions took the form of proposed treaties or required new legislation or appropriations, presidents would be required to persuade Congress of the wisdom of their initiatives.

Thus, in both the domestic and foreign policy spheres the Constitution contemplates deliberation not only within the Congress but also within the executive branch as well as between the Congress and the presidency. Yet while the new independent executive branch was to contribute to deliberative decisionmaking, its distinctive contribution to effective and competent governance was to come not through deliberation, but through *energy*. Hamilton's unapologetic defense of a strong presidency in the *Federalist Papers* hinged on the necessity for "energy in the executive," which he called "a leading character in the definition of good government."[100] An energetic executive was essential for national defense, the steady administration of the laws, the protection of property, and the security of liberty. "A feeble executive," Hamilton wrote, "implies a feeble execution of the government. . . . and a government ill executed, whatever it may be in theory, must be, in practice, a bad government."[101]

The energetic administration of the government requires the concentration of executive authority in a single person, for only a unified executive would be able to act with "decision, activity, secrecy, and dispatch." Conversely, a "numerous legislature" is "best adapted to deliberation and wisdom."[102] The contrast, and implicit tension, between energy and deliberation are reflected in the following passage from *Federalist* no. 70:

> In the legislature, promptitude of decision is oftener an evil than a benefit. The differences of opinion, and the jarring of parties in that department of the government, though they may sometimes obstruct salutary plans, yet often promote deliberation and circumspection, and serve to check excesses in the majority. . . . But no favorable circumstances palliate or atone for the disadvantages of dissension in the executive department. Here they are pure and unmixed. There is no point at which they cease to operate. They serve to embarrass and weaken the execution of the plan or measure to which they relate, from the first step to the final conclusion of it. They constantly counteract those qualities in the executive which are the most necessary ingredients in its composition—vigor and expedition.[103]

Genuine deliberation directed toward wise policies is often a slow, untidy, and contentious process in which "differences of opinion" and the "jarring of parties" play a central role. Yet these essential elements of sound deliberation would, if introduced into the executive branch, destroy the "vigor and expedition" that characterize an energetic executive. Whereas deliberation calls for a collegial institution in which those of roughly equal rank voice a variety of contrasting views as they argue and reason together to identify and promote common interests, the effective and energetic administration of the government, on the other hand, requires a hierarchical institution in which authority is concentrated in one set of hands that can act quickly, decisively, consistently, and often secretly.

There is, of course, deliberation within the executive branch. Presidents and their advisers reason about such matters as the merits of legislative initiatives, whether to sign or veto bills passed by Congress, whom to appoint to high-level executive positions, and what kinds of treaties to enter into with foreign nations. Nonetheless much, if not most, executive branch deliberation is of a special sort; for it is directed to, and bound by the necessities of, decisive, and often immediate, action. Consider the president's pardoning power. The principal reason, Hamilton argued, for vesting it in the president rather than Congress was the president's ability to act quickly and decisively during those "critical moments" that occur in the midst of insurrections or rebellions "when a well-timed offer of pardon to the insurgents or rebels may restore the tranquility of the commonwealth."[104] To wait for the legislature to convene and to debate the matter would likely forfeit the "golden opportunity," for "the loss of a week, a day, an hour, may sometimes be fatal."[105] Wise and timely pardoning decisions during periods of national crisis are more likely to result from the intense, highly focused, and secret deliberations of the executive branch than from a wide-ranging, unhurried, and public debate within the halls of Congress.

Executive branch deliberation directed toward decisive action necessarily sacrifices some of the qualities that ought to characterize the best sort of deliberation within legislative bodies. Time constraints dictated by the need for quick decisions may limit the range of opinions and views that come to bear on the decision or may result in actions whose consequences have not been well thought through. The hierarchical structure necessary for executive energy may limit the advice given the president to that of a small circle of advisers—perhaps like-minded advisers—or may inhibit those further down the chain of command from voicing objections to the plans of their superiors. Finally, the secrecy attendant to many executive branch decisions creates a barrier to discordant views both within the executive branch and outside, while also running the risk of losing public support for surprise policies that run counter to public desires or that have not been adequately explained to the citizenry.

Conversely, a full-fledged deliberative process within a legislative body is not well suited for the kind of immediate decisionmaking central to energetic administration. Even if the legislature is constantly in session (which was not the framers' expectation nor the early practice), the procedures that promote sound deliberation—hearings and debate before committees or subcommittees, the preparation of formal recommendations to the full body, floor debate, and the reconciliation of different versions of bills passed in a bicameral legislature, etc.—render legislative decisionmaking too slow to serve administrative exigencies. Moreover, the shifting coalitions over time or across issues that characterize large, collegial legislative bodies may foster inconsistent or even erratic decisions harmful to the dictates of effective administration. Finally, the open and public nature of legislative deliberations would be destructive of the secrecy necessary for at least some executive actions, especially, but not only, in time of war.

This is not to say that the two branches cannot adopt policies or procedures to try to embody some of the virtues of the other. Presidents, for example, may institute policy review procedures within the executive branch that promote a free exchange of diverse views; and Congress may create procedures for accelerating consideration of pressing issues, perhaps including nonpublic committee meetings or floor debate. Yet if the executive branch tries to become too much like the deliberative legislature, it risks undermining its capacity for effective and energetic administration of the government. And if the legislature tries too hard to emulate the executive's capacity for quick, decisive, and often secret action, it endangers its capacity for wide-ranging and public deliberation on national policy.

Thus, the contrast between these two essential principles of deliberation and energy creates a tension within the political branches as well as between them. The energetic executive must, if it is to function wisely, embody some of the elements of sound deliberation; the deliberative legislature must, if it is to be a full partner in the government, possess some ability to function expeditiously, consistently, and, perhaps at times, secretly. The tension that results between the branches is clearest when the president faces a real or perceived need to act quickly in the national interest. Misgivings about Congress's ability to respond decisively may lead the president to act unilaterally, perhaps trespassing upon the constitutional prerogatives of the legislature. On the other hand, if the president is solicitous of Congress's prerogatives and asks for its views, the need for immediate action may distort legislative deliberations by imposing severe and unnatural time constraints. It is perhaps not too strong to say that much of the conflict that separation of powers has caused in American government throughout our history represents a working out of this tension between deliberation and energy.

The Democratic Side of Deliberative Democracy

The framers' design for deliberative democracy was a response to the governmental inadequacies and the democratic excesses of the 1780s. Large, unchecked state legislatures whose members were elected from small districts and served short terms had failed to deliberate wisely and consistently on policies to promote the common good. Too rarely did decisionmaking in these bodies demonstrate the kind of reason, order, information, commonality of interests, and farsightedness essential to sound deliberation. The framers believed that this problem was not unique to the early state legislatures; rather it was endemic to the most democratic forms of decisionmaking—by mass assemblies of the people or by very large representative bodies. Through the various features of their institutional design, the framers sought to make democratic institutions more deliberative. We are led to ask whether making them more deliberative also made them less democratic.

At one level the answer is undoubtedly yes. When the Maryland Senate refused in 1785–86 to join the state's House of Delegates in enacting paper money laws, it was by all accounts resisting widespread public desires. Its position, if wiser and more deliberative than that of the popular branch, was certainly less democratic. Yet this institution with its five-year terms and indirect mode of election was much admired by the framers and served as a model for the national Senate. Indeed, the framers gave their Senate an even longer term and staggered elections, further enhancing its capacity to resist unwise, if popular, measures.

Madison could hardly have been more forthright in his discussion of the desirability, even the duty, of the new national Senate to resist some popular demands:

> . . . such an institution may be sometimes necessary as a defense to the people against their own temporary errors and delusions. As the cool and deliberate sense of the community ought, in all governments, and actually will, in all free govern-

ments, ultimately prevail over the views of its rulers; so there
are particular moments in public affairs when the people,
stimulated by some irregular passion, or some illicit advantage, or misled by the artful misrepresentations of interested
men, may call for measures which they themselves will after-
wards be the most ready to lament and condemn. In these
critical moments, how salutary will be the interference of
some temperate and respectable body of citizens, in order to
check the misguided career and to suspend the blow meditated by the people against themselves, until reason, justice,
and truth can regain their authority over the public mind? [106]

Certainly, during these "critical moments" when the Senate's deliberations lead it to resist unwise, and even dangerous, measures pushed by
the people (and presumably passed by the House of Representatives), it
is acting, in at least some sense, undemocratically. The same can be said
when the President acts in accordance with Hamilton's prescription in
Federalist no. 71: "When occasions present themselves in which the interests of the people are at variance with their inclinations, it is the duty of
the persons whom they have appointed to be the guardians of those interests to withstand the temporary delusion in order to give them time
and opportunity for more cool and sedate reflection." [107] Similarly, the
Supreme Court functions undemocratically when it acts "to guard the
Constitution and the rights of individuals from the effects of those ill
humors which the arts of designing men, or the influence of particular
conjunctures, sometimes disseminate among the people themselves, and
which, though they speedily give place to better information, and more
deliberate reflection, have a tendency, in the meantime, to occasion dangerous innovations in the government, and serious oppressions of the
minor party in the community." [108]

The Senate, presidency, and Supreme Court were all designed to
have the capacity to resist unsound popular inclinations. Their more informed and more thoroughly reasoned deliberations could lead them to
oppose the less deliberative impulses of the citizenry. Deliberation thus
serves to check the excesses of democracy; in this respect deliberative
democracy of the type created in 1787 is necessarily less democratic than
direct democracy.

Yet as the framers understood it, when deliberation checks democracy
it does so to serve a deeper democratic, or republican, principle: the rule
of deliberative majorities. When, as a result of passion, interest, or the
demagogic appeals of ambitious men, the people fall prey to "temporary

errors or delusions," their immediate desires, their unwise and possibly unjust inclinations, must be resisted by those in positions of public trust until these temporary errors give way to "better information, and more deliberate reflection" so that "reason, justice, and truth can regain their authority over the public mind." The point is not that citizens cannot know their own interests or that public judgments ought to be superseded by the greater wisdom and objectivity of elected officials, but rather that the ruling force ought to be "the cool and deliberate sense of the community," and not every immediate desire or inclination: "The republican principle demands that the deliberate sense of the community should govern the conduct of those to whom they intrust the management of their affairs; but it does not require an unqualified complaisance to every sudden breeze of passion, or to every transient impulse."[109] It is deliberative majorities expressing informed and reasoned public judgments that will best promote the people's true interests. And if deliberative majorities are to rule, they must be protected against the dangers of unreflective popular sentiments.

Thus, the theory of deliberative democracy that undergirds the American constitutional order rests on the central proposition that there are two kinds of public voice in a democracy—one more immediate or spontaneous, uninformed, and unreflective; the other more deliberative, taking longer to develop and resting on a fuller consideration of information and arguments—and that only the latter is fit to rule. The framers also expressed this point as a distinction between passion and reason—"[I]t is the reason, alone, of the public, that ought to control and regulate the government. The passions ought to be controlled and regulated by the government";[110] between prejudice and interest—the people may be misled by artful men "who flatter their prejudices to betray their interests";[111] or between interests and inclinations—"[O]ccasions present themselves in which the interests of the people are at variance with their inclinations."[112] It follows that the proper standard for evaluating the democratic character of deliberative democracy is how well the institutions of government foster the rule of informed and reasoning majorities rather than the rule of uninformed, passionate, or prejudiced majorities.

Although the framers recognized that the people of the United States would independently reach considered judgments on some pressing national issues, they believed that on most issues most of the time deliberative majorities would best be formed *through* the institutions of government, as the representatives of the people reasoned about public

policy for their constituents. Under a well designed representative system, Madison wrote, "it may well happen that the public voice, pronounced by the representatives of the people, will be more consonant to
the public good than if pronounced by the people themselves, convened
for the purpose."[113] The deliberations of representatives will in general
better promote the public good than the deliberations of the people directly both because representatives are more knowledgeable and experienced than their constituents and because they make decisions in an
institutional environment that fosters collective reasoning about shared
interests. The people at large, on the other hand, usually lack the time,
information, and instrumentality for reasoning together about common
concerns. Thus, deliberative majorities will not normally exist independent of the governing institutions themselves.

According to Madison's formulation, properly designed representative institutions do not displace public attitudes with the personal views
of elected officials, but rather "refine and enlarge the public views."[114]
The result can be called "the public voice" even though it is not pronounced by the people directly and even though it may differ substantially from public attitudes prevailing at any particular time. What may
appear to be an incompatibility between public opinion and public policy
may actually reflect the contrast between unreflective public sentiments
and deliberative public judgments actualized through representative institutions.

It must be admitted, nonetheless, that institutional arrangements that
protect governmental deliberations from unreflective public opinion
might also sever policymaking from public opinion simply. Thus, if this
governing system is to maintain its democratic character, the deliberations of the representatives must also be firmly rooted in popular interests and sentiments. If the representatives of the people share the basic
interests and desires of their constituents, then their deliberations should
result in policies that will approximate what the people themselves would
have chosen had they engaged in a similar process of reasoning about
the information and arguments presented in the national councils. The
chief mechanism for ensuring a reliable link between the deliberations
of representatives and the interests and desires of the represented is the
electoral connection.

The members of the House, with their two-year terms and direct
popular election, were the most firmly tethered to popular sentiments.
Madison maintained that a representative's sense of duty and gratitude
towards his constituents together with more selfish motives such as the

desire to be reelected would cr ate a "communion of interests and sympathy of sentiments" between the members of the House and those they represented.[115] Although senators, with six-year terms and an indirect mode of election, were intended to be somewhat more insulated from immediate public opinion, election by the democratic state legislatures helped to ensure, as noted earlier, that senators would share the basic sentiments and desires of their constituents.

Even the original electoral college mechanism for selecting presidents, though removed from direct popular vote, was expected to result in the election of individuals who possessed the confidence, and shared the basic values, of the citizenry. As Hamilton noted, "the sense of the people" would operate in the choice of the president because the people or their representatives in the state legislatures would choose the electors, and electors so chosen would likely share the interests and desires of the voters of their state.[116] Such electors, in turn, were likely to vote for someone for president who by reputation, accomplishments, or professed political sentiments had substantial popular support.

The particular virtue of the electoral college mechanism was that it combined "the sense of the people" with an "immediate election . . . made by men most capable of analyzing the qualities adapted to the station and acting under circumstances favorable to deliberation."[117] In this respect the electoral college was intended to combine democratic and deliberative elements in a way analogous to the design for the system as a whole. The democratic element was the selection of electors by the people themselves or by their representatives, virtually ensuring that the electors would reflect public sentiments. The deliberative element was promoted by the constitutional requirement that the electors meet together within each state before voting and by their freedom to vote for whoever they believed would make the best president. The intention was that electors who shared the interests and sentiments of the voters of their state would reason together about who would make the best president based on their own experience in public affairs and their knowledge of the virtues and capabilities of the major political figures in the nation. Their choice, though rooted in "the sense of the people" and presumably compatible with popular interests and values, would not necessarily be identical to what would result from a direct popular election.

As noted earlier, one also sees this conjunction of popular sentiment and deliberation in the election of senators by state legislators. No political institutions in the states or nation during the 1780s were more democratic, or closer to the people, than the state legislatures. Large, often raucous, bodies with many men from the "middling classes," they reflected public attitudes, and occasionally passions, with a fidelity that was at times unsettling to many of the leading statesmen of the day.[118] Yet it was in these bodies that the framers vested the choice of the members of the less democratic, or more high-toned, branch of the national legislature. Given their character, it was a good bet that when these bodies sat down to choose someone to serve in the United States Senate "the sense of the people" would operate in ways similar to what was expected for the electoral college. The individuals chosen for the Senate would likely possess the confidence and respect of the citizenry, even though a direct popular vote might have resulted in a different choice. The expectation was that state legislators, however close to the people, would exercise some degree of independent judgment in determining who would make the best U.S. senator. Thus would this selection method conjoin democracy and deliberation.

The original ratifying conventions present another illustration of the same principle. The popular election of delegates to the state ratifying conventions represented a kind of rough popular referendum on the proposed Constitution, as opponents and supporters of the new plan vied for election to the conventions. Yet the ratifying conventions were more than just mechanisms for tallying public preferences; they were also deliberative institutions in which proponents and opponents of the new Constitution argued and debated its merits with a view to persuading the majority of the wisdom of their position. The historical record indicates that if the conventions had merely reflected public opinion and not functioned as independent deliberative bodies some states that did ratify would have refused to do so. In New York, for example, Anti-Federalists outnumbered Federalists 46–19 when the convention began on June 17, 1788, but ratification was approved 30–27 six weeks later.[119]

The key to the conjunction of democracy and deliberation in the original constitutional design is that the representatives of the people must both share the deep-seated interests and desires of their constituents and be free to exercise some substantial independent judgment in making policy decisions. While rooted in popular inclinations, the deliberations of representatives must not be bound to only popularly acceptable positions. If the democratic principle becomes too intrusive—if, for example, representatives were recallable between elections (as they were under the

Articles of Confederation)—then a key requisite of sound deliberation would be undermined. If, on the other hand, the deliberations of representatives are cut loose from their moorings in public attitudes and desires, then the democratic principle is compromised and the rule of deliberative majorities threatened.

CHAPTER THREE

Deliberation, Democracy, and Policymaking

> Modern parliaments not only represent the "will" of the
> people, they also deliberate. . . . [T]hey endeavor to solve
> concrete problems of communal activity.
>
> Carl Friedrich, 1968[1]

The framing of the U.S. Constitution in 1787 was a single
episode in the historical development of liberal democracy in
the West. It represents one particular institutional design for
conjoining deliberation and democracy. Others were and are
possible. Indeed, over the years most major Western democracies developed or adopted parliamentary institutions, rather
than the American separation of powers system. Although the
statesmen and theorists of liberal democracy have disagreed
as to how to fashion institutions that would best promote
sound deliberation while preserving democratic principles,
there has been, at least until the present century, substantial
agreement regarding the nature of the problem and the importance of the task.

The classic early statement of the issue was made by Edmund Burke in his famous Speech to the Electors of Bristol
in 1774. Having just been elected to Parliament from a city in
which he did not live, Burke delivered a speech to the voters
confronting the growing public sentiment that representatives
ought to be bound by authoritative instructions on public
matters issued by the electorate. Though well known, it is
worth quoting here at some length.

> Certainly, gentlemen, it ought to be the happiness
> and glory of a representative to live in the strictest
> union, the closest correspondence, and the most
> unreserved communication with his constituents.
> Their wishes ought to have great weight with him;
> their opinion high respect; their business unre-
> mitted attention. It is his duty to sacrifice his re-
> pose, his pleasures, his satisfactions, to theirs—

and above all, ever, and in all cases, to prefer their interest to his own.

But his unbiased opinion, his mature judgment, his enlightened conscience, he ought not to sacrifice to you, to any man, or to any set of men living. . . . Your representative owes you, not his industry only, but his judgment; and he betrays, instead of serving you, if he sacrifices it to your opinion.

. . . If government were a matter of will upon any side, yours, without question, ought to be superior. But government and legislation are matters of reason and judgment, and not of inclination; and what sort of reason is that in which the determination precedes the discussion, in which one set of men deliberate and another decide, and where those who form the conclusion are perhaps three hundred miles distant from those who hear the arguments?

. . . Parliament is a *deliberative* assembly of *one* nation, with *one* interest, that of the whole; where, not local purposes, not local prejudices ought to guide, but the general good, resulting from the general reason of the whole.[2]

Although representatives have an obligation to prefer the interests of their constituents to their own personal interests, they have an equally important obligation to exercise their independent judgment as to what policies would best promote the good of their constituents and of the nation. This judgment will be informed by the discussion and debate that occur *within* the legislative body; for only those who are directly exposed to the arguments can reach wise decisions. Burke, like the framers of the U.S. Constitution, believed that people's inclinations and interests do not necessarily coincide. The task of representatives is to reason together to ascertain and foster the people's true interests.

Across the Atlantic, early American statesmen besides the framers recognized the importance of deliberation to the success of democracy. The two most famous and important American founders not present at the Constitutional Convention were undoubtedly John Adams and Thomas Jefferson. For Adams one of the great virtues of local self-government was that it taught Americans "the habit of discussing, of deliberating, and of judging public affairs."[3] Jefferson similarly emphasized the importance of deliberation to democracy. In defending the trade embargo with Europe during his presidential administration, he described it as "an appeal to the deliberate understanding of our fellow citizens."[4] In letters written from retirement Jefferson criticized European monarchies for their insulation from "the peaceful deliberations and collected wisdom of the nation"; praised bicameralism in the American states because "experience has proved the benefit of subjecting questions to two separate bodies of deliberants"; and proposed the creation of small political units, called "wards," in which "the voice of the people would be thus fairly, fully, and peaceably expressed, discussed, and decided by the common reason of the society."[5]

In his lengthy and detailed analysis of American government and society, the Frenchman Alexis de Tocqueville frequently discussed the importance of political deliberation within the governing institutions or among the citizenry to the success of American democracy. Characteristic is his discussion of what is meant by the term "republic" in the United States: "It is an orderly state really founded on the enlightened will of the people. It is a conciliatory government under which resolutions have time to ripen, being discussed with deliberation and executed only when mature."[6]

Some decades later the English political theorist John Stuart Mill systematically analyzed the deliberative capacities of representative assemblies. In *Considerations on Representative Government* Mill, like the framers of the U.S. Constitution, agreed that legislatures were not well suited for the business of administration, a task that ought to be vested in a single set of hands. Rather, "what can be done better by a body than an individual is deliberation. When it is necessary or important to secure hearing and consideration to many conflicting opinions, a deliberative body is indispensable."[7] Mill went beyond the framers, however, in arguing that large representative bodies were not only poor administrators, but also poor drafters of legislation: "a numerous assembly is as little fitted for the direct business of legislation as for that of administration."[8] By relegating the essentially technical business of drafting legislation to a special body of "professional legislators," a Commission of Legislation, the representatives would be able to focus their efforts on broad policy issues, instructing the Commission on the kinds of bills they wanted drafted and then voting on its recommendations. (Here Mill's position is similar to that of Jefferson and Hamilton a century before that the Congress under the Articles of Confederation ought to free itself from excessive attention to details to focus on broad policy matters.)

In fashioning the broad outlines of public policy, Mill's legislature would serve the nation as its "Congress of Opinions":

> an arena in which not only the general opinion of the nation, but that of every section of it, and, as far as possible, of every

eminent individual whom it contains, can produce itself in full light and challenge discussion; where every person in the country may count upon finding somebody who speaks his mind as well or better than he could speak it himself—not to friends and partisans exclusively, but in the face of opponents, to be tested by adverse controversy; where those whose opinion is overruled feel satisfied that it is heard, and set aside not by a mere act of will, but for what are thought superior reasons, and commend themselves as such to the representatives of the majority of the nation.[9]

Mill's representative assembly is in all crucial respects a deliberative institution. The views of all major segments of society are publicly voiced and debated, and decisions are the result of "superior reasons," not the mere force of numbers or an act of will.

A few years later political scientist (and future president) Woodrow Wilson applied the same interest in deliberation to his classic study of the U.S. Congress, *Congressional Government.* Wilson particularly faulted Congress for its failure to engage in the kind of open and public debate on major national issues that would foster community-wide discussion and reflection and thereby elevate public opinion throughout the nation. His point was not that deliberation was absent from Congress, but that it was hidden from view behind the closed doors of the standing committees: "the House virtually both deliberates and legislates in small sections."[10] It "delegates not only its legislative but also its deliberative functions to its Standing Committees."[11] Revenue and appropriations were an exception; for on these "Congress acts with considerable deliberation and care. . . . [Q]uestions of revenue and supply are always given full measure of debate."[12]

This same attention to deliberation characterized Wilson's later lectures on American government, published as *Constitutional Government in the United States* in 1908. As in the earlier work, Wilson criticized the House of Representatives for the absence of wide-ranging public debates on matters of national concern. "The nation," he maintained, "does not look to it for counsel [but] . . . has come to regard it as what it is, a piece of lawmaking machinery, but not a deliberative assembly in whose debates it may expect to find public questions clarified, disputed matters settled."[13] He acknowledged, however, that "there is oftentimes genuine common counsel in the committee rooms of the House."[14] The Senate fared better. Its tradition that the full body ought to reach independent judgments on major issues remained strong. "The Senate is a deliberative assembly," Wilson affirmed.[15] It is, *"par excellence,* the chamber of debate."[16]

Whatever the differences in the detailed views of these various political actors and thinkers (and others could be cited), a central belief of leading statesmen and theorists of liberal democracy in the eighteenth and nineteenth centuries was that for political democracy to be successful it must provide means and mechanisms by which public opinion would be, in Madison's words, "refine[d]" and "enlarge[d]" through informed and dispassionate reasoning about common concerns. The great danger to democracy was the rule of uninformed, passionate, or prejudiced opinion; the great challenge was to devise laws and institutions that would foster the rule of deliberative majorities.

Within the bounds of this fundamental agreement, however, lie quite distinct views as to where and how deliberative majorities should be formed. At one pole is the view that the essential and guiding deliberation should take place among the citizens themselves. The prototypical example is the New England town meeting, or perhaps Jefferson's ward democracy. Citizens, it is maintained, ought to come together and reason with each other to discern their common interests and to devise the appropriate means for achieving them. Sometimes called "classical republicanism," this is what Jane Mansbridge describes as the "older understanding of democracy": "In that older understanding, people who disagree do not vote; they reason together until they agree on the best answer. Nor do they elect representatives to reason for them. They come together with their friends to find agreement."[17] Advocates of such direct citizen deliberation are usually suspicious of distant representative institutions and are likely to hold that (1) as much governmental power as possible should be exercised by the people directly or by the institutions closest to them (and thus closest to their deliberations) and (2) when representatives must make decisions they should, to the extent possible, defer to the deliberations of their constituents. Over the years a variety of proposals have been advanced to promote direct citizen deliberation, including town meeting forms of government, neighborhood assemblies to discuss public issues, the initiative and referendum process of direct citizen lawmaking, and, more recently, the use of electronic media, such as two-way television, to establish a kind of electronic democracy.[18]

At the opposite pole is the view that policy deliberations ought to be entrusted entirely to the representatives of the people. Burke's Speech to the Electors of Bristol seems to say as much. In this it parallels Montesquieu's view that "the great advantage of representatives is, their capacity of discussing public affairs. For this the people collectively are extremely unfit, which is one of the chief inconveniences of a democracy."[19] Perhaps the modern theorist who most clearly articulates this argument is Willmoore Kendall. In Kendall's view, the voters choose the most virtuous citizens for political office and these virtuous officials then "arrive . . . at policy decisions through a process of deliberation."[20] The American constitutional system was based "on the ability of the people, i.e., at least a majority of the people, to make sound judgments regarding the virtue of their neighbors, not on the ability of the people to deliberate on matters of policy."[21] Thus, for Kendall, there is no need for the citizens to deliberate about public policy either during election campaigns or between elections. Having chosen the most virtuous to deliberate for them, they can trust their leaders to make reasoned decisions in their interest.

As the discussion in the previous chapter indicates, the original plan for the American constitutional system lies somewhere between these two poles. Contrary to those who put their faith in direct citizen deliberations, the framers were persuaded by the history of republics as well as by their own experiences that sound political deliberation could only be reliably achieved through carefully crafted institutions. On the other hand, they did not see their system as simply displacing citizen deliberations with those of the wise and virtuous. It was, after all, the rule of the "cool and deliberate sense of the community" that the framers claimed to promote, not simply the rule of the most virtuous within the community. Representatives, according to Madison, would pronounce "the public voice," not merely their own enlightened judgments. Indeed, following Kendall's formulation it is hard to see what relationship would necessarily exist between the deliberations of the virtuous and the wishes of the community.

The problem with applying an essentially Burkean (or perhaps neo-Burkean) view of representation to the American system is that it vastly underestimates the role that policy issues would necessarily play in campaigns for national office. Why would—or should—citizens restrict their considerations to the identification of the virtuous when in a diverse and dynamic political community the virtuous themselves will disagree about many of the most important matters facing the nation? This disagreement among the virtuous will likely mirror similar disagreement among the voters themselves. If the citizens of a democracy (a form of government that purports to give the decisive governing power to the majority) care about public issues, they will hardly ignore the policy positions of candidates for high office. Indeed, it is the very discussion of policy issues during an election campaign that ensures that those selected to positions of authority will share the basic interests, dispositions, and attitudes of the citizenry. As long as candidates are not forced to commit themselves to specific policy proposals (especially nonincumbents who have yet to study the salient issues in a legislative setting) and as long as representatives are not recallable between elections (which would subject them to control by unreflective public opinion) then policy discussion throughout a campaign will not foreclose subsequent deliberation on the details of legislative policy.

While the framers put great faith in the principle of representation, it would be a mistake to overstate the independence of representatives from majority sentiment in the system they designed. Elections are more than a mechanism for choosing deliberators. They also ensure that deliberations within distant institutions are rooted in popular interests and desires. The framers sought to create not merely a deliberative government, but a deliberative democracy.

Deliberation Defined

The deliberation that lies at the core of the kind of democracy established by the American constitutional system can be defined most simply as *reasoning on the merits of public policy.* As commonly and traditionally understood, deliberation is a reasoning process in which the participants seriously consider substantive information and arguments and seek to decide individually and to persuade each other as to what constitutes good public policy. Thus, deliberation includes a variety of activities often called "problem solving" or "analytic": the investigation and identification of social, economic, or governmental problems; the evaluation of current policies or programs; the consideration of various and competing proposals; and the formulation of legislative or administrative remedies. In any genuine deliberative process the participants must be open to the facts, arguments, and proposals that come to their attention and must share a general willingness to learn from their colleagues and others.

So defined, the proximate aim of a deliberative process is the conferral of some public good or benefit. Such a benefit need not necessarily be national in scope (such as a healthy economy or a sound national defense); it may instead be a locally oriented good (such as a flood control project or a new highway), a good directed toward a broad class of citizens (as with civil rights laws or labor legislation), or even transnational in its reach (such as foreign aid). Thus, the existence of deliberation does not turn on the distinction between local and national interests. An overriding desire to serve one's local constituents does not in itself close a legislator to the persuasive effects of information and arguments, although such a legislator will respond to different kinds of appeals than one who seeks to promote national interests. This is true even if the desire to confer local benefits results directly from self-interested calculations, such as the representative's desire to be reelected; for the legislator who seeks singlemindedly to be reelected may well find that in some situations this goal requires him to give real consideration to the merits of legislative proposals designed to benefit his constituents. (More on this issue in chapter 5.)

Although legislators may deliberate about local, or partial, interests as well as those of a national dimension, there remains a relationship between the likelihood and nature of deliberation in Congress and the scope of the public benefits that legislators seek to confer. Consider, for example, legislators who deliberate about how to promote the well-being of specific interests. If such legislators see their job essentially in terms of doing good for external groups, they will be inclined to accept the groups' determination as to how this should be done; for who knows the groups' interests better than they do. The narrower and more specific the group (wheat farmers, auto workers, coal miners, etc.) the less difference of opinion or conflict there will be and therefore the less need for such a legislator to consider different arguments or to reason about alternative proposals. However, as the scope of the legislator's concerns widens, to encompass more or broader interests, the more difficult it will become to defer to the interests themselves for guidance. A variety of differing and often conflicting opinions will highlight the complexity of the issues at stake and place a greater obligation on the lawmaker to exercise some independent judgment. For the legislator who seeks to promote the national interest, personal deliberation will be essential; insofar as other legislators share the same goal, collective deliberation will be pervasive.

Personal deliberation by individual legislators does not require that others in the lawmaking body share the same goals. A member of the House, for example, could deliberate in a serious way about how the federal government could solve a transportation problem within his or her district even if no other House members shared the same concern. Collective deliberation, however, necessarily requires some sharing of goals, purposes, or values. If legislators are to reason together about the merits of public policy, there must be some common ground for the arguments and appeals essential to deliberation. Whether the shared goal is quite specific and well defined (e.g., a national health insurance plan along the British model) or much broader and even somewhat vague (e.g., a healthy economy or a sound national defense), it will provide the basis for legislators, who may have little else in common, to share information and to reason and argue together about public policy.[22]

Although the geographically based representation of the American system of government has a tendency to elevate localized interests and needs over broad programmatic concerns, district and state representation also provides a solid basis for the sharing of goals within Congress. Similar kinds of constituencies are likely to have common interests and needs and therefore similar desires or expectations for national policy. Inner-city residents throughout the nation are likely to have similar desires regarding social welfare policy. Farmers from the Midwest, South, and West are likely to agree on the need for price supports. Blue-collar workers in threatened industries across the country are likely to desire high tariffs or other protectionist measures. Those elected to Congress to represent these kinds of constituents will soon discover that many of their colleagues represent similar electorates and thus share many of the same policy goals. In some cases such like-minded legislators institutionalize and promote their shared policy interests through an informal caucus which helps them to share information and ideas and to coordinate policy efforts.

In describing what deliberation is, it is important to clarify what it is not; for policy deliberation is not just any kind of reasoning involved in the policy process. As understood throughout this book, policy deliberation necessarily involves reasoning about the substantive benefits of public policy, reasoning about some *public* good—some good external to the decisionmakers themselves. "Reasoning on the merits" of public policy means reasoning about how public policy can benefit the broader society or some significant portion thereof. Thus, there is a sharp analytical distinction between deliberation and merely self-interested calculations (however complex the relationship between these two in practice). Similarly, deliberation does not include reasoning about legislative tactics, such as drafting a bill to facilitate its referral to a sympathetic committee or determining how to use the rules of the House or Senate to greatest advantage during the legislative process.[23]

Although a deliberative process is per se rational or analytical, the values or dispositions that the participants bring to bear on the determination of good public policy may reflect a host of diverse influences: general upbringing, parental values, personal experiences, the views of friends and acquaintances, influential teachers, partisan attachments, social class, economic status, etc. Thus, it is not surpising that different individuals often reach quite opposed conclusions about the merits of policy proposals even when exposed to the same information and arguments. Such disagreement is not in itself evidence of the absence of deliberation.

Deliberation, as defined here, may take a variety of forms. It may be a largely consensual process in which like-minded individuals work together to fashion the details of a policy they all desire; or it may involve deep-seated conflicts over fundamental issues or principles. It may result in unanimity of view, where no votes are necessary; or it may reveal sharp disagreements that require formal voting to determine the majority view. It may range from private reflection in the quiet of an office or study to an emotionally charged exchange on the floor of the House or Senate. It may take the form of open and public discussions preserved in official records or of private exchanges hidden from public view. It may involve direct discussions among elected officials themselves or, perhaps more frequently, conversations among their staff. It may be limited to those who hold formal positions in the government, either elective or appointive; or it may include the ideas and opinions of interest groups, trade associations, national organizations, or the scholarly community.

Nonetheless, however diverse the various manifestations of deliberation, every deliberative process involves three essential elements: information, arguments, and persuasion.

INFORMATION

"[I]nformation is the weaponry, the ammunition of legislative battle."[24] Reasoning on the merits of public policy requires at a minimum that serious consideration be given to pertinent substantive information on policy issues. Such information may include basic facts and figures on some social, economic, or national security issue (such as unemployment rates, housing conditions and needs, or the military capabilities of other nations), scientific or technical information (such as the impact of airborne pollutants on public health), details and evaluations of current or past legislative or administrative policies (possibly including experiences at the state and local level or in other countries), and the content and likely consequences of proposed policies. Other kinds of information, such as knowledge of parliamentary procedures or estimates of upcoming votes, do not bear on the merits of an issue and therefore are not elements of the deliberative process itself, however important such information may be to the outcome of the policy process.

Both Congress and the executive branch have invested heavily in the collection, analysis, and dissemination of substantive, policy relevant information. It has even been argued that "[g]athering and processing information is perhaps the central activity in the operation of Congress."[25] Over the years Congress has created four distinct agencies whose main purpose is to generate and analyze information for policy purposes: the Congressional Research Service, the General Accounting Office, the Congressional Budget Office, and the Office of Technology Assessment. In addition, some thousands of committee and personal staff in Congress are heavily occupied with collecting and distilling information for their superiors. Much of this congressional investment in information is of fairly recent origin and results from the widespread perception within the House and Senate in the 1960s that Congress was overmatched by the information resources of the executive branch.

Within the executive branch the generation of policy relevant information is widely dispersed among the two-million-member bureaucracy. It is also concentrated within specific agencies whose main business is the production of statistical data for use by policymakers. These include, among others, the Bureau of the Census, the Bureau of Labor Statistics, the National Center for Health Statistics, and the Bureau of Justice Statistics. Numerous other agencies fund, monitor, and evaluate empirical research into issues of direct policy relevance.

In addition to governmental agencies and personnel, an equally important source of policy relevant information is interest groups and their lobbyists. Organizations that represent the interests of specific groups such as farmers, labor, or business or that have broader ideological goals such as a clean environment or tax reform are a major source of highly focused information on the issues of concern to them. Such organizations have both the interest and the resources to generate detailed information and to put it into a form that is useful to policymakers. As William K. Muir, Jr., noted about lobbyists who tried to influence the California state legislature, "[t]he task of the lobbyist . . . was to provide basic information 'quickly' and intelligibly."[26] That the same characterization would apply to lobbyists of the U.S. Congress is supported by the conclusions of a political journalist who spent two years in the mid-1970s studying the Senate through special access to Senator Edmund Muskie (D., Maine) and his staff: "it may come as a surprise that more than ninety-nine per cent of lobbying effort is spent not on parties, weekend hosting, and passing plain white envelopes, but trying to persuade minds through facts and reasons."[27] This is not to deny, of course, the problem of bias when interested individuals and groups bring information and arguments to bear on the legislative process.

Information may serve a variety of distinct purposes in a deliberative process. First, it may educate policy advocates themselves as they fashion specific administrative or legislative proposals. Second, policy advocates (or opponents) may use information to try to persuade other decision-makers of the merits (or shortcomings) of proposed policies. Finally, the contestants in the policy process may gather, distill, and disseminate information in order to mobilize support for, or opposition to, a policy initiative outside of the governing institutions themselves, among, for example, the media, state and local officials, interest groups, or the broader public.

ARGUMENTS

"Very few facts are able to tell their own story, without comments to bring out their meaning."[28] Information alone is not enough to determine appropriate courses of action; for it is necessary also to connect mere facts with desirable goals. This is the function of arguments. Those who propose new policies will not only produce information describing the nature of pressing social, economic, or national security problems but will also fashion arguments explaining how their proposals will ameliorate the existing problem at a reasonable cost. Opponents, who may or may not dispute the factual claims of the advocates, will fashion contrary arguments purporting to show how the new policies will not accomplish their aims, will do so only at great cost, or will have other unacceptable consequences. Although closely joined in practice, information and arguments are analytically distinct elements of deliberation.

Arguments on the merits of policy proposals constitute the bulk of the formal decisionmaking process within the U.S. Congress. Such arguments are found in (1) oral and written testimony presented at congressional hearings by representatives of the administration, members of Congress, or outside individuals and groups; (2) formal committee reports submitted to the full bodies (often including both majority and minority opinions); (3) debate on the floor of the House and Senate; and, where applicable, (4) conference committee reports and (5) veto messages. Moreover, policy arguments may constitute an important element in the informal stages of the deliberative process, such as private meetings involving legislators, staff aides, interest group representatives, or officials of the administration. Whether presented in formal or informal arenas, policy arguments may range from narrow technical issues to the broadest political principles.

The kinds of arguments advanced in a body like Congress depend not only on the quality of the arguments themselves, that is, their intrinsic persuasiveness, but also on the audience to which they are addressed. Note, for example, how farm lobbyists opposed to a reclamation bill modified their arguments for different kinds of legislators: "We talked to eastern economy-minded congressmen about spending the taxpayers' money on big corporation subsidies. We talked to southern congressmen about monopoly, and we talked to congressmen in reclamation states about the threat to all future reclamation projects if this bill were passed."[29] Because different groups of legislators share distinctive interests and beliefs, some kinds of arguments are more likely to be successful with one group than with another.

In some situations, however, the arguments advanced during public phases of the legislative process may be directed less to the legislators in attendance than to the broader public. This is quite common, for example, during a highly publicized committee hearing on some new or controversial issue when witnesses and committee members seek to generate favorable publicity and thus to promote public interest and support. Similarly, legislators who engage in extensive floor debate (particularly in the Senate where the rules are more flexible) may be seeking less to persuade their colleagues than to influence public opinion for or against the matter at hand. It should not be surprising if arguments addressed to the broader public are, at times, of a quite different nature from those addressed directly to other legislators—more "rhetorical," moralistic, simplistic, or perhaps demagogic. An interesting question, to which we shall return, is how arguments addressed to outside audiences, facilitated by the opening up of the legislative process to public scrutiny in the past several decades, affect the nature and quality of deliberation within Congress. (This is not to say, of course, that arguments addressed to the people by legislators, presidents, or others cannot be deliberative, that is, cannot enhance the public's reasoned understanding of public policy issues. This is addressed in chapters 7 and 8.)

PERSUASION

"[P]ersuasiveness is the most underrated resource in politics."[30] Deliberation requires more than the mere existence of information and arguments; it requires also that these have a real persuasive effect. Persuasion, then, is the final stage, and the singular mark, of a deliberative process. Persuasion occurs when information and arguments on the merits of an issue lead a participant in the policymaking process to take a substantive position that he or she had not taken prior to engaging in the process. It thereby involves some kind of change or development in the policymaker's understanding.

In some cases a member of Congress may actually change his or her mind on an issue after considering the relevant information and arguments. Legislative case studies of Congress report a variety of such examples. During the Eisenhower administration, Republican Representative Stuyvesant Wainright decided to oppose the President's school aid bill even though he had originally sponsored it in the House: "Wainright conceded that he had introduced the administration's school bill at the request of the Secretary of Health, Education and Welfare. 'Then we had four months of testimony, and I changed my mind.'"[31]

In the early 1960s Democratic Representative Kenneth Roberts, who chaired the Subcommittee on Health and Safety of the House Committee in Interstate and Foreign Commerce, switched from strong opponent of giving the federal government enforcement authority over air pollution, a key feature of the administration's proposed Clean Air Act, to a vigorous supporter.

> The chief factor [in Roberts's change of mind] was that he simply began to see the problem of air pollution in broader terms than he had before. He had become increasingly aware of the serious problem in Birmingham, near his home. In discussions with Dr. Prindle of the Division of Air Pollution [of the Public Health Service] he learned more about the killing smog in London in December 1962, which Prindle had observed first-hand. He became convinced both that the problem was a truly national one and that it offered an immediate threat to the health of millions of Americans.[32]

When opponents of the bill confronted him during the House hearings with his earlier opposition to federal enforcement, "Roberts responded immediately with the proverbs, 'Consistency is a hobgoblin of little minds' and 'The wise man changes his mind and the fool never does.'"[33]

During the Nixon administration Democratic Representative Wilbur Mills, Chairman of the House Ways and Means Committee, moved from initial opposition to the president's proposed reform of the welfare program, titled the Family Assistance Plan, to energetic support after several months of committee hearings and executive sessions. A month after the committee voted to report a bill, Mills "went before the House Rules Committee to obtain clearance for the legislation to go to the floor, and recounted his 'personal conversion' with a zeal—passion would not be too strong a term—that the Capitol had not before seen in the chairman of Ways and Means."[34] Before the full House Mills explained why he relented on his earlier opposition to including the "working poor" in the bill: "I became convinced that this was the right thing to do."[35] Although it is impossible to determine how often legislators are moved by facts and arguments to change their minds, such persuasion may well be more common than is usually believed.

Genuine persuasion, however, need not result in an actual change of mind; for often representatives and senators have no initial preferences on an issue, or at best only broad dispositions. If a policymaker without a detailed initial position reaches a firm decision on a legislative matter as a result of reasoning through the merits of the issue, this would also constitute persuasion. Although this kind of persuasion is more difficult to identify than a clear change of mind, it is equally the sign of deliberation.

Although newly elected members of Congress may carry with them into the legislature policy preferences on some subjects, they will face many issues there for the first time. It is unlikely that their prior experience will have exposed them to the range and breadth of issues they will be forced to confront in Congress, especially in the areas of foreign and military policy, which have no direct corollary in state and local government or in the private sector. Moreover, even veteran members of Congress are forced to address new issues as they move to new committees or as the legislative agenda changes over time. For example, in 1980 Representative Dan Quayle (R., Indiana) was elected to the U.S. Senate after serving four years in the House. As a member of the new majority party, he became chairman of the Employment Subcommittee of the Committee of Labor and Human Resources during his first year in the Senate. In his study of Quayle's Senate career, Richard Fenno writes that "[Quayle's] first task as chairman was to learn something about 'the way the world is' in the tangle of issues encompassing manpower, employment, and training. He was totally unfamiliar with the policy area and with the issue networks that had formed over time to shape policy making in that area."[36] Election to the Senate, appointment to specific committees, and chairmanship of one subcommittee forced Quayle to confront unfamiliar issues on which he did not have specific preexisting preferences.

Thus, the members of Congress are often required to make decisions in areas where they do not have settled views. Unless the representative or senator simply defers to others on these new issues, he or she must become sufficiently informed to make reasoned decisions in committee or on the floor. The information and arguments made available in committee hearings and reports, during floor debates, and through the activities of staff and interest groups will in most cases provide legislators with ample material for reaching informed judgments.

Even when preferences already exist in the relevant subject area, they may be little more than broad goals or values that provide little guidance for making specific legislative decisions. A desire, for example, for social justice, a healthy economy, or a sound national defense will not give the legislator sufficient direction on how to vote on the highly detailed bills and amendments that come before committees and the full bodies. Even a preference for something as specific as national health insurance will not help much in formulating the actual details of a program or in choosing among a variety of competing alternatives. Here more is required than the mere existence of a preference if the legislator is to make an informed decision. What is called for is a careful analysis of the nature of the health problem in the United States, the extent of existing insurance coverage, experiences in other countries, and the costs, feasibility, and likely consequences of the various alternative approaches.

When legislators develop reasoned judgments on legislative matters about which they originally had no opinion or only broad preferences, they are as much "persuaded" by the information and arguments brought to their attention as when they change their mind from a previously affirmed position. There may be a tendency to assume that because the members of Congress often end up on the side expected, the reasoned consideration of information and arguments played no part in getting them there. Persuasion in these circumstances is less obvious, though probably much more common, than that resulting in a clear change of mind. As Senator Muskie once commented on a Senate floor debate, "The debate didn't change my mind. It made up my mind."[37] It is in making up minds rather than changing minds that we are likely to observe the main persuasive impact of information and arguments.[38]

Deliberation Eclipsed

Deliberation, as here defined and as addressed by leading eighteenth- and nineteenth-century theorists and practitioners of liberal democracy, has not been the focus of the attention of scholars of American democracy throughout most of this century. Powerful alternative interpretations of legislative and governmental decisionmaking have replaced the earlier focus on the deliberative functions and capacities of governing institutions.

BARGAINING AND GROUP THEORIES

No idea is more responsible for this development than the view that politics reduces to the struggle of group interests. If groups and their interests are what really matter in politics, then there must be some mechanism through which partial interests can be aggregated into national policies. Bargaining generally, and especially logrolling—when individuals trade support for each other's proposals—seems the natural means for achieving this aggregation. No one presented this view more clearly and forthrightly than Arthur Bentley in his famous treatise, *The Process of Government*:

> Logrolling is, . . . in fact, the most characteristic legislative process. When one condemns it "in principle," it is only by contrasting it with some assumed pure public spirit which is supposed to guide legislators, or which ought to guide them, and which enables them to pass judgment in jovian calm on that which is best "for the whole people." . . . [But] when we have reduced the legislative process to the play of group interests, then log-rolling, or give and take, appears as the very nature of the process. It is compromise. . . . It is trading. It is the adjustment of interests. . . . There never was a time in the history of the American Congress when legislation was conducted in any other way.[39]

This accommodation of conflicting interests by logrolling, however, is not readily apparent to those who observe the formal workings of Congress. On the contrary, the members of Congress appear to reason and deliberate about broad national interests. But this is deceptive, for "along with all this log-rolling in all its forms goes great activity of reasoning, theorizing, and argument, and at times the argument seems to be the cause of all that is happening. In this latter case as in the others it merely provides a technical agency for the transaction."[40] Thus, the reality of the legislative process lies not in the presentation of information and arguments in public hearings, in a committee's reasoned defense of its proposals in a formal report to the full body, or in debate and persuasion on the floor of the House and Senate, but rather in the orchestration of deals, the trading of votes, and the hard-headed compromises that are arranged off-stage or through subtle manipulation of the formal process itself.

Although Bentley's work was not immediately influential, it was the inspiration for the "group theory," or pluralist interpretation, of American politics that gained prominence in the 1950s and 1960s. Like Bentley, the proponents of this view emphasized the importance of log-rolling and bargaining as devices for reaching collective decisions (although most did not go as far as Bentley in seemingly reducing all politics to trading). David Truman, for example, in his influential work, *The Governmental Process*, defined logrolling as "a group's giving support to a proposal that may bear no relation or only the most tenuous relation to its own objectives; in return it receives similar support from the group it has assisted."[41] Echoing his mentor, he defended logrolling as a legitimate and necessary means for reaching collective decisions in Congress: "fundamentally . . . the trading of support is a technique for the adjustment of interests. These interests must be adjusted in some fashion. . . . The very essence of the legislative process is the willingness to accept trading as a means."[42] As Theodore Lowi concluded in his critique of group theories, "[pluralism] provided a theoretical basis for giving to each according to his claim . . . . In other words, *it transformed access and logrolling from necessary evil to greater good.*"[43]

In its emphasis on vote trading and bargaining among conflicting groups rather than collective deliberation about shared interests, the group theory of politics had a wide-ranging influence on theories or interpretations of policymaking in American national government, and particularly in Congress. No institution, it is argued, better recreates the conflict of interests present in American society or is more suited for the peaceful resolution of this conflict through bargaining than the U.S. Congress. The geographical basis of representation, independent elections, the formal equality of the members, and a decentralized policy-making process all foster decision by bargaining:

> Bargaining . . . is particularly suited to a decision-system in which every man has some influence, no man or group has undivided control over important resources of influence, and in which men who are in a formal sense equals must bring a common interest out of a diversity and conflict of interests. Such a system is built for bargaining.[44]

The legislative process in Congress requires a succession of majority votes—by subcommittees, committees, and the full bodies—before a bill becomes a law. Majorities must be built anew at each stage of the process. This puts a premium on the techniques of coalition building: "The congressional *modus operandi* is one of fragmentation and decentralization. . . . In such circumstances, congressional politics becomes coalition politics. That is, proponents of various proposals seek, through bargaining, compromise, negotiation, or 'logrolling,' to assemble fragments of power into winning coalitions."[45]

The bargaining interpretation has been widely accepted by students of Congress. It is emphasized in many of the leading studies on Congress and congressional policymaking, including works on procedures,[46] roles,[47] leadership,[48] budgetary policymaking,[49] and defense policy.[50] Although it is not generally argued that bargaining is the exclusive means for reaching collective decisions in Congress, many of the leading interpretations clearly reflect the view that bargaining is the predominant or characteristic way in which conflict is resolved and majorities built. One recent work calls bargaining "a ubiquitous feature of the legislative process" and cites "the widespread belief that bargaining is endemic to the legislative process."[51] Indeed, a few scholars have gone so far as to identify legislative behavior with bargaining simply:

> [B]argaining . . . is a political situation *par excellence*. It is distinguished . . . by imperfectly shared goals and widely distributed resources. . . . If those who find themselves in such a situation are to maximize their goals, they must engage in a little politicking: That is, they must trade off their goals and resources. . . . We refer to such bargaining as legislative in character, whatever its institutional focus.[52]

Three types of bargaining are often distinguished: the logroll, the compromise (or splitting the difference), and the use of side payments.[53] As the above selections suggest, the *logroll* is the most frequently discussed. A logroll occurs when two or more members of Congress trade support for each other's bill or proposal. It may occur at any stage in the legislative process and involve either a small number of members or large groups. Logrollers may trade support for different provisions or features to be contained in a single statute, such as a public works bill which distributes benefits in discrete packages throughout the nation, or they may trade their votes on several different bills, not necessarily bearing any substantive relationship to each other.

One prominent example of a classic logroll involving unrelated bills is the passage of the Food Stamp Act of 1964 (to be examined at greater length in the next chapter). In the spring of 1964 liberal Democratic supporters of the Food Stamp bill in the House of Representatives, most representing northern urban districts, faced solid Republican opposition and likely defections by conservative, mostly southern and rural, Democrats. On the eve of the vote, supporters were still some votes short of a majority. They knew, however, that their votes would be needed for the passage of the pending wheat-cotton farm bill, much desired by southern and rural Democrats. Thus evolved the strategy of tying the votes on the two bills together: northern and urban Democrats would trade their support for wheat-cotton in exchange for southern and rural Democratic support for food stamps:

> Gradually during March it became clear that the trade would involve the food stamp bill and the wheat-cotton bill. No formal announcement was made of such a trade. Indeed, no formal meeting was held at which leaders of urban and rural blocs agreed on it. Instead, and this is typical of the operations of the House, it was a matter of a favorable psychological climate. The more the individual members and the press talked about a specific trade of rural votes on food stamps for urban votes on wheat-cotton the more firmly the exchange became implanted in the minds of the members.[54]

To ensure that the trade was carried out, the leadership of the House arranged to have the wheat-cotton debate and vote immediately after the vote on food stamps. This kept the House in session until well after midnight on the night of April 8. According to the leading interpretation, vote trading ensured the passage of both bills: food stamps, 229–189, and wheat-cotton, 211–203.

The *compromise*, unlike the logroll, requires the participants to moderate their demands or goals. Two or more irreconcilable positions are put forward and resolution is reached by splitting the difference. This type of bargaining is said to be especially characteristic of conference committee decisionmaking. For example, when the House and Senate differ over an appropriation level, the natural resolution is to split the difference by agreeing on a figure midway between the two positions. Moreover, when the two branches propose different features or provisions for the same bill, they may reach agreement by trading off provisions, which may be simply another way of splitting the difference. Consider the following account by a Senate aide of the efforts by House and Senate staff to reach a conference committee resolution of the two versions of the Clean Air Act amendments of 1976:

> We [the Senate staff] met with the House staff . . . and agreed
> that reconciliation of all issues from both bills is impossible. I
> suggested we try a trade-off approach. We put together pack-
> ages from both bills side by side that seemed to lend them-
> selves to trade-off from a viewpoint of neatness of bartering,
> if not from a viewpoint of policy.[55]

Here the actual bargaining was, in effect, delegated by the members of
the conference committee to their staff. As in all compromises neither
side ended up with all it wanted. Those faced with the prospects of compromise are always forced to decide whether "half a loaf is better than
none."

The third type of bargaining, the *use of side payments*, is characterized
by the inducement of a non-policy reward or punishment to influence a
legislator's behavior. It is usually engineered by someone in a leadership
position with control over resources or perquisites. A popular president,
for example, employs this technique when he induces support for his
legislative program from legislators of the other party by promising not
to campaign actively against them in the next election. There were reports in President Ronald Reagan's first term that he made such a promise to some southern Democrats in Congress in return for their support
of his major tax cut in 1981. Similarly, the Speaker of the House or the
Majority Leader in the Senate may use their influence over such items
as committee assignments, office space, and congressional delegations
to foreign nations to influence the legislative behavior of the members.
Outright bribery is perhaps the starkest example of the use of side payments. Although it is probably quite rare in Congress, there have been
several documented cases in recent decades.

As these definitions illustrate, none of these forms of bargaining necessarily involves reasoning on the merits of legislative proposals. What is
controlling in a bargain is not a judgment on the merits of an issue, but
a hard-headed calculation that support for a bill must be "purchased"
with something of value to other legislators, such as a vote on an unrelated matter or a non-policy benefit of some sort. In a pure bargain the
merits of an issue are quite irrelevant to the process of reaching a collective decision, however important the merits may be to the advocates of
each position. In the logroll on the food stamp and wheat-cotton bills in
1964, for example, advocates of each bill, presumably convinced of the
wisdom of their own proposal, traded their support for a proposal they
otherwise would have opposed in exchange for votes for their bill. Indeed, it was precisely because many northern Democrats were uncon-

vinced of the merits of wheat-cotton and many southern Democrats of the merits of food stamps that a trade was necessary. If, on the other hand, an appeal to the merits of a proposal is effective in garnering support from others, then something other than bargaining must be involved; for here the legislator appealed to is moved not by the expectation of receiving something of value in exchange for his support but by his judgment that the proposal at issue will promote good public policy. Thus, bargaining and deliberation are analytically distinct activities, however difficult to distinguish in practice.[56]

Of the several types of bargaining, making side payments is the easiest to distinguish from deliberation; for the offer of non-policy rewards or punishments to influence legislative behavior involves appeals that are quite distinct from those that are effective in a deliberative process. When logrolling is involved, distinguishing bargaining from deliberation can be complicated by the fact that one legislator may seek to arrange a logroll by arguing its "merits" to another. That is, one legislator may try to show another that the logroll will truly serve his particular interests as well. Yet this kind of persuasion is not the same as that involved in deliberation, as here defined. The difference is that in a deliberative process one legislator appeals to another by arguing the substantive merits of his own proposal. In a classic logroll, on the other hand, the merits of one legislator's proposal is irrelevant to the others; for each side seeks only a marriage of convenience as a device for building a majority in support of its particular goals. Of course, the prospective logroller may, prior to entering a deal, reason about the merits of his own proposal, as we would expect the legislator from a wheat-producing district to work with his constituents, organized agricultural interests, and other legislators from similar districts to fashion a proposal that will genuinely benefit wheat farmers. This kind of deliberation, however, should not be confused with logrolling itself, which would occur later and, *qua* logrolling, would not involve appeals to the merits of the proposal to benefit wheat producers.

Compromise, or splitting the difference, is the type of bargaining most difficult to distinguish from deliberation. This is because some compromises are strictly bargains while others may be the result of a deliberative process. The former occurs when the parties to a dispute believe so strongly in the merits of their respective positions that persuasion of one side by the other is impossible. It may happen, for example, that the Senate approves an increase in the appropriations for some federal program at the same time that the House votes a decrease. In the conference committee the representatives of each branch may ably and vigorously argue the case for their respective bodies, but persuasion may be impossible. At some point it will become clear that if a bill is to be passed some kind of compromise, some splitting of the difference, will be necessary. The result may be a public agreement, such as maintaining appropriations at existing levels, with which neither side is very satisfied. Such a compromise is a straightforward bargain, since it involved no element of persuasion.

Other compromises, however, may result from a judgment on the merits of the issue at hand. Consider, for example, a conference committee decisionmaking process in which a dozen or more provisions of a bill are in dispute between the House and Senate. In all likelihood each branch will win some and lose some in conference as a condition for reaching agreement. Although the result may look like a simple bargain, or splitting the difference, deliberation may play a large role in determining *what* each side wins and loses through reasoning about the merits of the specific provisions or about the soundness of the package as a whole. It would be a mistake to categorize the "compromise" that results in this case as a mere bargain and thus confuse it with the kind of compromise in which deliberation and persuasion are absent.

Compromise through deliberation may also occur when legislators serve, in effect, as arbitrators in a conflict among external interests. Congress, for example, may have to resolve the competing claims of conservationists and of mining and lumber companies to the use of federally owned land. One kind of resolution to such a conflict is a mere trade-off designed to appease powerful political interests; but another may involve Congress's independent assessment of the merits of each side's claim. Members of Congress may seriously weigh the arguments of each side with a view to how to promote a broader public interest in the use of the land. They may conclude that the public will be best served by limited and controlled exploitation of the resources in a way that will preserve the land's conservationist value. Again, the result is a compromise of the claims of the respective parties, but it is not a mere bargain.[57]

The more recent proponents of the bargaining interpretation of Congress have not, on the whole, demonstrated the analytical clarity of Arthur Bentley's work in distinguishing bargaining from reasoning on the merits of public policy. For Bentley the formal argumentation in Congress was little more than a sham; the real action was the favor-trading occurring behind the scenes. This view thoroughly rejects the notion that Congress is a deliberative institution and, consequently, that the American governmental system is a deliberative democracy. Bentley's intellectual progeny, however, have not confronted this issue squarely. Bargaining has been accepted and presented as the characteristic mode of collective decisionmaking within Congress—as "endemic to the legislative process"—with little if any attention to how it differs from deliberation, to what its limits are in explaining congressional behavior, and to the broader implications for understanding the nature and purpose of Congress in the American democratic system.

REELECTION AND POLITICAL AMBITION

Though enormously influential, bargaining interpretations have not been solely responsible for the demise of deliberation as a subject of inquiry in studies of the Congress and of American government in general. Another theme in recent interpretations undermines deliberation by focusing on the motivations and actions of legislators. Most simply put, this is the view that the members of Congress are disinclined to expend much effort in the reasoned consideration of public policy because such activity carries few if any political rewards. The members come to learn that the public has little interest in broad national issues and that pursuing a detailed policy agenda runs the risk of creating as many enemies as friends. The political payoff—particularly reelection—comes not through serious lawmaking, but rather through the various forms of constituency service: answering mail, meeting with delegations from the home district or state, and intervening for constituents with the departments and agencies of the federal government (from tracking down a social security check to trying to influence the location of a federal project). Every hour devoted to such constituency service—an hour that might otherwise be spent on legislative work—results in a net political benefit. Thus, those who serve in the House and Senate simply lack powerful personal incentives to engage fully in the often slow and tedious process of formulating complex legislation for a complex society. Deliberation suffers as the members of Congress prosper.

In recent decades this argument has been most fully developed by David Mayhew and Morris Fiorina.[58] Both argue that the reelection incentive is the key to understanding and explaining congressional behavior. Ambition for reelection directs congressional attention away from policymaking and programmatic concerns and toward much more politically useful activities such as pork-barreling and casework (Fiorina) or advertising, credit claiming, and position taking (Mayhew). With their eyes rigidly fixed on the next election and their activities geared to enhance their standing back home, the members of Congress have every incentive to do those things that foster a pleasing public image but little reason to expend valuable hours and staff resources promoting good public policy. The legislative process necessarily suffers. There is a general lack of interest in legislation that does not provide particularized benefits; little effort is devoted to mobilizing support for broad policy initiatives; and, worse still, little attention is paid to the content or implementation of legislation: "members display only a modest interest in what goes into bills or what their passage accomplishes."[59] Congress does, of course, pass legislation of broad national scope. Such legislation, Mayhew argues, serves mainly a symbolic purpose; for "in a large class of undertakings the electoral payment is for positions rather than for effects."[60] Congress is quite willing to enunciate and promote great and noble goals, but it "does not act (in legislating or overseeing or both) so as to achieve them."[61] Fiorina's conclusion is no more encouraging: "Public policy emerges from the system almost as an afterthought. The shape of policy is a by-product of the way the system operates, rather than a consciously directed effort to deal with social and economic problems."[62] In the end, "the general, long-term welfare of the United States is no more than an incidental by-product of the system."[63]

If this view is correct, then there is currently a radical disjunction between deliberation and democracy in the American political system. The electoral connection, which is nothing less than the linchpin of American democracy and which was originally intended to ensure that the deliberations of representatives would be firmly rooted in popular interests and sentiments, has become the chief enemy of deliberation. Electoral considerations have generated massive disincentives for the members of Congress to spend their time reasoning together about broad national concerns. The more efficient Congress has become as an engine for the reelection of its members, the less it bears the character of a deliberative institution and the less the system as a whole can be characterized as a deliberative democracy.

Mayhew and Fiorina make a compelling case that mere self-seeking by the members of the House and Senate can result in behavior that is harmful to genuine deliberation. They show that there is no necessary congruence between what is good for individual legislators and what is good for the institution in which they serve and the nation it governs. This reminds us, as the founding generation learned during the first decade of independence, that sound deliberation is not something that automatically occurs whenever a body of legislators assemble.

Mayhew's work in particular is extraordinarily helpful in identifying the variety of nondeliberative activities in which the members of Congress may engage throughout the legislative process and the nature of the incentives that so incline them. Some of these activities, such as advertising or credit claiming, are not likely to be confused with genuine deliberation. Such, however, may not be the case for "position taking": "the public enunciation of a judgmental statement on anything likely to be of interest to political actors."[64] According to Mayhew, position taking is something like pure rhetoric: "The congressman as position taker is a speaker rather than a doer. The electoral requirement is not that he make pleasing things happen but that he make pleasing judgmental statements. The position itself is the political commodity."[65] Put somewhat differently, genuine reasoning on the merits of public policy—the attention to detailed information and arguments and the careful fashioning or assessment of policy alternatives—should not be confused with the posturing and rhetoric so common to committee hearings and floor debate.

It remains here only to make one point about the relationship of bargaining theories to those that focus on reelection incentives. This is the perfect congruence of these two explanations of congressional behavior; for the focus on reelection in explaining individual preferences and behavior neatly complements the emphasis on bargaining to account for collective decisions. If the members of Congress seek only their personal well-being, then collective reasoning about broad public matters will serve no purpose. Yet there remains the need to reach collective decisions; no proposal, after all, including pork-barrel legislation, can become law without the votes of a majority of the members of the House and Senate. Bargaining, especially logrolling, would seem to be the natural mechanism for aggregating hundreds of individual preferences. Indeed, Fiorina makes the point explicitly:

> [I]n order to attain reelection, congressmen focus on things that are both more recognizable in their impact [than broad national policies] and more credible indicators of the individual congressman's power—federal projects and individual favors for constituents. In order to purchase a steady flow of the latter, congressmen trade away less valuable currency—their views on public policy. The typical public law is simply the outcome of enough individual bargains to build a majority.[66]

Conversely, if arguments about the merits of pending proposals are utterly without force in Congress, then even the most public-spirited legislator may soon be moved by a deepening cynicism of his job and his institution to give up on public goals and salvage whatever private benefits he can.

The next two chapters will assess the adequacy of bargaining and the reelection incentive in accounting for lawmaking in Congress. The issue is not whether bargains occur and whether the reelection incentive sometimes leads to nondeliberative activities (this is not contested); rather, the immediate question is *how much* do bargaining and reelection explain and how much do they leave unexplained. What conclusions about the relative importance of deliberative versus nondeliberative behavior follow from a fair review of what we know about lawmaking in Congress, particularly from detailed case studies, and what we know about the goals and behavior of legislators, particularly from careful profiles of representatives and senators?

 CHAPTER FOUR

Bargaining and Collective Decisions:
The Limits of Explanation

> [T]his could be politics in the best sense, the rational dis-
> cussion of issues . . . .
>
> Stewart Udall, 1971

Is bargaining, as is widely believed, the prevalent mode of
reaching collective decisions in Congress? Is it the characteristic way in which the preferences of the members of the
House and Senate are aggregated into public policy? Is "[t]he
typical public law . . . simply the outcome of enough individual bargains to build a majority"?[1] Logrolls, compromises,
and side payments certainly occur in the House and Senate,
but how much do they explain and how much do they leave
unexplained?

Bargaining and Case Studies

In assessing the prevalence and importance of bargaining
in Congress, we can do no better than to begin with the dozens of detailed case studies of lawmaking in Congress for the
very period when bargaining interpretations gained ascendancy: in the decades after World War II. Focusing on the
formation and passage of domestic legislation (where bargaining is thought to be more prevalent than in the national security and foreign policy fields), I have identified for the
period 1945–70 twenty-nine case studies written more or less
contemporaneously covering (1) twenty-seven national laws,
(2) three congressional statutes successfully vetoed by presidents, and (3) three proposals rejected by Congress. (See the
Appendix for a list of the case studies.) Excluded are very
brief accounts, merely journalistic reviews, and broad studies
of national policymaking that do not explicate the details of
the legislative process.[2]

A few of the case studies, such as Stephen K. Bailey's *Congress Makes a Law* and Raymond Bauer, Ithiel deSola Pool, and

Lewis A. Dexter's *American Business and Public Policy,* are among the best-known works on American government and politics during this period.[3] These and other studies trace the legislative history of some of the major domestic policy enactments of the postwar period, including the Employment Act of 1946, the Reciprocal Trade Act of 1955, the National Aeronautics and Space Act of 1958, the Landrum-Griffin Act of 1959, the Food Stamp Act of 1964, the Economic Opportunity Act of 1964, the Elementary and Secondary Education Act of 1965, and the Medicare Act of 1965. Other studies trace some of the early legislative efforts in fields such as civil rights (the Civil Rights Bill of 1956 and the Civil Rights Act of 1960) and environmental protection (the Water Pollution Control Acts of 1956 and 1960 and the Clean Air Act of 1963) where the major national policy innovations were to come later. A few of the case studies deal with rather obscure bills that seemed to have little national importance. These include the San Luis Reclamation Bill of 1960 and the Bill Disposing of the DesPlaines Public Hunting and Wildlife Refuge Area of 1960. Since the selection of case studies is weighted toward particularly important, and even landmark, legislation—hardly a representative sample of lawmaking in Congress—the insights that can be gleaned from the studies of lesser bills take on added importance.

What, then, do these diverse legislative case studies reveal about the prevalence of bargaining in Congress? Perhaps surprisingly, these case studies, written at a time when pluralist interpretations of American government and bargaining interpretations of Congressional decisionmaking were dominant, have rather little to say about bargaining. Indeed, only four of the twenty-nine case studies attribute any particular importance to bargaining as a mechanism by which decisions were reached in the cases analyzed. These are Roger Davidson's studies of the Area Redevelopment Act of 1961 and the Emergency Employment Act of 1971, Randall Ripley's account of the passage of the Food Stamp Act of 1964, and Theodore Marmor's history of the Medicare Act of 1965.[4] Brief descriptions of the kinds of bargaining involved in each case follow.

Davidson's two studies describe coalition building through logrolling in the Senate. In both cases proponents of new policies, which did not initially garner majority support, broadened their bills in order, in effect, to purchase the support of originally recalcitrant legislators. In bargaining terminology, some senators traded their support for the entire bill in exchange for a provision or concession of special interest to them.

In his account of the early history of the Area Redevelopment Act, Davidson shows how in the Eighty-fourth Congress (1955–56) Senator

Paul Douglas (D., Illinois) engineered majority support for a bill that was originally designed to assist the decaying industrial areas of the North and East. When Douglas discovered that his proposal had too narrow an appeal, he twice broadened it to include substantial aid to depressed rural areas. This tactic, according to Davidson, ensured the success of the Douglas bill in the Senate: "By promising 'aid to the country cousins' the [revised] proposal was able to attract support from influential rural legislators as well as those from older industrial areas."[5] Resistance in the House and the executive branch, however, prevented passage of depressed areas legislation until the Eighty-seventh Congress (1961–62).

Similarly, Senator Gaylord Nelson (D., Wisconsin), chairman of the Subcommittee on Employment, Manpower, and Poverty of the Senate Committee on Labor and Public Welfare, refashioned in several different ways what was to become the Emergency Employment Act of 1971 in order to gain the support of a majority of his subcommittee. After negotiations within the subcommittee, he added a variety of special provisions to build his majority: "special provisions were added for mid-career and elderly people (Jennings Randolph of West Virginia and Harrison Williams of New Jersey); for Indians (Edward Kennedy of Massachusetts); and for Spanish-speaking people (Ralph Yarborough of Texas) . . . . By engaging in the time-honored tactic of logrolling, Nelson and his staff . . . managed to build an unshakable coalition of the subcommittee's majority party members."[6]

Randall Ripley's account of the logroll on the passage of the Food Stamp Act in the House of Representatives in 1964 (with votes traded between supporters of the food stamp and wheat-cotton bills) was briefly described in chapter 3. This was preceded, according to Ripley, by another logroll at the committee stage. In the early months of 1964 the administration's efforts to secure passage of a permanent food stamp plan were thwarted when a coalition of Republicans and southern Democrats on the House Agriculture Committee defeated the bill by a vote of 19–14. Liberal Democrats within the House responded by using their influence within the Rules Committee to prevent the granting of a rule on a tobacco research bill previously reported from the Agriculture Committee and of special interest to the committee's chairman, Harold Cooley (D., North Carolina). Although Cooley had earlier voted to report the food stamp bill, the liberal Democrats did not trust him and blamed him for the committee's failure to act favorably. According to Ripley, the implication was clearly communicated to Cooley that there would be no rule on the tobacco research bill until a food stamp plan was reported. Within a few weeks the Agriculture Committee reversed itself and reported an amended version of the administration plan by an 18–16 vote. Three southern and border state Democrats switched from opponents of food stamps to proponents, providing the margin of victory. Shortly thereafter, the Rules Committee reported the tobacco research bill.

Theodore Marmor's history of Medicare proposals through the passage of the 1965 act is the only one of the case studies examined here that applies several well-formulated models of the policy process to the legislative events. Employing Graham Allison's typology, from *Essence of Decision*,[7] of "rational actor," "organizational process," and "bureaucratic politics" (or bargaining) models of decisionmaking, Marmor argues that (1) the first best explains the decision by elites in the early 1950s "to narrow the focus of federal health insurance bills from the general population to the aged, and to restrict benefits to partial hospitalization coverage";[8] (2) the second fits the pattern of responses by interest groups to medicare proposals from 1952 to 1964;[9] and (3) the third best describes the enactment of Medicare in 1965:

> The enactment of Medicare was treated in earlier chapters primarily as the result of a bargaining game in which none of the relevant executive, legislative, or pressure-group players could fully control the outcome. The key actors—Mills and Byrnes of the Ways and Means Committee, Cohen of HEW, Long and Anderson of the Senate Finance Committee, the AMA and the labor leaders—all had different conceptions of the problem at hand. They had different stakes in the outcome of the legislative struggle and different terms on which they were willing to compromise.[10]

One example of bargaining on Medicare is the conference committee's resolution of more than five hundred differences between the House and Senate versions of the final bill: "Most of the changes were made through the standard bargaining methods of *quid pro quo* and splitting the difference."[11]

Assume that each of these accounts is completely accurate. What are we to conclude? Simply this: that on *some* bills bargaining explains the votes of *some* legislators at *some* stages of the decision process. In the Eighty-fourth Congress some votes in the Senate were won over to Douglas's plan to assist depressed areas through an implicit logroll. In 1971 Senator Nelson secured some votes on his subcommittee for the passage of an employment act through an explicit series of deals. In 1964 three votes on the House Agriculture Committee and some number of votes on the floor of the House were brought around to support food stamps through logrolling involving different bills. Marmor is less precise in detailing specific bargains during the passage of Medicare in 1965. Nonetheless, if he is right, bargaining at the very least accounts for how the conference committee resolved the hundreds of differences between the House and Senate versions.

The question that must be asked in these and like cases is how many votes in Congress are the result of bargaining at each decision stage and how many must be explained on other grounds, such as judgments on the merits. Indeed, even if bargaining is decisive for building a majority, it may only explain a small number of votes. Theoretically, it is possible that a legislative body could divide evenly on the actual merits of a proposal, with a last-minute bargain creating a one-vote majority for the bill. Would we conclude in this case that bargaining was decisive to the passage of the bill because without the bargain the bill would have been defeated; or would we conclude that bargaining was dwarfed by deliberation, since every legislator but one voted on the merits? Both conclusions are valid. To focus on the first and ignore the second would result in an obviously deficient account. Thus, to prove the importance of bargaining in this hypothetical case in no way refutes the dominance of deliberation.[12]

In the food stamp case, for example, the two logrolls identified by Ripley—which apparently account for 3 votes in the House Agriculture Committee and some fraction of the 229 floor votes for food stamps—do not explain: (1) why Republicans in the House, both those on the committee and in the full body, remained solidly and nearly unanimously opposed to food stamps throughout; (2) why most House Democrats favored food stamps even without the added inducement of the wheat-cotton bill; or (3) why the Senate passed the bill with only minimal opposition. Ripley, himself, does not claim otherwise. Yet his emphasis on the importance of bargaining to the passage of food stamps, as reflected in his title—"Legislative Bargaining and the Food Stamp Act, 1964"— gives bargaining a weight perhaps greater than it deserves in a comprehensive explanation of why Congress passed a permanent food stamp program in 1964. (We return to this particular case below.)

Another issue in evaluating the prevalence of bargaining in Congress is whether behaviors attributed to bargaining could be as well, or even more persuasively, explained on other grounds, including reasoning and judgments on the merits of legislation. Have analysts been too quick to see bargaining in cases where deliberation is a sounder explanation?

Consider, for example, Marmor's description of the conference committee's decisionmaking on the Medicare Act: "Most of the changes were made through the standard bargaining methods of *quid pro quo* and splitting the difference."[13] This suggests a mere trade-off, with each branch getting roughly half of what it wanted. But with five hundred issues in dispute, what determined which particular provisions survived? Granted that the conferees for each side knew that they could get only about half of what they wanted, how was this half decided? It is certainly possible that an appeal to the merits of alternative provisions and to the need to construct a coherent and workable package as a whole played some role in determining the conference outcome. With the Medicare conference closed to the public, this possibility cannot be dismissed without evidence. Thus, the mere fact that each branch wins some and loses some in conference does not prove the absence of deliberation. The roughly equivalent influence of the conferees from each branch—with each delegation retaining an absolute veto over the product—may simply establish the limits within which reasoning on the merits assists in fashioning an acceptable bill.

A similar problem of interpretation arises in Marmor's explanation for the surprising behavior of Congressman Wilbur Mills, Chairman of the House Committee on Ways and Means, in calling for an expansion of the administration's Medicare plan, a radical switch in Mills's position. Throughout the Kennedy administration, Mills and his committee had steadfastly opposed proposals for federally supported health care for the aged. Marmor argues, however, that this opposition was likely to cease after the 1964 election brought a lopsided Democratic majority into the House. The election results virtually assured that some health insurance bill for the elderly would be passed by the Eighty-ninth Congress.

In this revised context the Ways and Means Committee began hearings shortly after the new Congress convened. Three plans were before it: (1) the administration plan providing some hospitalization and nursing home insurance benefits financed through the social security system; (2) the American Medical Association's "Eldercare" plan, which offered a wider range of benefits, including physicians' fees and drug costs not included in the administration plan, but only to needy individuals; and (3) a plan sponsored by the ranking Republican on the committee, John Byrnes, which provided benefits similar to the AMA plan to voluntary enrollees with the financing split between the participants and the federal government.

Midway through the hearings Chairman Mills suggested to a "stunned" and "initially suspicious" Wilbur Cohen, secretary of the Department of Health, Education, and Welfare, that a plan be devised combining features of both the administration bill and the Byrnes bill.[14] This suggestion resulted in a Medicare program of much wider scope than the administration's original proposal. According to Marmor, the expanded program "assumed a form which no one had predicted in the post-election certainty that some type of social security health insurance was forthcoming."[15] "What had changed Mills," Marmor asks, "from a Medicare obstructionist to an expansion-minded innovator?"[16]

As noted earlier, Marmor argues that the behavior of Mills and the other key actors on Medicare was the result of the "bargaining game" in which they found themselves: "[Mills] could in 1965 be a reluctant bystander or an adroit manager of legislation which in another setting he would have preferred to block. Mills had always adjusted to legislative certainty and tried to take charge of the form which the inevitable takes."[17] Because Mills did change after the 1964 election from opponent to proponent of federally supported medical care for the aged, this explanation has a certain plausibility. But does it adequately explain why Mills acted to expand the administration's plan in so dramatic a way?

Mills, after all, could certainly have exercised his influence in fashioning and managing the legislation without calling for such a major expansion. The new provisions had their source in the Republican plan offered by Byrnes, but these had been offered as an *alternative* to the administration plan, not as an addition to it. When Mills and the administration instead joined a part of the Republican plan to the original administration bill, this was not done to gain Republican votes. Indeed, not a single committee Republican voted to report the expanded bill. Given that, as best we can tell, all the influential actors pushing for a bill—the administration, committee Democrats, and Democrats in the full House— would have been satisfied with the original proposal, how can we explain why Mills, who we are led to believe would have preferred no bill at all, recommended that the administration proposal be expanded well beyond its original dimensions?

Contrary to Marmor's bargaining explanation to account for Mills's behavior, a deliberative explanation seems to fit better with the observed facts. It could be argued that once Mills became convinced that some measure was going to pass, he focused his attention and considerable

legislative skills on getting the soundest bill possible, carefully considering the arguments advanced at the hearings for the various alternative
proposals. Seeing merit in both the administration plan and Byrnes's
proposal and recognizing that these were not mutually exclusive, he proposed the fashioning of a combination program superior to either single
plan. Indeed, even if Mills would have preferred the Byrnes bill simply
over the administration's plan, his action in recommending the joining
of portions of both could be said to be a combination of hard-headed
political calculation—some version of the administration bill clearly was
going to pass—*and* deliberation—there was merit in the Byrnes proposal
and it deserved to be part of the legislative package.

To summarize to this point: First, only a few of the more than two
dozen case studies of domestic policymaking in Congress during the
1945–70 period place any particular importance on bargaining as a
means for aggregating collective decisions in the House or Senate. Second, as these few studies illustrate, even when bargaining is decisive to
legislative outcomes, it may only explain a small fraction of votes in committee or on the floor. Third, some legislative behaviors attributed to
bargaining may be better explained by deliberative interpretations.

Greater light can be shed on these issues by following in some detail
the process by which a particular legislative proposal moves through
Congress, achieving success in committee and on the floor. Here it is
useful to focus on a "worst case" from the point of view of deliberative
interpretations, that is, a major legislative initiative whose success has
been quite emphatically attributed to deal making rather than reasoned
persuasion. The passage of the Food Stamp Act by the House of Representatives in 1963–64, one of the pillars of Lyndon Johnson's Great
Society program, provides a particularly fruitful case study of the interaction and relative importance of bargaining and deliberation in the lawmaking process.

Bargaining and Deliberation on Food Stamps

The first federal food stamp program had been in operation from
1939 to 1943. It was administered under authority of amendments
passed in 1935 to the Agriculture Adjustment Act. These amendments
provided that the secretary of agriculture could set aside a certain portion of the tariff receipts on agricultural products to finance programs
that would encourage the consumption of surplus commodities. After
the discontinuation of this program in 1943, there were periodic attempts to reestablish the program on a permanent legislative basis.

Success was nearly achieved in 1958 when the House Agriculture Committee, previously the principal roadblock to congressional passage of a food stamp program, reported a bill in early August. The bill went to the floor under suspension of the rules. The required two-thirds majority was not achieved, but a simple majority did vote to pass the bill, 196–187. In the following year the House and Senate passed legislation authorizing the secretary of agriculture to establish a program for a two-year period. The language of the bill was permissive rather than mandatory, and the Eisenhower administration never exercised the authority. Shortly after John Kennedy became president in 1961, the new administration instituted a pilot food stamp program on the authority of the 1935 legislation.

SYNOPSIS OF LEGISLATIVE HISTORY, 1963–64

Early in 1963 the Kennedy administration requested legislation authorizing a permanent food stamp program. The full House Agriculture Committee conducted hearings on the administration's bill on June 10, 11, and 12, 1963. Several months later a special subcommittee was appointed to give the matter further consideration. It met in executive session on August 7, 8, and 15 and agreed on the main lines of a plan. A new bill incorporating the subcommittee's recommendations was introduced, but in executive session on October 30 the full committee could not reach agreement. Some months later, on February 4, 1964, the full committee formally acted to table action on food stamps. On March 3 another revised bill was introduced. Several days later the Agriculture Committee amended the bill in executive session and reported it to the floor on an 18–16 vote. Debate began under an open rule on April 7. Late in the evening of the next day the House passed the food stamp bill by a roll call vote of 229–189.

The House bill went to the Senate, where the Committee on Agriculture and Forestry held hearings on June 18 and 19, 1964. On June 29 the committee voted 14–2 to report the House bill with minor amendments. After perfunctory debate on June 30, the Senate passed the bill on a voice vote. The House agreed to the Senate amendments on August 11.

On August 31, 1964, President Lyndon Johnson signed into law a bill establishing a permanent food stamp program at an authorized cost of $375 million for the first three years of operation. The new program would allow needy families in participating areas to exchange a specified percentage of their income for a greater dollar value of stamps with which to purchase food at regular retail outlets. It was intended to be a more dignified and efficient alternative to the program it replaced: direct distribution of surplus commodities, such as milk and cheese, to needy individuals. Ostensibly, it would continue to serve the two main purposes of direct distribution: (1) to decrease the supply of surplus commodities, and (2) to help meet the nutritional needs of the poor.

ANALYZING THE LOGROLLS IN THE HOUSE

In 1964 the House Agriculture Committee had thirty-five members, twenty-one Democrats and fourteen Republicans. Thirty-three of these voted on the tabling motion on February 4. The Republicans on the committee were joined by five southern or border state Democrats to constitute a majority to hold up the bill. Food stamp proponents had expected opposition from all the Republicans and two Democrats. The three surprise Democratic votes supplied the margin of defeat: Paul Jones of Missouri, George Grant of Alabama, and E. C. Gathings of Arkansas. One month later these three reversed positions and voted to report a food stamp bill. According to Ripley, the three Democrats "were persuaded by the impending defeat of the tobacco bill [held up by liberal Democrats on the Rules Committee] to join Cooley and the other Democrats in voting to report the bill." [18] The result was an 18–16 majority in the committee for food stamps.

As noted earlier, this logroll, by which liberal Democrats on the Rules Committee traded their support for the tobacco research bill in exchange for the food stamp votes of conservative Democrats on the Agriculture Committee, at best explains three of thirty-four votes on the committee. The other thirty-one committee members were not involved in this deal and thus voted as they did for reasons unrelated to the fate of the tobacco research bill. If Ripley's account is accurate, then, this logroll had a limited, though decisive, effect. It is not entirely clear, however, that even these three votes were purchased for reasons wholly unrelated to the merits of the food stamp plan; for the bill passed by the Agriculture Committee in early March was not identical to the bill tabled in February, raising the possibility that it was the amendments made to the earlier version, not merely the prospects of the tobacco bill, that brought the three Democrats around.

The bill passed by the Agriculture Committee in March of 1964 differed in at least four respects from the one the committee had tabled the month before: (1) it provided that for budgetary purposes food stamps would be listed as a "welfare," not agricultural, expenditure; (2) it included new language emphasizing that one of the program's main purposes was to reduce food surpluses; (3) it decreased the authorized expenditures from a total of $550 million for four years to $400 million; and (4) it added the requirement that the states pay one-half of the cost of the coupons. Although Ripley's account does not assess the impact that these changes had on the three Democrats who switched position, one may wonder why these changes were made in the first place if the logroll on the tobacco bill was itself enough to switch the three votes. All the changes, after all, and especially the last two, were in the "conservative" direction. Why would the liberal Democrats on the committee approve a weakening of the program at this stage if they could get the three extra votes they needed in committee through a bargain unrelated to the merits of the program itself? Thus it seems highly likely that these changes in the substance of the bill were intended to help bring around the three southern and border state Democrats who had once been thought to be possible supporters. If so, a judgment on the merits of the bill contributed to the switch of the three crucial votes.

This episode displays some of the complexity of sorting out the relative contribution of bargaining and deliberation in the legislative process. By holding up the rule on the tobacco bill, food stamp supporters were putting added pressure on their more conservative Democratic colleagues on the Agriculture Committee. Yet these committee members had their own judgments about the merits of the administration's plan. They may have told Chairman Cooley that some concessions would be necessary if they were to change their votes, in particular that the costs be reduced and that the states be forced to contribute to the program. In a pure logroll these merit issues would be simply irrelevant. In this respect this episode is not unlike the situation that faced Wilbur Mills on Medicare. External events created pressure on the congressman to switch from opponent to proponent. But this pressure in itself did not blind him to issues regarding the merits of the legislation.

The second logroll, as we have seen, involved a trade between supporters of the food stamp bill and the wheat-cotton bill. The evidence is compelling that some kind of trade was involved in floor voting on these two bills. As noted earlier, the leadership kept the House in session until after midnight on the evening of April 8 so that the debate and vote on wheat-cotton could be held immediately after passage of the food stamp bill, strongly suggesting some kind of deal. Moreover, the deal was itself an issue in the debate on food stamps. Republicans criticized the unsavory arrangement by which the food stamp bill was offered as a "sweetener" to urban Democrats to win their support for wheat-cotton.[19] Republican John Saylor of Pennsylvania, a supporter of food stamps, virtually conceded the existence of a deal by arguing that vote trading was nothing new. The practice dated back even to the First Congress when Alexander Hamilton, "one of the great statesmen of all times," arranged a trade between southerners, who wanted to move the national capital south to the banks of the Potomac, and northerners, who wanted the federal government to assume the state debts incurred during the Revolution (more on this bargain in chapter 7).[20] Finally, the independent source *Congressional Quarterly* reported that

> HR 10222, the food stamp bill, and HR 6196, the administration's cotton-wheat bill, were brought to the House floor together April 8 under a log-rolling arrangement worked out by the Democratic leadership. Under the arrangement, both bills were passed the same day, with the food stamp bill, supported mainly by Northern Democrats, taking precedence over the cotton-wheat bill, supported mainly by Southern Democrats.[21]

The purpose of a logroll of the kind described here is to generate greater recorded support for two distinct bills than either would receive if considered alone. On each bill some individuals vote in favor who would otherwise abstain or vote against the proposal. Thus, the votes recorded in favor of the bills are not accurate reflections of "true" support. This is the thought behind the Republicans' criticism of the deal on food stamps and wheat-cotton: each bill should be considered separately on its merits so that true support can be measured. It follows that in assessing the importance of the logroll to the passage of food stamps, we would like to know how many of the 229 "aye" votes (with 418 voting on the bill 210 were needed for passage) came from those who would have abstained or opposed food stamps in the absence of the logroll.

Although this figure cannot be precisely determined, the evidence suggests that only a very small fraction of the food stamp supporters on the House floor would have been opponents if no logroll had been involved. First, it must be acknowledged that the food stamp program would not benefit only the urban poor; for its reach would extend to the rural poor as well. Indeed, the Kennedy administration's pilot program had "include[d] both urban and rural areas."[22] Thus, it cannot simply be presumed that southern Democrats, who represented predominantly rural areas, would necessarily be inclined to oppose food stamps. In fact, earlier food stamp plans had drawn considerable support from southern

Table 1. Democratic Votes in Favor of Food Stamp Bills:
House of Representatives, 1958–64

Democrats	1958		1959		1964	
	N	%	N	%	N	%
Northern	112	98%	144	97%	141	99%
Southern	57	62%	66	74%	75	76%

Note: All percentages are based on those voting on final passage.
Source: Compiled from *Congressional Quarterly Almanacs: 1958*, pp. 408–9; *1959*, pp. 384–85; and *1964*, pp. 618–19.

Democrats. As table 1 shows, both in 1958 and 1959 clear majorities of southern Democrats voted for food stamp programs.

In 1958, 62 percent of southern Democrats had supported the bill for a permanent food stamp program reported by the House Agriculture Committee; and in 1959, 74 percent had supported legislation granting the secretary of agriculture discretionary authority to establish a food stamp program.

Although northern Democrats were more supportive of the earlier plans than their southern colleagues, there is nothing in the votes of 1958 and 1959 to suggest to food stamp advocates in the Eighty-eighth Congress that most southern Democrats would oppose the administration's plan. Conversely, there is no evidence in these figures that large numbers of southern Democrats voted "aye" in 1964 who absent a deal on wheat-cotton would have opposed food stamps; for only 9 more southern Democrats supported food stamps in 1964 than in 1959, and 18 more than in 1958. At first glance this would seem to be the range of votes attributable to the logroll.

A more precise way to estimate this figure is to compare on an individual basis the votes of southern Democrats in 1964 with their earlier votes on food stamps. This is shown in table 2.

Of southern Democrats who voted in favor of food stamps in 1964, only 7 clearly switched positions, having voted only against food stamps on the earlier occasions, and another 8 were ambiguous switchers, having voted once in favor and once against the earlier bills. Assuming that there were no other reasons for changing votes, an arbitrary assumption friendly to the logrolling interpretation, we can posit that the deal on the wheat-cotton bill accounted for 7–15 aye votes in 1964 from southern Democrats who had voted on food stamps before. By making the further

Table 2. Comparison of Southern Democratic Votes on Food Stamps in 1964 with Votes in 1958 and 1959

Food Stamp Votes in 1958 and 1959	1964 Vote by Southern Democrats: Number Voting Aye
Did not vote in 1958 and 1959	19
Voted in 1958 and/or 1959	56
Voted only aye in 1958 and 1959	41
Voted aye once and nay once in 1958 and 1959	8
Voted only nay in 1958 and 1959	7
TOTAL	75

Source: Compiled from *Congressional Quarterly Almanacs: 1958*, pp. 408–9; *1959*, pp. 384–85; and *1964*, pp. 618–19.

assumption that the group of 22 southern Democrats who voted on food stamps for the first time in 1964 (19 voted in favor and 3 against) would have supported the earlier bills in rough proportion to their colleagues—in the range of 62–74 percent, or approximately 14–16 supporters—then perhaps 3–5 of the 19 who voted for the 1964 bill also participated in the trade.

As best we can determine, then, a maximum of 10–20 southern Democrats traded their votes to become nominal supporters of food stamps in 1964. Given that a shift of fully 20 votes would have been necessary to defeat the bill, it is likely that the logroll did not even supply the margin of victory. Ripley himself admits as much at the conclusion of his study: "It is likely that the food stamp bill could have passed the floor without being attached to any rurally oriented bill."[23]

Indeed, it appears from Ripley's account that the logroll was engineered principally with wheat-cotton in mind. Wheat-cotton was "more costly and controversial" than food stamps.[24] In the last few weeks before the vote "it became evident that the wheat-cotton bill was in much more danger of defeat than the food stamp program."[25] A poll taken by the leadership showed 212 Democrats intending to vote for food stamps, ordinarily enough to win on the floor, but only 197 likely to vote for wheat-cotton, "clearly not enough if Republican lines held solid."[26]

> Thus, in the closing hours the main efforts of the speaker, the majority leader, and the whip, as well as of the [Agriculture]

department and the President, were aimed at getting more
Democratic votes for the wheat-cotton bill. The appeals were
directed especially at urban Democrats and stressed that passage of the food stamp legislation could be assured if they
would help to get the wheat-cotton bill through.[27]

In the end wheat-cotton passed by the narrow margin of 211–203. If as
few as four northern Democrats, inclined to oppose the bill, traded their
support as part of a deal on food stamps, then the logroll here *was*
decisive.

The picture that emerges is that although the food stamp plan was
likely to pass without the logroll, its success could be "assured" if urban
Democrats agreed to support the wheat-cotton bill. The real impetus for
the bargain stemmed from the impending defeat of wheat-cotton. Nonetheless, whether one takes food stamps or wheat-cotton, the issue is the
same: How does one sort out the relative importance of bargaining and
deliberation as means for building majorities at the various stages of the
legislative process? From the results of the leadership's poll, it appears
that at least 212 Democrats were prepared to vote for food stamps and
197 for wheat-cotton even in the absence of a logroll. If the logroll involving the two bills was *not* responsible for so many votes for the two
bills, what was? Conversely, what explains the 189 negative votes on food
stamps and the 203 on wheat-cotton, mainly from Republicans?

The following account details the elements of the deliberative process
that moved food stamps through the House of Representatives in 1963
and 1964. This deliberative explanation provides a much more comprehensive and persuasive account for why the House passed a permanent
food stamp program than does legislative bargaining.

THE MERITS OF FOOD STAMPS

In assessing the contribution of deliberation, or reasoning on the merits, to the passage of the Food Stamp Act of 1964, it will be useful to
analyze the legislative history in terms of three key components: (1) the
proponents' case for food stamps; (2) the House Democrats' support for
the administration's plan; and (3) House Republican opposition to food
stamps.

The Case for Food Stamps. The case for a permanent food stamp program was formally made before the House Agriculture Committee in
hearings on June 10, 11, and 12, 1963. Representatives from the administration were the lead witnesses, followed by six members of the House

from both parties and one public witness. All the witnesses testified in favor of a new permanent food stamp program.

Secretary of Agriculture Orville Freeman presented the administration's case for the bill. His testimony consumed nearly the entire first day of hearings. The following sketches the key elements of the administration's case for food stamps:

- "Every American citizen should have an adequate, nutritious diet. . . . This is both a spiritual and moral principle."
- We can achieve this goal because "today this country produces more than enough food to meet the needs of every man, woman, and child."
- However, "some 13 percent of the American people have serious nutritional shortages."
- The reason for inadequate nutrition "is simply that the distribution machinery is not as effective as it should be."
- To improve the mechanics of food distribution the Department of Agriculture since 1961 has (1) expanded the direct distribution of surplus commodities to low-income families and (2) "been testing in urban communities—in rural areas—and in various combinations of both rural and urban populations, a new piece of food distribution machinery— the food stamp program, designed to supplement the food budget of low-income families."
- Although the direct distribution program "is doing an enormous amount of good," its "inherent weaknesses . . . are becoming more obvious." These include: the creation of a separate food distribution system paralleling the regular wholesale and retail system, resulting in waste and inefficiency; the opportunities for violations and misuse, which could not be eliminated without a "cumbersome" administrative machinery; and a limited number of commodities, usually no meat products, fruits, or vegetables.
- The food stamp system solves each of these problems. It is particularly superior to direct distribution in that it allows participating families to purchase any food items they wish through regular retail outlets.
- Experience with the pilot food stamp program has been "uniformly good." It has increased retail food store sales in pilot project areas; it has markedly improved the diets of participating families; and it has been well received by participants and welfare workers.
- The successful experience of the pilot program justifies the establishment of a permanent food stamp program.[28]

Freeman presented the issue as simply one of finding an effective way to solve the serious national problem of inadequate nutrition. The established program to meet this problem was the direct distribution of surplus commodities to needy families. An alternative program designed to avoid the defects of direct distribution had been tested and shown to be a more effective solution to the nutrition problem. It should be made permanent national policy.

In making his case, Freeman emphasized the consensus that already existed within the nation on the principle of assuring all Americans adequate nutrition. His intention was not to open up the whole issue of a direct federal role in this area:

> I know the Congress speaks with the same voice—witness the appropriation in this current fiscal year of more than $600 million to finance various programs to share our food abundance more widely—through school lunch, special milk, institutional feeding, direct distribution, and other programs.[29]

The food stamp plan was a tested and proven instrument, or means, to achieve common goals. The administration's aim here was to narrow the issue before Congress to the advantages of food stamps over direct distribution, thereby focusing attention on the operation of the pilot program and deemphasizing large principled issues regarding the appropriateness of direct federal aid to increase the food purchasing power of the poor.

The principal congressional sponsor of food stamps, Representative Leonor Sullivan, made her case for the bill at the start of the second day of hearings. Her argument closely followed the administration's. The main issue was simply "whether the food stamp plan of distribution is preferable to the direct distribution system."[30] The answer lay in the evaluation of the pilot program: "The experience in the pilot plan areas proves that it is preferable, without any doubt whatever. . . . [T]he plan does work, and works exceptionally well to bring decent, American-standard, nutritious, enjoyable diets to families long denied such a blessing."[31]

During subsequent questioning Representative Sullivan introduced another element in defense of food stamps over direct distribution, what one witness called the "humanitarian" aspect of the bill:

> I think the arguments that were used against it [direct distribution], ever since I appeared before this committee in 1954,

are still valid. In letters to me many of the Congressmen bring
out the fact that people have to stand in line to receive this
food once a month under all kinds of weather conditions, and
so forth, and it has not been a very—maybe "dignified" is not
the word to use, but when you receive charity you still have
some dignity, and you do not want people to lose that and to
have to stand in line and gather this food as they do once a
month. That has been very, very hard for older people and
the handicapped, particularly.[32]

This argument, that the food stamp plan respected the dignity of recipients, would be repeated many times throughout the ensuing debate.

Of the other five members of the House who testified in person, three
were Republicans. Two of these, Charles Mathias of Maryland and James
Fulton of Pennsylvania, defended the food stamp proposal on the basis
of traditional Republican principles. Mathias expounded the merits of
the plan in supporting, rather than competing with, the normal market
system:

I believe that it is entirely possible that this food stamp program would increase the sale of farm products through normal channels. I am very much interested in this, because I
think that the millers, the retailers, the people who handle
farm products, will benefit if the food can be handled through
normal commercial channels, rather than through the give-
away program.[33]

Fulton's appeal to his fellow Republicans was even more explicit, as these
excerpts illustrate:

I favor this legislation for expansion of the Federal food
stamp program. I believe that every Republican as well as
Democrat should favor it, because this is the private enterprise approach to food distribution as distinguished from the
public and relief method which is the surplus food direct distribution. This plan gives private enterprise in the regular
channels the method of distributing.[34]

The point is that the Federal food stamp program is so
placed that it operates in conjunction with local State customs,
practices, usages, and legislation and so I favor it strongly. I
think that all Republicans should simply for that reason. If the
State or local community does not want the program, they do
not have to participate.[35]

These market-oriented appeals eventually proved unsuccessful; for nine months after the hearings ended, the fourteen committee Republicans voted unanimously to oppose the committee bill, and on final passage only thirteen Republicans, 7 percent of those voting, supported food stamps.

This near unanimous Republican opposition to food stamps, however, was not a foregone conclusion in June of 1963. At the time there were several reasons for thinking that more than a few Republicans might embrace food stamps.

First, the floor votes in the House in both 1958 and 1959 had shown significant, if small, minorities of Republicans splitting with their colleagues to support food stamp plans: 15 percent and 18 percent, respectively. If similar proportions could be persuaded to support food stamps in 1964, this would amount to 26–32 Republican votes, a number well worth shooting for on a closely divided issue. The fact that the 18 percent Republican vote for food stamps in 1959 was cast in the face of unanimous opposition by the twelve Republicans on the Agriculture Committee shows that some number of the Republican contingent in the House were not decisively influenced by their colleagues on the committee. The appeals by Mathias and Fulton may have been directed more to them than to the committee Republicans.

Furthermore, there was a possibility in June of 1963 that even some committee Republicans could be persuaded to support the administration's bill. Although it is true that Republicans on the committee had unanimously opposed the 1959 bill, and therefore that the nine who were still serving in 1963 could probably be expected to oppose food stamps again, in the interim five new Republicans had joined the Agriculture Committee (over a third of the party contingent). These five had not formally reviewed the food stamp issue since coming to the committee, and thus their views were probably less settled than those of their more senior colleagues. One sign that the Republicans on the committee did not all enter the hearings dead set against the proposal is Chairman Harold Cooley's remark during floor debate on the bill that Republican opposition coalesced *after* the hearings ended, just prior to final committee action.[36]

Finally, it must be acknowle{ }ed that there *was* a legitimate case {o be made for the preferability of f{ }d stamps over direct distribution on the basis of traditional Republican {rinciples; for unlike direct distribution, the food stamp program would utilize the normal commercial channels of food distribution and thereby support the market system. Thus, there is every reason for believing that the appeals by Mathias and Fulton were genuine efforts to persuade their party colleagues, either on the committee or in the full body, that food stamps were more in keeping with traditional Republican principles than was the existing direct distribution system.

In the absence of witnesses opposed to the food stamp bill and with only modest opposition voiced by committee Republicans, the hearings served less as an arena for debating the merits of the bill than as a forum for the administration and the congressional friends of food stamps to make their best case. Although the food stamp issue was not a new one to the committee, fourteen of its thirty-five members (nine Democrats and five Republicans) had joined the committee since it last considered food stamps in 1959. Forty percent of the committee membership, then, probably had little detailed knowledge of the issue. And even the other twenty-one members were required by the administration's initiative to evaluate a plan that differed in important respects from earlier proposals.

Given that two-fifths of the committee members were new to the food stamp issue and that even veteran committee members had not previously considered the specific kind of program proposed in 1963, it is not surprising that committee members used the hearings to gather basic information on the mechanics, coverage, and cost of the new program. Questions ranged from the very specific—such as whether food stamps could pay for the state sales tax on food items and how the stamps would be distributed to the recipients—to broader policy matters—such as why imported foods were eligible for purchase and how the new program would affect the established direct distribution system.

Because much of the administration's case rested on the purported success of the pilot program begun in 1961, committee members wanted to learn more about the operation of the program and the evidence of its superiority to direct distribution. This kind of questioning worked to the benefit of the administration; for it was well prepared to use the results from the pilot program to support its case. For example, it was not obvious that increasing the food purchasing power of the poor would necessarily lead to more nutritious diets. Food stamps might be used to purchase low nutrition items, or they might be hoarded for future use. Congressman Edward Hutchinson raised the latter point with Secretary Freeman: "Then how can you be assured, Mr. Secretary, that the coupons are going actually to be used for an increased nutritionally adequate diet?" To this Freeman replied, "Our projection on this is based on our studies and surveys of the communities in question."[37] In the absence of an independent evaluation of the pilot program, there was little basis for challenging the administration's positive interpretation of the evidence. That interpretation lent powerful support to the administration's case.

Although not all questions asked at the hearings were of a straightforward information-seeking type—some by Republicans were clearly critical in intent (discussed below)—in the main the three days of hearings served the basic function of informing the committee as to the contents of the administration's proposal and the evidence and arguments supporting its enactment. The high levels of attendance and of participation in the questioning indicate that the members had a real interest in what the witnesses had to say. Nearly two-thirds of the thirty-five members were present for at least some part of each day's testimony, and approximately two-thirds of those present participated in the questioning during the first and second sessions. Altogether, twenty-nine members attended at least one session, and throughout the three days of hearings a total of eighteen members questioned the witnesses. This is precisely what one would expect from an information-gathering exercise.

House Democratic Support for the Administration Plan. Nine months after the hearings ended, eighteen of the Agriculture Committee's twenty-one Democrats voted to report an amended version of the administration's proposal. All fourteen committee Republicans and two Democrats opposed the bill. (One Democrat did not vote.) This sharp partisan division carried over to final passage where 89 percent of voting Democrats were opposed by 93 percent of voting Republicans. Although thirteen Republicans voted "aye" on final passage, the Democratic vote alone (216) would have been sufficient to pass the bill.

The Democratic majority of the Agriculture Committee formally gave its reasons for endorsing food stamps in the committee report issued on March 9, 1964. The committee report explained the principal features of the program and argued the bill's merits. As we have seen, three of the eighteen Democrats who supported the bill may have also been responding to pressure generated by the refusal of the Rules Committee to act on the tobacco research bill. But this pressure was not a factor for the fifteen Democrats who supported food stamps throughout the committee's consideration.

The committee report began by deemphasizing the novelty of the proposal: "The purpose of this bill is to bring under congressional control and enact into law the rules under which food stamp programs are to be conducted in local areas throughout the country."[38] The committee did not propose a wholly new program but simply one that "improves, expands, and makes permanent the food stamp program that is now operating successfully on a pilot and experimental basis."[39] The report then included a seven-page detailed description of the pilot program, demonstrating that the "pilot food stamp program has proven to be an effective means of expanding farm markets and of improving the food consumption and nutrition of low-income households."[40] The results of the pilot program justified expanding the food stamp program and making it a permanent element of national policy.

In its report to the full House of Representatives the committee majority in effect restated the administration's case for the bill. But in so doing they addressed an issue largely ignored by the administration in its original case to the committee: a comparison of food stamps and direct distribution with respect to (1) the kinds of foods consumed and (2) their impact on farm income. Republicans had voiced concern during the hearings that the food stamp program would not meet one of the original purposes of the direct distribution program: to increase consumption of surplus agricultural products and thereby strengthen the agricultural economy. Administration witnesses had replied that consumption of the surplus feed grains would be stimulated indirectly by the increased consumption of meat, dairy, and poultry items. Republicans were skeptical, and this remained the weakest part of the administration's case. In the committee report, however, a major effort was made to show, using the results of a detailed study of one pilot program, that food stamps led to *greater* consumption of feed grains than direct distribution and provided a greater economic benefit to the farmer. In this way the committee report shored up a weakness in the administration's original case, thereby responding to and anticipating Republican objections.

If the majority report was an accurate reflection of the beliefs of most committee Democrats, then it is evident that they were persuaded by the case made at the hearings. They may have been disposed to favor food stamps from the beginning, but the record shows that most knew little about the details of the administration's bill when the hearings opened. The hearings provided those inclined to favor food stamps with information about the program and evidence and arguments to support it.

As will be discussed more fully in chapter 6, the committee's obligation to explain and justify its actions through a formal report to the full body signifies the deliberative aspect of the division of labor effected through the committee system. In principle, the committee does not merely act, or will, for the parent body, but reasons, or deliberates, for it. The full House or Senate then reviews the outcome of the committee's deliberations. The report serves the committee as an instrument for informing and persuading nonmembers, and it serves the full body as the basis for passing judgment on the committee's work. Although we do not know how many representatives (or their staff assistants) read the House Agriculture Committee's report on the food stamp bill, it should be noted that the fifty-four-page report (majority views, seventeen pages; supplemental view, one page; minority views, thirty-two pages) was particularly well designed for efficiently communicating basic information on the background and mechanics of the administration's proposal and the principal arguments on both sides.

One example of how the committee report was intended to serve this information function is the way it handled the committee-passed amendment, introduced by Republican Albert Quie, requiring 50 percent state matching of the cost of the coupons (the cost to the government being defined as the difference between the nominal value of the coupons and the amount paid for them). The amendment had been passed by a coalition of Republicans, who opposed the bill entirely, and conservative Democrats. It did not represent the views of the Democratic majority responsible for the bill as a whole. Consequently, in the majority report the state matching provision was mentioned but not defended,[41] and appended to the report was a one-page separate view signed by committee Chairman Harold Cooley prominently titled, "State matching provision would destroy the food stamp program."[42] Thus it was made clear to the reader that this particular provision was not a recommendation of the supporters of the bill.

As will also be addressed in chapter 6, if the report is the committee's explanation and defense of its actions in print, then floor debate is in large part the committee's explanation and defense in speech. Committee members on opposing sides of the issue usually dominate floor debate, addressing their colleagues in a public forum to argue and debate the merits of the committee's proposal. Although this is termed "general" or "open" debate, it is debate that is very much structured by what has gone on before, by the information and arguments brought to bear on the subject during committee consideration and by the issues that have developed in this earlier stage. Accordingly, the prior committee consideration of food stamps was central to the case made by the bill's supporters during floor debate on April 7 and 8. The floor debate, for example, was filled with references to prior committee consideration of key issues and to the information and arguments contained in the committee report. Committee chairman, Harold Cooley, who led the debate for food stamps, cited the committee report in his opening speech: "I commend our report to you setting forth the purposes of the bill."[43] Throughout the floor debate he and other proponents specifically referred to evidence in the committee report showing greater consumption of surplus food items under food stamps than under direct distribution. Moreover, during the second day of debate the proponents repeatedly argued that various proposed amendments should be voted down by the House because the Agriculture Committee had previously rejected them after careful and serious consideration. For example, in opposing an amendment to prohibit the purchase of foreign foods with food stamps, Congressman Hagen argued that "this amendment or something very similar to it was considered judiciously in our committee and rejected."[44] We return to a discussion of the House floor debate below.

House Republican Opposition to Food Stamps. The Republican dissent on food stamps was formulated sometime after the Agriculture Committee hearings ended. As we have seen, the Republicans did not use the hearings as a forum for a sustained attack on the administration bill. Nonetheless, the core of their opposition was anticipated in the very first question asked by a Republican in the hearings, that of ranking minority member Charles Hoeven to Secretary Freeman: "What was the original purpose of the food stamp plan?"[45] Hoeven went on to argue that the new plan would fail to meet one of the original purposes of direct distribution and earlier food stamp plans: "to get rid of surplus agricultural commodities."[46] He maintained that it "would have practically no effect whatsoever on the surpluses of wheat and corn and other surplus commodities,"[47] that "when you boil it all down, so far as the reduction of the surplus agricultural commodities are concerned, this food stamp plan is just infinitesimal."[48] A few minutes later fellow Republican Clifford McIntire drove home the point:

> Then the real connection between the program and the disposal of surplus commodities is incidental, and it rests in the choice of the person who holds this certificate.
>
> In reality, the program does not direct itself to the removal of surpluses. It directs itself to the volume of food purchasing

in which the purchaser is not limited as to the food items that this certificate will be used for.[49]

The purpose of Hoeven's and McIntire's remarks was to paint the administration's proposal as a radical new departure in public policy. This was a wholly new kind of plan, in Hoeven's words, "a strictly welfare program."[50] On the House floor Hoeven argued that this was the decisive issue: "This is the issue, in the last analysis: Shall we now embark on a complete welfare program, or shall we go back to our original intent and try to do something to get rid of surplus agricultural commodities. That is the issue."[51] Once identified as a straight social welfare program, food stamps could be attacked on traditional Republican grounds: that it would not accomplish what it set out to, that it was excessively expensive and therefore fiscally irresponsible, and that it undermined state and local authority and responsibility.

The Republicans made two arguments regarding why the new plan would not accomplish its purposes. In their dissenting views in the committee report, the Republicans on the Agriculture Committee held that "with the adoption of this legislation, State governments will be much less inclined to increase benefits to the needy people in their States. . . . Why . . . should States now increase these benefits if the Federal Government is going to undertake to meet a major portion of the food needs of its welfare recipients?"[52] This argument, however, was not pursued during floor debate.

The second and more actively debated point was that fewer needy people would be served under food stamps than under direct distribution. This pattern had been observed in the pilot programs when food stamps replaced direct distribution. In the minority report on the committee bill the Republicans introduced evidence to show that in some of the pilot program sites fewer people participated in the food stamp program than had previously been receiving surplus commodities through direct distribution.[53] This was a rare case where the minority was able to use the results of the pilot program against the bill's supporters. Republicans made a special point of raising this issue on the floor. For example, Representative Sullivan, one of the floor leaders for food stamps, was pressed on the decline in participation from 63,000 to 12,000 when a pilot food stamp program replaced direct distribution in her St. Louis district.[54] Shortly thereafter Republican Catherine May introduced figures showing a decline from 10,032 to 3,281 in the number of participants in the state of Washington's pilot project.[55]

The issue of cost was another major theme in the Republican opposition. The opponents charged that the food stamp program would end up being enormously more expensive than its supporters would admit. Committee Democrats, relying on a study conducted by the Department of Agriculture, had estimated the net additional federal cost of a national food stamp program at $80–175 million per year. The Republicans, however, citing an earlier Department of Agriculture study, this one conducted in 1957 during the Eisenhower administration, estimated the cost of a national program at something between $600 million and $2.5 billion per year depending on the scope of the program. This was an expense, the committee Republicans charged, that "our country cannot afford . . . in a period of chronic deficits."[56]

Finally, the Republicans opposed the food stamp program as an unwarranted federal infringement upon state and local authority. It was "a fundamental principle of our Federal-State welfare programs that the primary responsibility for welfare should rest with those units of government closest to the people." If the federal government does act to help meet local needs, then "the State and local governments should bear at least half of the burden."[57] Thus, if there must be a permanent food stamp program, the Republicans argued, one-half of the cost of the coupons should be borne by state and local governments, a provision they had managed to insert in the committee-passed bill (Quie amendment). In a statement included in the committee report, Representative Quie described state matching in social welfare programs as a "time-honored and time-tested principle that has been historically and successfully followed . . . to give the State and local governmental bodies the opportunity to share in both the benefits and the responsibilities of federally sponsored programs."[58] Quie defended the principle of state matching during both days of floor debate.

The Republicans' indictment of the administration's bill is best summed up in the following language from the minority report:

> . . . the establishment of a national food stamp plan is not needed; it would be extremely expensive and inefficient; it would destroy the rights and usurp the responsibilities of local and State governments; it would aggravate the problems of commodities now held in surplus stocks by the Government; it would add hundreds of new employees in the Department of Agriculture; it would give the Secretary of Agriculture new broad and sweeping powers; it would be adverse to the needy

people it is designed to help; and it would be of little benefit
to the U.S. farmer.[59]

Like their counterparts on the other side of the issue, only a small
fraction of Republicans in the House actively participated in the debate
on food stamps during the Eighty-eighth Congress. The handful of Republicans on the Agriculture Committee carried the burden of the case
against the bill. The character of their arguments indicates that they directed their appeal principally to party colleagues in the House. That
93 percent of Republicans opposed food stamps on the House floor is
evidence of the persuasiveness of these conservative appeals among fellow party members in the House.

There was, however, one element of the Republican strategy that was
directed not to other Republicans but to southern Democrats. This was a
concerted effort, begun in the hearings and carried through the committee report and floor debate, to raise the civil rights implications of the food
stamp act, suggesting that the South might be cut out of the program by
administrative action because of segregated commercial establishments.

Republican Paul Findley surfaced the civil rights issue in his questioning of Secretary Freeman on the first day of the hearings: "The President
has been giving a lot of attention to segregation recently. I was wonder-
ing whether in the operation of the pilot food stamp program you limited it to stores which are racially nondiscriminatory?"[60] After Freeman
responded that the bill prohibited discrimination in the distribution of
stamps, Findley continued: "How about the store itself—do you limit the
programs to stores which operate on a racially nondiscriminatory basis?
That subject has been in the papers a lot of late. I notice that the President would like to end segregation. Would this not be a way to put a
financial incentive into this, moving toward a nondiscriminatory basis
in the operation of grocery stores."[61] Fellow Republican Delbert Latta
made the point very clear on the final day of hearings in his questioning
of Howard Davis of the Department of Agriculture:

> Let me preface my question by saying that since I have
> been a Member of Congress I have supported civil rights leg-
> islation and I probably will support civil rights legislation if
> any is presented in this session, but the way this bill is written
> and if it is passed the way [it] is written, would it not be pos-
> sible to enforce civil rights legislation by withholding foods
> from needy areas until they did whatever was directed by the
> Justice Department? . . .

It gives the Federal Government one more lever or one more club to use in its drive toward complete integration in the South.[62]

By the time the Committee's report on food stamps was issued, the House had passed its version of the Civil Rights Act of 1964. In the minority report on the food stamp bill the Republicans described the provisions of title VI of the civil rights legislation—"Nondiscrimination in Federally Assisted Programs"—and concluded with the statement: "We are confident, therefore, that if H.R. 10222 [food stamp bill] should become law, the provisions of title VI would be enforced under the food stamp program."[63] Although the Republicans did not elaborate on what this would mean for the South, their clear intent was to heighten the concerns of southerners in the House.

This effort to split off southern Democrats from their colleagues on food stamps was carried one step further when at the very beginning of the second day of floor debate the first Republican speaker, H. R. Gross, asked whether food stamp funds could be withheld from a state found to be in violation of its citizens' civil rights. This set off a lengthy exchange between Chairman Harold Cooley of the Agriculture Committee, Majority Leader Carl Albert, several southern Democrats, and several Republicans. Nothing much was settled, and the debate did not seem to leave a marked impression on southern Democrats.

This persistent effort by Republicans to raise the civil rights issue may not have been intended to foster the highest kind of deliberation on the food stamp bill, but it *was* designed to persuade southern Democrats that from their point of view the bill suffered from serious defects, either alone or in conjunction with the pending Civil Rights Act. The introduction of this issue by Republicans at each stage of the legislative process—during the hearings, in the committee report, and during floor debate—demonstrates their belief that the arguments and issues they raised in the formal legislative channels might be efficacious.

The two sides of the food stamp controversy confronted each other in a highly active debate on the floor of the House on April 7 and 8, 1964. On the first day twenty-eight members of the House participated, fourteen on each side. On the second day forty-five members debated various proposed amendments to the committee bill. The discussion on both days bore the marks of a real exchange among the opposing parties. The principal debaters on each side showed themselves well versed on the major issues and prepared to meet their opponents' arguments. Few speeches were completed without interruptions—some intended to assist the speaker in making his best case, but most aimed at exposing weaknesses or errors in the speaker's presentation. As noted earlier, at the end of the second day of debate, the food stamp bill passed by a vote of 229–189. The bill was supported by 89 percent (216) of voting Democrats and only 7 percent (13) of voting Republicans.

A DELIBERATIVE EXPLANATION FOR THE PASSAGE OF FOOD STAMPS

This brief review demonstrates the vitality of argument that characterized the House consideration of food stamps in 1963 and 1964. At every stage the principal parties felt compelled to defend their positions with empirical information and reasoned arguments and to respond to charges from the other side. The arguments on both sides were honed throughout the process, as supporters and opponents sought to construct the most persuasive case for their position. By their behavior the legislative antagonists showed that information and arguments on the merits of food stamps mattered to the fate of the bill. Indeed, the legislative record on food stamps displays none of the lifelessness that one would expect from a merely formal rhetorical process if all the "real action"—power plays and wheeling and dealing—was occurring behind the scenes.

To be more specific, the record reviewed here displays much that one would expect to find in a true deliberative process in Congress, including
• the function of the committee hearings in providing a basic working knowledge of the administration's proposal and in bringing forth the evidence and arguments in its defense;
• a high degree of attendance and participation at the hearings, indicating that the members were genuinely interested in learning about the issue before them;
• the attempt during the hearings by the few Republican supporters of food stamps to appeal to their party colleagues on the basis of traditional Republican principles;
• the consistent effort by Republican opponents to persuade their party colleagues that the new proposal violated long-standing Republican principles;
• the effort by Republican opponents to persuade southern Democrats to oppose food stamps because of the civil rights implications of the bill;
• the action by committee Democrats to strengthen the administration's case for the bill in the committee report by detailing evidence of

the consumption of surplus commodities in the pilot food stamp program;
• the opponents' attempt to challenge the results of the pilot program by
presenting figures to show substantial declines in participation when
food stamps replaced direct distribution; and
• the lively debate among the opposing parties on the floor of the House.

In light of this evidence of deliberation in the House consideration of
food stamps, I suggest the following explanation for why the House of
Representatives passed the Food Stamp Act of 1964.

When the House Agriculture Committee opened hearings on the administration's food stamp proposal in June of 1963, most committee
members were familiar with the general issues but not with the details of
the new proposal nor with the experience under the pilot program. The
Democrats were generally disposed to support the administration. From
what they knew about food stamps they considered it a sensible way to
improve the diets of low-income families without the indignities and in-
convenience of direct distribution. The more they learned about the administration's program in the hearings, the more certain they became
that it was a good program that should be expanded and made permanent. They were especially attracted to the feature, absent from earlier
food stamp plans, that made all food items eligible for purchase with the
stamps. The breaking of the direct connection between food stamps and
surplus commodities that this entailed was not especially troublesome;
for most committee Democrats were more interested in the social welfare
aspects of the program than in its impact on the agricultural economy,
or they were persuaded that the new plan would indirectly stimulate consumption of surplus commodities.

The committee Republicans, on the other hand, were skeptical when
the hearings opened and inclined to oppose the administration's bill.
They were particularly interested in aiding the farmers by increasing the
demand for surplus food products, and this goal remained primary.
They had long believed that the direct distribution of surplus products
to needy persons was the most logical way both to relieve the surplus and
to improve nutrition. Food stamps appeared to them as a complicated
and inefficient scheme designed more to appease liberal sensibilities than
to dispose of farm surpluses. As the features of the new plan were spelled
out in the hearings, these Republicans became convinced that the administration proposal represented a fundamental break with the past, that it
was a straight social welfare program that would have minimal effect on
the disposal of surpluses. After the hearings ended the Republicans cau-

cused to find widespread agreement on the defects of the legislation. They were convinced that direct distribution was a better program and voted unanimously to oppose the committee bill.

The committee Democrats, in the meantime, faced defections within their own ranks. Four southern congressmen and one from Missouri were less attracted to the program than their northern colleagues and initially opposed it. Two remained steadfast, but the other three, faced with the possible defeat of a tobacco research bill in the Rules Committee and propitiated by further amendments in the food stamp bill, changed their minds. This constituted a majority of the committee, which reported an amended bill to the full House.

The bill's success in the committee virtually assured that the body of liberal northern Democrats would support it. Food stamps was a recognized liberal issue. Even those who knew little of the details of the program understood that the direct distribution of large quantities of surplus items to persons who waited in long lines through all kinds of weather would be replaced by a system providing for the purchase of additional food through regular retail outlets. This alone was enough to dispose most liberal Democrats to support food stamps. And as for the details of the bill, most were willing to trust the combined judgment of the administration, the liberal Democrats on the Agriculture Committee, and long-time sponsor Congresswoman Sullivan.

Southern Democrats in the House were more ambivalent, reflecting the ambivalence of the southerners on the Agriculture Committee. Many had supported the earlier plan and were inclined to support the new one. Others were simply disposed to follow the Democratic administration. Some, however, were clearly opposed to the plan. In order to attract as many southern votes as possible the leadership devised the strategy of tying the votes on the food stamp bill and the wheat-cotton bill together. Southerners were keenly interested in the cotton provisions of the latter bill, and the assurance that it would pass if food stamps passed convinced perhaps a dozen or more of them to support the administration.

Republicans in the full House, however, had received a clear signal from their colleagues on the Agriculture Committee: all had voted against the committee bill. Like their committee colleagues Republicans in the House tended to favor direct distribution over food stamps. If the federal government was to be involved in feeding the needy, they preferred to see this done specifically with the overproduction of the agricultural sector rather than as part of a general program to increase the purchasing power of the poor. Once they learned that the pending proposal, unlike earlier plans, was not directly tied to surplus commodities and that it included other features unattractive to those who espoused Republican principles, most determined that it was a bad bill.

In this atmosphere the food stamp bill came to the House floor on April 7 and 8, 1964. Most congressmen had probably already decided how to vote. It is unlikely that many attended the debate in a strictly neutral frame of mind, equally open to arguments on both sides. Some, however, inclined to vote one way or the other, may have attended to hear the case on each side before making a final decision. Even at this late date many congressmen, occupied with their own committee work and constituency service, may not have had a chance to review the principal issues and arguments. The two days of debate provided this opportunity. The floor debate produced no surprises. Those inclined to vote on each side of the issue would have heard good arguments to follow through on their original inclinations. Accordingly, the bill passed.

☆

If this account is broadly accurate, then what explains the passage of the Food Stamp Act by the House of Representatives in 1964 is not "enough individual bargains to build a majority" but rather the reasoned judgment by the vast majority of Democrats in the House that the administration's program constituted good public policy. By improving the nutrition of the poor and by removing the indignities that attended direct distribution, it was the just and humane thing to do. The vast majority of Republicans, on the other hand, remained unconvinced of the merits of food stamps. They opposed such a substantial expansion of the federal welfare function, were much less bothered by the indignities of direct distribution, and were principally concerned with disposing of surplus agricultural commodities. If butter, cheese, and milk were in oversupply, then the best policy would be simply to continue the program of distributing the surplus directly to the poor.

It seems evident that the ideas and beliefs of the members of Congress mattered to the outcome of the decision process on food stamps. Indeed, the whole formal legislative process—including the hearings, the committee report, and the floor debate—can be viewed as an effort to link those ideas and beliefs to this specific bill. This, as best we can tell, is how the majority was built for food stamps, both on the committee and in the full body (with partial assists from logrolls involving other bills).

Once we concede the existence of broad policy preferences among those who serve in the U.S. Congress, hardly a heroic assumption, then the argument for the necessity of bargaining to build majorities collapses and the importance of the formal legislative process comes into focus. If the proponents of a bill can, through reasoned appeals, persuade a majority on a committee or in the full body that their policy goals will be served by a particular legislative proposal, then wherein lies the necessity to bargain? Reasoned appeals, of course, may well fall short of fashioning an ironclad majority, as was apparently the case on the wheat-cotton bill. At such times additional votes may be sought through nondeliberative means.

Lawmaking as a Rational Effort to Do Good

The food stamp case serves as a window on the broad issue of the interaction and relative importance of bargaining and deliberation in the legislative process. In so far as the lessons from this case are more generally applicable, as evidence in this and the following chapters will support, the following generalizations seem valid:

- The members of Congress bring with them to the institution and/or develop while they serve a variety of beliefs, preferences, or dispositions regarding public policy.
- These beliefs, preferences, and dispositions provide an independent basis for how members vote in committee and on the floor.
- In many, and perhaps most, cases preexisting policy preferences are too general and imprecise to stipulate specific decisions within Congress.
- Hence, the principal purpose of the formal legislative process is to link general policy preferences to a specific course of action: that is, to persuade legislators through information and arguments to support, amend, or oppose a particular legislative initiative.

The very existence of policy preferences—of ideas and beliefs about what government should or should not do—inclines legislators to be receptive to information and arguments. House Democrats in 1964 genuinely wanted to ameliorate hunger in America. When the administration told them that it had a plan for doing so, they naturally wanted to learn the details, to find out how the new program would work, and to study the results of the pilot program that ostensibly worked so well. House Republicans, on the other hand, genuinely wanted to restrain the growth of the welfare state. They were disposed to oppose the new program from the beginning, and the more they learned about it the more convinced they became that their initial dispositions were well founded.[64]

This is, of course, a very different picture of Congress from the one painted by the bargaining theorists. Instead of the wholesale trading of votes, we observe legislators reasoning about the merits of a new policy initiative and seeking to persuade their colleagues for or against the measure at hand with pertinent information and arguments. Persuasive rhetoric in the form of arguments about the public good had an importance throughout the legislative consideration of food stamps and an actual impact on the results in a way that no pure bargaining theory could explain. Instead of hundreds of private preferences being aggregated through bargaining mechanisms, the legislative process on food stamps can best be described as a rational effort to do good, in the face of two competing understandings of the good.

Given the dominance of theoretical formulations that seemingly deny any real importance to reasoning about the public good in Congress, it is striking how many case studies describe the lawmaking process in the House and Senate as largely a rational effort to do good. Six such studies are briefly summarized here.

In his study of the passage of the Federal Aviation Act of 1958 Emmette Redford presents the history of the act as an intelligent and serious attempt by Congress to meet the growing problem of air safety caused by an increasingly congested airspace and the advent of jet transportation. It became clear to Congress that air traffic control systems had to be upgraded, including increased coordination of civil and military air traffic. The Federal Aviation Agency was Congress's answer to the growing problem: "A consciousness of need arose and . . . Congress met this need by passing a law."[65] In his conclusion Redford distinguished his findings from the usual interpretations of how Congress legislates:

> Much attention has been given [by others] . . . to decision-making as a process of choice from among alternatives, and to the making of choices in a setting of conflict in which warriors are struggling for contending interests and viewpoints. There was necessity for choice and there was conflict among parties in the instance of the Federal Aviation Act, but there was also unity of purpose and congruences of interests which led to cooperation in search for solutions and to accomodation of rival needs in order to achieve the consensus necessary to enact a law. . . . [There was] a core of common interest which bound the parties and which seemed to accord with the general needs of the public and the nation.[66]

Another important federal initiative in the same year as the Federal Aviation Act was the National Aeronautics and Space Act. In her study of the creation of NASA, Alison Griffith presents a similar picture of Congress as a rational problem-solving body. Here the problem to be confronted was Soviet ascendancy in space exploration, signaled by the successful Sputnik launch of October 4, 1957.

In the ten months following Sputnik "Congress educated itself so as to act competently and legislate thoroughly."[67] Special committees were set up in the House and Senate to consider the Eisenhower administration's proposal to establish a National Aeronautics and Space Agency. Members were selected "who would work hard," and an able staff was assembled.[68] Staff reports proved especially valuable to the committees in outlining the issues and providing essential background data. The members of the two committees exhibited "a dedicated spirit and a determination to do the best job possible."[69] The House and Senate hearings "differed considerably, but in the end they tended to complement each other."[70] Two different but broadly similar bills emerged from the two bodies; the differences were settled in conference where the "best of each bill tended to be chosen."[71] In the end the congressional product was a distinct improvement over the administration bill: "Congress legislated creatively, with the bill as it finally emerged a considerable improvement over the initial proposal. Many of the provisions had been strengthened and clarified, and much new material had been added."[72] Griffith's overall assessment was that information was decisive: "The Act seems to have been a triumph of research and fact finding. No one can examine the quality of testimony in the hearings or the comprehensiveness and excellence of the staff reports without being aware that here was probably the determinative factor."[73]

These two studies remind us that not all legislative proposals excite sharp partisan, ideological, or regional conflicts. Consensus on goals, such as the safe and efficient use of airspace or American ascendancy in space exploration, supports a cooperative decisionmaking process. In an effort to meet a pressing national problem the members of Congress may engage in a process of instrumental reasoning, a rational assessment and comparison of alternative proposals in search of the most effective remedy.

A less consensual deliberative process is described by Daniel Patrick Moynihan in his insider's account of the Nixon administration's Family Assistance Plan, passed by the House of Representatives in early 1970 but defeated in the Senate some months later. Regarding the role of deliberation at the various stages of the policy process, Moynihan's major point is that reasoned consideration of the nature of the rapidly escalating welfare problem (mushrooming welfare rolls and therefore growing dependency) led the Nixon administration to formulate and the House of Representatives to approve a major departure in social policy: income supplements to the working poor and a federally financed income floor for all welfare recipients, i.e., a guaranteed income. The plan then failed in the Senate, Moynihan argues, because the Senate Finance Committee was institutionally incapable of giving the complex issue the serious attention it deserved.

Moynihan especially praises the work of the House Ways and Means Committee and its chairman, Wilbur Mills. Where other political institutions were "much concerned with the symbols of politics, Ways and Means was almost totally taken up with its substance."[74] This was particularly true of its chairman. Mills "was pragmatic: above all, open to information. As he learned more about welfare he more and more came to feel that something had to be done."[75] (Mills is profiled at some length in chapter 5.) In working through the welfare problem and formulating an amended version of the administration's plan, the Ways and Means Committee in effect deliberated for the full House. The House "was perfectly willing to trust to the competence and prudence of the committee to offer the course of action that seemed best. The traditions of Ways and Means, in turn, dictated a process of careful deliberation and judicious compromise aimed at furthering the business at hand."[76] In sum, "the committee had done the work of the House, *for* the House. . . . This was deference to reasonable, moderate men."[77]

Unlike bargaining interpretations of how collective decisions are reached in Congress, deliberative explanations hold that ideas about the public interest, like the Nixon administration's argument that a guaranteed income would reduce welfare dependency, can build majorities in the House and Senate. This is, for example, part of the explanation given by T. R. Reid, who closely followed the progress of the Waterway User Charge Act in Congress in 1977–78, for why Congress passed a law charging the barge companies for the first time for use of the inland waterway system. Although opposed by powerful interests and given little likelihood of passage when introduced by first-term Republican senator Pete Domenici, this fundamental redirection in long-standing national policy became law in part because "the force of a good idea is a powerful influence. From the beginning of his uphill fight to pass the waterway bill, Pete Domenici benefited from the general perception, at least among those members [of Congress] not closely allied with the barge industry, that it was a good idea to end the barge lines' free ride."[78]

Similarly, in their study of the deregulation of the airlines, trucking, and telecommunications industries between 1975 and 1980, Martha Derthick and Paul Quirk conclude by emphasizing the importance of ideas about the good to flow from deregulation in overcoming the political opposition of the affected interests. "Elite opinion," including that of economists, policy research organizations, and political leaders, had "converged in support of reform."[79] During the congressional debates those advocating reform "managed to provide simple and vivid cues on the merits of the issues . . . and to make a rhetorical connection between deregulation and larger concerns of the general public."[80] The deregulation movement demonstrated "[a]s vividly and impressively as possible . . . the role that disinterested economic analysis can play in the formation of public policy."[81] In the end the decision to deregulate airlines and trucking (and to a lesser extent telecommunications) "was reached through a process of orderly deliberation in which symbolism played some, but not a dominant, role."[82]

One of the most widely read case studies of recent years is Jeffrey Birnbaum and Alan Murray's study of the major domestic initiative of President Ronald Reagan's second term, the Tax Reform Act of 1986. This is a highly detailed and nuanced account of the constellation of forces and personalities that came together to produce a radical restructuring of a system of tax preferences that was vigorously defended by many of the most powerful interests in American society. In assessing the reasons why tax reform passed, the case study authors give full credit to such nondeliberative factors as political pressure and private ambition. Yet they acknowledge that "[r]eform was also achieved because it combined goals that were important to both political parties." Democrats, or at least some of them, had long wanted to end tax loopholes for the rich. Supply-side Republicans "were passionately committed to lowering tax rates." This combination created "an impressive bipartisan coalition" attracted to tax reform for broad ideological reasons.[83] In the end, Birnbaum and Murray conclude that tax reform "was a heroic effort to address a profound and pervasive social and cultural problem that had been ignored for too long. For all its faults, the Tax Reform Act of 1986 was the rough-hewn triumph of the American democratic system."[84] Or as Albert Hunt put it in the introduction to the book, "[a]bove all, this is a drama about a powerful idea whose time arrived to the surprise of many so-called insiders."[85]

Although these are some of the clearest examples, many other case studies could be brought to bear to demonstrate the importance of ideas in general or of information, arguments, and persuasion in particular in building majorities in the House and Senate. Without in any way denying that bargains of various types occur for some bills among some legislators at some stages in the decision process, the empirical evidence simply does not support the view that bargaining is "the most characteristic legislative process . . . . [or] the very nature of the process,"[86] that it is "[t]he very essence of the legislative process,"[87] that it is "a ubiquitous feature of the legislative process . . . . [and] endemic to the legislative process,"[88] or that "[t]he typical public law is simply the outcome of enough individual bargains to build a majority."[89] Moreover, not only is the dominance of bargaining unsupported by the empirical evidence, there is, as we have seen, no theoretical necessity for bargaining as a device for reaching collective decisions in Congress. There is nothing about the nature of Congress as such that requires bargaining to build majorities in subcommittees, full committees, or on the floor. Indeed, the empirical evidence reviewed here makes a stronger case for the view that reasoned persuasion through the use of substantive information and arguments is the more powerful force throughout the legislative process.

One final point about bargaining versus deliberation is worth addressing. The presumption of deliberative democracy is that better decisions will result when legislators reason together about the merits of proposed policies than when they simply bargain with each other. Yet some pluralist and rational choice theorists defend bargaining as a positive good, as a useful device in a large heterogeneous society for aggregating the diverse and often conflicting preferences of legislators, interest groups, or geographically defined constituencies. Such mutual accommodation helps the various parts of the whole to satisfy their interests, while mitigating the potential divisiveness of trying to reach principled judgments in Congress about "what is good for the nation."

Two points can be made about this positive defense of bargaining. First, the evidence reviewed here suggests that national laws in the United States are not, as a general rule, fashioned by aggregating through bargains the preferences of the hundreds of legislators necessary to pass bills. As noted earlier, twenty-nine case studies of lawmaking in Congress written at the very time when pluralist interpretations of American government were dominant revealed only a handful of examples where bargaining seemed to be at all important in the decisionmaking process. Thus, those who attribute to bargaining some of the virtues of the American governmental system are relying on an activity that is not nearly so characteristic of lawmaking in Congress as they suppose. If

American government is to be praised for moderate policies and the accommodation of diverse interests, the explanation must lie elsewhere than a bargaining machine at the heart of the U.S. Congress.

Second, whatever the advantages of bargaining in dispersing discrete public benefits, such as water projects, throughout the nation, how could bargains among hundreds of different legislators help Congress to make wise decisions on such great national issues as how large a military force and of what type to maintain in the post-Cold War era; whether to continue funding the Strategic Defense Initiative; whether and where to support American military intervention overseas; whether and how to restructure the nation's health care system; whether and how to reform federal welfare programs; how to tend for the wellbeing of the environment without unduly impairing economic growth; how to define equal rights and whether to embrace affirmative action policies to redress past discrimination; how to improve the nation's schools; or how to reduce crime? There are, after all, better and worse answers to these questions, better and worse policies that Congress might embrace. The task of the national lawmaker is to find the better answer, to fashion the better policy. How else are the nation's legislators to do so responsibly but by reasoning together on the merits of proposed approaches, informed by the best information and arguments available?

CHAPTER FIVE

Interest, Ambition, and the Character of Lawmakers

> For some members, the purpose of serving in the Senate was to remain there. Keeping in touch with home, taking care of constituents, and tending sacred cows was a full-time occupation. They performed these tasks so that they might be retained to perform them again.
>
> But for most senators, these were only requirements, not purposes. For them, a senator's purpose was to legislate on matters of concern to the country.
>
> Harry McPherson[1]

> If they're there only to get reelected, what's the purpose of it? If you aren't going to contribute your own judgment, anybody can do the job and there isn't any real issue as to which person could do it better, or is more qualified, or has higher personal character and integrity, or anything else.
>
> Senator John Culver[2]

As noted at the end of chapter 3, bargaining and reelection theories are the two great pillars that support the widespread contemporary view that Congress is not a deliberative institution (at least in any fundamental sense) and, by implication, that American democracy is not a deliberative democracy. We have seen in the previous chapter how little support the case studies of policymaking within Congress provide for the belief that bargaining is the predominant device for reaching collective decisions in the House and Senate. What, then, of the reelection incentive as the principal explanation for individual desires and actions? No one can dispute the analytical attractiveness of *assuming* its dominance, but what does the empirical evidence tell us, fairly reviewed?

We must be careful how we frame the issue. The question here is not whether the reelection incentive matters in Congress. The vast majority of those who serve in the House and Senate give every indication that they desire to remain in office (although some voluntarily resign at each election). Thus, it is reasonable to call the reelection incentive an established fact. This incentive, then, inclines the members of Congress to engage in behaviors helpful to future electoral success. As we have seen, such behaviors are not limited to formal campaigning. They may occur throughout a legislative term (it is not unusual to hear House members complain about campaigning for reelection all the time) and may include activities that are clearly nonlegislative in character, such as tracking down missing social security checks, posing for photographs with delegations from home, and the like. That those who serve in the House and Senate devote a certain amount of their time and resources, especially staff time, to nonlegislative activities that will promote reelection is beyond dispute.

Thus the issue here is not whether the members of Congress pursue reelection but rather whether the reelection incentive squeezes out deliberative activities in a way that undermines, or even destroys, Congress's character as a deliberative institution. This could occur in two ways. First, reelection-oriented activities could so consume the time and resources of the member that nothing is left for serious reasoning about public policy. Second, the reelection incentive could intrude upon formal legislative activities in such a way as to distort otherwise deliberative behavior. For example, the committee member who single-mindedly plays to the cameras during some hearing on a controversial matter because it is good politics has allowed his private interests to overcome his deliberative responsibilities.

While it is certainly possible for the reelection incentive to undermine deliberation in these two ways, it is not necessary. The fact that the members of Congress do certain things to promote their reelection is hardly proof that they do not do other things to reach reasoned judgments about the merits of public policy. Indeed, as noted earlier, those who designed the American Congress saw no necessary incompatibility between the reelection incentive and deliberation. The framers believed not only that the legislator's desire to return to Congress would not disable him from engaging in genuine deliberation about national laws, but also that the reelection incentive was the vital link between deliberations in Congress and popular interests and attitudes. Indeed, to argue that the system of public accountability in the modern Congress makes genuine deliberation impossible is virtually the equivalent of saying that deliberation and democracy, as presently constituted in the United States, are incompatible.

It follows, then, that in assessing Congress as a deliberative institution the issue is not so much whether the reelection incentive is a powerful motive in influencing congressional behavior, but rather whether and to what degree legislators in the U.S. Congress embrace and act upon the independent desire to promote good public policy, the end for which deliberation is the means. How much evidence do we have that the ambitious and reelection-seeking members of Congress actually care about and work to promote good public policy? And if the evidence supports the notion that the goal of good public policy influences congressional behavior in important ways, what can we say about the relationship of good public policy to reelection or to other self-interested goals?

How Many Goals; How Do They Matter?

In his 1973 book on committees Richard Fenno postulated that the members of the House of Representatives pursue three "basic" goals: "They are: *re-election, influence within the House, and good public policy.* . . . All congressmen probably hold all three goals. But each congressman has his own mix of priorities and intensities—a mix which may, of course, change over time."[3] Why these three goals? Because when Fenno asked 179 members of the House who served on six different committees why they wanted to serve on their particular committee, these were the goals they described. The six committees in the study fell into three pairs, with one goal dominating for the members of each of the pairs. Not only did these goals explain which committees the members sought, but coupled with the "environmental constraints" that faced the committees they also went quite far in explaining how these committees functioned and the kinds of decisions they made. Thus, in Fenno's study the members' goals and environmental constraints were the "independent variables" and the procedures and decisions of the committees were the "dependent variables."

For present purposes the importance of Fenno's study lies in his two central claims regarding the goal "good public policy": (1) that all members of Congress probably possess this goal to some degree (a proposition not further developed in Fenno's book) and (2) that for a significant portion of the membership this goal was the dominant one. With respect to the latter point it is useful to recall Fenno's characterization of the House members who served on the Education and Labor and the Foreign Affairs committees:

They emphasize a strong personal interest in and a concern for the content of public policy in their committee's subject matter; in short, they want *to help make good public policy*. Congressmen who seek membership on these two committees do so, they say, because these committees deal with "interesting," "exciting," "controversial," and "important" subjects.[4]

There are, it appears, some Congressmen who want to serve on whatever committees happen to be dealing with the most pressing, controversial, national problems of the time.[5]

The distinctive, dominant member goal on Education and Labor and Foreign Affairs is) help make good policy in an area of substantial personal int est.[6]

When Fenno looked at the equivalent committees in the Senate—the Labor and Public Welfare and the Foreign Relations Committees—he found a similar devotion to promoting good public policy: "for those members positively attracted to the Senate Labor and Public Welfare Committee, the dominant motivation is the promotion of their policy interests. . . . [T]he dominant goal of most members [of the Senate Foreign Relations Committee] remains participation in the making of good foreign policy."[7]

In a footnote to his Introduction, Fenno explained that "goal seeking" by the members of Congress was "a keystone" of his analysis. In this respect he was rejecting the emphasis on committees as social systems that had characterized his previous work on the appropriations committees of Congress, for "[a]ll committees are not pre-eminently social systems."[8] There are two points to note here. First, goal seeking appeared to be a more fruitful analytical approach than a social-psychological one. Second, one of the goals with substantial explanatory power was the desire to promote good public policy. Thus, to say that the behavior of the members of Congress results more from independent goal seeking than from the pressure of social and psychological forces is not to say that the goal seeking must be of a narrowly self-interested sort. Indeed, Fenno's work can be viewed as a persuasive demonstration of the importance of good public policy—and not simply reelection or power and prestige within Congress—as an independent force in explaining congressional behavior. More recent work on the goals that influence committee selection in the House and Senate has confirmed the continued validity of Fenno's findings.[9] There is a certain irony in the fact that within a few years of Fenno's work demonstrating the power of all three goals in Congress, the leading edge in congressional studies came to focus almost exclusively on the reelection incentive.

Legislative Portraits

Over the past two decades the literature on the United States Congress has been enriched by a number of detailed portraits of those who serve in the House of Representatives and Senate. What do these descriptions of the work and thoughts of the members of Congress tell us about their motives and goals? What do the nation's legislators actually do with their time and resources? What gives them satisfaction in serving in the U.S. Congress?

In the following pages we look in some detail at descriptions of three legislators whose goals, activities, and character cannot be accounted for in terms of narrow self-interest: former Representative Wilbur Mills, former Senator Edmund Muskie, and Senator Pete Domenici. There follows a briefer sketch of three other legislators whose behavior in Congress also cannot be understood without ceding the importance of public-spirited goals and deliberative means. As will be seen, the picture of legislative character that emerges from the studies of these legislators is much closer to Fenno's more complex typology of congressional goals than to the view that the members of Congress pursue only reelection.

WILBUR MILLS

Wilbur Mills (D., Arkansas) served as chairman of the Ways and Means Committee in the House of Representatives from 1958 to 1974. Prior to his fall from power for sexual improprieties and alcohol dependency, he was by all accounts one of the most powerful and respected members of the House. John Manley's book-length study of the Ways and Means Committee, which focused on the period of Mills's chairmanship, Daniel P. Moynihan's study of the Nixon administration's Family Assistance Plan, and Fenno's book on committees present a coherent and consistent portrait of the chairman of the House's tax-writing committee.

According to Manley, Mills insisted that his committee do a "workmanlike job on . . . legislation":

> Mills believes that part of the Committee's job is to examine carefully all policy proposals it actively considers. Given the complexity of tax law and fiscal policy and the need to protect the actuarial soundness of the social security system, he makes

sure that the Committee is painstakingly thorough in the mark-up stage of the legislative process, that it studies the alternatives before reaching conclusions, and that it proceeds cautiously to lessen the chances of adversely affecting the economic status of the country, corporations, or individuals.[10]

Accordingly, Mills's preeminence within his committee was based on "influence" rather than "power": "influence is, in essence, a means of *persuasion* that involves giving reasons or justifications for doing certain things and avoiding others, whereas power may be taken to mean the communication of decisions that activate obligations." Mills was "a leader whose style . . . [was] that of persuasion." Key to Mills's successful persuasion of his colleagues was his "great expertise in the abstruse areas considered by the Committee." Committee members who were "unsure of the answers to complex questions . . . [could] rely on his judgment and expertise."[11]

A Republican member of the Ways and Means Committee attributed Mills's influence to "[h]is knowledge, the fact that he does his homework." Another Republican, in language that future events would prove ironic indeed, attributed his influence to his total devotion to legislative issues: "He's so single minded, never goes out, no social life or cocktail parties. He's thoroughly absorbed, goes home and thinks about the legislation." Democratic committee members shared a similar view of the chairman:

> They see him as a man who has put years into the study of Ways and Means business ("work is his hobby"), knows more than they do ("takes the experts, the specialists who have spent 40 years in the subject, apart"), has great natural ability ("best mind on the Committee"), understands the material ("isn't anything in taxes he fails to understand or fails to relate to what has gone before and tie it into today"), and who, with all of this, is fair and considerate in his relations with them.[12]

The main features of Manley's portrait of Mills—the openness to information, development of expertise, hard work, seriousness of purpose, dedication to good policy, and use of reasoned persuasion—were reiterated by Daniel Patrick Moynihan in his account of the failure of Congress to pass Nixon's Family Assistance Plan (FAP) in 1969–70. As Nixon's Assistant for Urban Affairs, Moynihan was principal author of this major welfare reform and income redistribution proposal. Although Moynihan himself cites the influence of Manley's book on his own thinking, his account of Mills and his committee draws heavily upon his own involvement in the legislative history of FAP.

According to Moynihan, Mills and his committee approached the administration's proposal with an openness to the arguments for reform and a willingness to learn from administration witnesses. As the administration made its case for reform in extensive hearings before the committee, "[t]he hearing began to become a dialogue."[13] It soon became clear that "Mills was struggling with himself and the subject. . . . He was pragmatic: above all, open to information. As he learned more about welfare he more and more came to feel, as had the president, that something had to be done."[14] Mills was "of all things, lawyerlike"; he "led his committee but did not coerce."[15] In the end the committee voted 21–3 to report an amended FAP to the full House. The committee endorsement

> reflected, more than any other single factor, the judgment of the House that 'something' had to be done about welfare; it was perfectly willing to trust to the competence and prudence of the committee to offer the course of action that seemed best. The traditions of Ways and Means, in turn, dictated a process of careful deliberation and judicious compromise aimed at furthering the business at hand. . . . [T]he committee, under Mills's leadership, had established a record of thoroughness and prudence in the execution of its highly technical and consummately important work.[16]

As noted in the example of persuasion in chapter 3, Mills recounted to his colleagues on the House floor how he had been converted from skeptical opponent of the guaranteed income provisions of FAP to vigorous supporter of the key elements of the administration's plan. In a word, Mills had been persuaded by the merits of the administration's case for reform. He, like President Nixon, "was of an analytical frame of mind, and each saw his role as one of decisionmaking."[17] Both "were trying to respond to a specific problem they felt to be serious enough to warrant large risks."[18]

Neither of these accounts of Mills and his contribution to the important legislative business of the House of Representatives attempts to explain his behavior in terms of reelection incentives. Why did Mills work so hard on the taxation, welfare, and other matters that came before his committee? Why did he develop the kind of expertise, especially on taxation issues, that was unchallenged and unsurpassed within the Washington community? Why was he so open to information and arguments from others and so fair-minded and deliberative in how he ran his committee? Can any of these essential features of the legislative character of the longtime chairman of Ways and Means be fairly described as behaviors designed to enhance reelection prospects? Would Wilbur Mills, possessor of one of the safest of the safe seats in Congress (running unopposed in eight of the nine general elections between 1958 and 1974) have been any less likely to be reelected from the Second District in Arkansas if he had been somewhat less hardworking, somewhat less knowledgeable about taxation, somewhat less open to persuasion, or somewhat less evenhanded in running his committee?

What emerges from these portraits of Mills is the strength, not of the reelection incentive, but rather of two very different goals: power and prestige within Congress and good public policy. In his mapping of goals to committees, Fenno argued that the gaining of power and prestige was actually the dominant goal for most members of Ways and Means. (Fenno did not specifically describe Mills's personal goals.) About this, however, two things can be said. First, the record contains substantial evidence that even apart from his power and prestige, Mills was devoted to fashioning good public policy. He was committed to protecting the tax code from irresponsible, if popular, revisions; to preserving the integrity of the social security trust fund; and to reducing dependency on the welfare system. Indeed, on the two great domestic issues to come before his committee in the 1960s—Medicare and Family Assistance—Mills's behavior is more readily explained as promoting good public policy than as enhancing his power and prestige. As noted in chapter 4, he could easily have endorsed the administration's Medicare plan, preserving his prestige within Congress, without expanding it in the dramatic way he proposed. Moreover, given the absence of pressure from the full House in 1969–70 to embrace Nixon's Family Assistance Plan, Mills could likely have quietly killed the proposal in his committee with no loss of power or prestige. I suggest, then, that any comprehensive explanation of the behavior of this key congressional figure—called by Moynihan at the time "the second most powerful man in Washington, following only the president"[19]—must include good public policy as a goal of independent weight and explanatory power.

Second, as Fenno particularly makes clear in his treatment of Mills in his book on committees, the two analytically distinct goals of power and prestige within Congress and good public policy were mutually reinforcing. To put it simply, Mills was able to achieve power and prestige within the House by developing a reputation for the kind of subject matter expertise, hard work, openness to argument and persuasion, and thoroughness of analysis that was necessary to produce sound legislation. By promoting a careful deliberative process within the committee, Mills was able to earn the trust and respect of his committee colleagues. The committee, in turn, by embodying the same deliberative qualities that characterized the chairman, was able to earn the trust and respect (and therefore the votes) of the full House. As a top executive official explained:

> When congressmen see Wilbur Mills bringing out a bill, they know certain things. They know Wilbur Mills has done his homework. They know the Ways and Means Committee has worked on the bill. And with the closed rule and all, they can be sure the Committee has the situation well in hand.[20]

A similar sentiment was expressed by a member of the House Committee on Interior and Insular Affairs, commenting on the floor success of several House committees:

> There are some committees that start with anywhere from a 20- to 50-vote edge. There are three committees that, when they come to the floor, the House knows they have probably done their work. Ways and Means, first of all. Mills . . . . Then, in order, Interstate. Oren Harris . . . . Then [Wayne] Aspinall [chairman of the Interior Committee]. He has the respect of the House and they know once a bill has gone through our process, chances are it's okay. Wayne's a master of the subject.[21]

Fenno also found that the House Appropriations Committee shared with Ways and Means and Interior the same norms of hard work, subject matter expertise, and careful deliberation. Its reputation for embracing such qualities translated directly into success on the House floor.[22] To put the point only slightly more directly than did Fenno himself, the House committees and their chairmen who most displayed "thoroughness of deliberation"[23] in their operations were the ones that earned the most power and prestige in the full House and thus achieved the greatest success on the House floor.

Two conclusions, then, seem warranted from this brief analysis of the legislative character of Wilbur Mills. First, Mills's legislative career cannot be fully understood without ceding the independent importance of the goal of good public policy; and second, Mills's desire to earn power and prestige within the House was served by exhibiting the very qualities that promote good public policy. To rephrase the latter point, Mills's self-interest (his desire to achieve power and to be esteemed and respected by his colleagues) was promoted by demonstrating his devotion to the nation's interests (responsible tax policies, the soundness of the social security system, the health of th᠎ elderly and the poor, and the redu tion of welfare dependency). That   is connection between self-interest and public interest was possible pre   mes, of course, that the members of the House, who held the key to the ,toreroom of power and prestige, did in fact care about good public policy. We shall return to this connection between private interest and public interest below.

EDMUND MUSKIE

Edmund S. Muskie (D., Maine) served in the U.S. Senate from 1959 to 1980. In 1975 and 1976 Muskie gave political journalist Bernard Asbell virtually unencumbered access to his legislative activities, including private meetings with staff and senatorial colleagues, as well as to strategy sessions for his 1976 reelection campaign. During this time Muskie served as chairman of three Senate institutions: the Budget Committee, the Environmental Pollution Subcommittee of the Public Works Committee, and the Intergovernmental Relations Subcommittee of the Government Operations Committee. Muskie's principal legislative preoccupations during these two years were the reauthorization of the Clean Air Act of 1970 (not finally passed until August of 1977) and the defense of the new congressional budget procedures.

By the mid-1970s Senator Muskie and his subcommittee had been grappling with the complexities of air pollution for more than a decade. Years of exposure to pollution issues through the legislative process combined with innumerable hours of private study and reflection had made Muskie an expert on the subject. In the words of his Administrative Assistant, "thinking is cumulative. Over the course of these markups on the Clean Air Act, which he's been doing for twelve years, he's become one of the country's experts on this whole business."[24] Another staff aide attributed the Clean Air Acts of 1963 and 1965 to Muskie's substantive dominance of the issues: "They were primarily the Senate going along with the hard work of Ed Muskie. He dug into the issues like he does every other goddamned thing, and he dug and dug and dug. It's one of the reasons he sometimes gets bored with it now, because nobody's caught up with him. He still knows more than most people, including me."[25]

As Asbell makes clear, Muskie's hard work to master the issues under his jurisdiction did not end with each day's session of the Senate. Commenting on Muskie's preparation for an important markup in 1975 on the Clean Air Act, Asbell writes: "Last night—as he does every night before a major meeting—Muskie took home a black loose-leaf briefing book. It contains summaries of the main factual information brought out in hearings and studies, and [an aide's] advisory memos synthesizing the issues. Muskie often hits his briefing book before breakfast; in fact, before dawn."[26] Consequently, Muskie's aides were not reluctant to "send a lot of stuff home with him" even in the face of his "constant complaints." "But the thing is," one aide noted, "he'll read it. He's very good. Every night, a briefing book on the issue of his hearing or markup the next morning."[27] Muskie's own account was similar: "The staff keeps saying that I'm such a quick and thorough study. They don't know I have to sit up every night reading all their damned stuff."[28] Indeed, according to Muskie, the crush of his evening or early morning homework was the reason why he and his wife cut down their Washington socializing "to the bone":

> [Although it was good for the ego for a while], it kills you. It kills your health and kills your time and your energy and your ability to do your job. Too often when I go to an embassy party or somewhere else, all during the evening I'm worried about that bill that I'd like to be working on, or a problem I'd like to be tackling. When I get home and go to bed, I pile the books up beside it and read until I fall asleep. Well, that's no way to do business. Or get up at five-thirty in the morning.[29]

Just as he worked to build up his personal expertise on the issues thrust before him, so did Muskie seek to educate the subcommittees he chaired. He described his Environmental Pollution Subcommittee as "a well-educated committee," something he "tried to encourage over the years."[30] Committee hearings were designed to generate "dialogue, debate. Questions are raised so the committee understands the underlying complexities."[31] What was sought was "full and free discussion at the subcommittee level."[32] Asbell, for example, was quite surprised at how open Muskie was to the policy arguments of James Buckley, the subcommittee's ranking minority member:

> I'm not adverse, just because he's a conservative, to having Jim Buckley influence my judgment on pieces of legislation. He's going to have good ideas on this issue. . . . When he makes a point it usually has intellectual integrity, so if I don't accept his point of view—my previous view may be eliminated by

what he has to say—I might alter my point of view to meet the objections he's raised. Why should I lose the benefit of that? If he's found a weak point and attacks it, and his attack is credible intellectually, then I'm challenged to grapple with it. And I think you just come out with sounder legislation.[33]

Muskie's goal throughout was to enhance "committee credibility" within the full Senate: "some committees more than others develop a reputation for thoroughness, or comprehension, or reliability for fairness and accuracy, and for good judgment. That may be the most important—a reputation for good judgment."[34]

What was the practical effect in the Senate of all of Muskie's hard work to educate himself and his subcommittee on issues such as air pollution? If the senator, his staff, and other observers are to be believed, the hard work and substantive expertise translated directly into power to move legislation through the Senate. One "veteran and keenly observant staff man" offered the following assessment: "The work of the Senate has thrust on him certain issues, which he may not have chosen, but he's never been heard to complain that they aren't glamorous enough. He knows more about those issues than anybody else . . . . On his issues, especially the environment, he's towering, overpowering, impossible to ignore."[35] Muskie himself forcefully argued that the development of substantive expertise was the surest route to real power in the Senate:

"Power, power," says Muskie impatiently. "People have all sorts of conspiratorial theories on what constitutes power in the Senate. It has little to do with the size of the state you come from. Or the source of your money. Or committee chairmanships, although that certainly gives you a kind of power. But real power up there comes from doing your work and knowing what you're talking about. Power is the ability to change somebody's mind. That is power around here. . . . The most important thing in the Senate is credibility. *Credibility! That* is power." . . .

"When someone gets up to say something is so, and if you can have absolute reliance that he's right, *that* is credibility. And that is power. If you've done your homework and know what you're talking about, that is power. It takes time to build up. Over the years that is one thing that has not changed in the Senate."[36]

This is clearly the portrait of a serious-minded, public-spirited legislator, of someone who cares about the substance of legislation, who works hard to learn the subject matter, who is open to persuasion from others, and who takes seriously his responsibility to persuade others of the merits of his approach to the issues under his jurisdiction. This is hardly the mere showman who thirsts only for reelection and the opportunity to continue to enjoy the perquisites of high office. (Muskie's explanation for why he cut down his Washington socializing is very telling in this regard.) Indeed, as Asbell relates, in several ways during 1975 and 1976 Muskie took actions that he knew would result in significant political costs even though he faced an election in 1976.

One such action was in continuing to insist that the Clean Air Act provide detailed auto emission standards for hydrocarbons, carbon monoxide, and nitrogen oxide. According to one lobbyist who used to work for Muskie's committee, the Clean Air Act and the Water Pollution Control Act were "two of the most detailed statutes ever written by the Congress. The reason is because Muskie insists on it." It would, of course, have been much easier to pass broad statutes that simply delegated the key decisions to the bureaucracy. But by this growing practice of "writing more and more general statutes," Congress had "abdicated its responsibility" and "remove[d] people from the political process. Muskie feels that way." On the other hand, to write detailed statutes takes "an incredible amount of time and effort" and results in "more political risks."[37] If, as political scientists often argue, reelection or other self-interest motives explain why Congress passes vague statutes that leave the details to the bureaucracy or the courts, then other goals or purposes must be operating when some in Congress insist on detailed legislation.

Another action that highlighted Muskie's willingness to take political risks for the sake of good policy was his stubborn defense, as chairman of the Senate's Budget Committee, of the new budget process and its spending guidelines against politically popular proposals. In 1975 the new procedures created by the Congressional Budget and Impoundment Control Act of 1974 were in a trial period (to become mandatory in 1976). In the spring of 1975 the full Senate had endorsed a Budget Committee recommendation specifying total spending, divided among seventeen broad categories. By July, however, the Senate was being asked to expand the school lunch program by $200 million, a violation of the previously approved spending targets. This put Muskie in a particularly difficult position. "He's never opposed school lunches in his life," the Budget Committee's Chief Counsel told Asbell. "The program is very important to Maine, and to him. He's caught between his Maine interests and his committee interest."[38]

Despite the political attractiveness of supporting the expansion in the school lunch program, Muskie forcefully defended the spending limits on the floor of the Senate. "*Discipline* is *discipline*," he exhorted his colleagues. "It cannot be directed only at the defense budget—or only at the space budget—or only at those programs that have no relevance to our own states and our own needs. Discipline has to be across the board."[39] After a floor debate that drew more attention than usual from the members of the Senate, Muskie's position was affirmed by a roll call vote of 61–29. As Asbell described the scene, "The gallery buzzes. The Senators who did the amendment in, still milling, seem slightly awed by something imponderable they have just witnessed: the Senate, *this* Senate of the overwhelming Democratic and liberal majority, *does not defeat school lunch bills.*"[40] Less than a month later the spending targets were threatened by a conference committee report on military procurement. Again Muskie stubbornly resisted spending in excess of the budget resolution and again he won: "Amazing," commented Asbell, "[t]he Budget process wins over the military, 48 to 42!"[41]

It is clear from this portrait that Senator Edmund Muskie was not satisfied simply to serve in the Senate. Mere service and the honor it bestowed were not enough; he was not satisfied simply to *be* a senator, to enjoy the perquisites of office and the prestige of title. Rather his deepest satisfactions came from using his position for good ends, for accomplishing important national goals, such as a cleaner and healthier environment and a more responsible budget process.

In the following quotations from the Asbell book, Muskie describes what motivated and satisfied him in his public life:

> The pleasure in this job, if there is any, is the challenge it gives to your ability to think, to create, to innovate, to put things together.[42]

> [On his high school years:] I wanted to be recognized, to let people know, you know, what I could do. That I was someone who had thoughts, someone of substance. . . .
> I just had this drive for achievement, . . . never satisfied.[43]

> [On law school and the practice of law:] I didn't find law the kind of fulfillment I was really looking for, although I thought I did at the time, and I think I had a potential for being a very good lawyer. But I suppose the same thing that made me want to become class president eventually drew me into politics.[44]

In the [Maine state] legislature I did my homework and I was beginning to learn that I had a capacity to influence others that people thought was unusual at that time, even when I was a freshman legislator.[45]

[A]round here there's only one essential thing—and that's power. I don't mean that in an invidious way. I mean that the Senate and the House together are the power to legislate policy for a great world power. The United States of America is a great power. I'm not saying that in the sense of selfish power. I'm talking about very real, practical power.
    —The thing that draws people to this level of political office is the power to influence great events, great issues. We are deciding issues. There's a personal satisfaction in that—but also a heavy responsibility to do it right, the accountability for which is very real. . . .
    —And that's *the* great satisfaction out of a political life.[46]

The words and actions reported by Asbell are clearly not those of someone whose character is principally explainable in terms of narrow self-interest, such as reelection. The senator portrayed here had higher goals in mind. He wanted "to create, [and] to innovate"; to be recognized as "someone of substance"; to achieve personal "fulfillment"; "to influence others"; and "to influence great events, great issues." He was attracted to political life and to the U.S. Senate because it provided an opportunity for achievement and personal fulfillment that other careers did not offer. In the end one cannot account for the career and the legislative behavior of the Edmund Muskie portrayed here without positing the importance of good public policy as a central, perhaps overriding, goal. As Asbell related Muskie's assessment of the 1977 reauthorization of the Clean Air Act: "Muskie himself is satisfied that the law has located itself at that magical point of political balance: the boldest feasible act in the public interest that takes into account the relative political strengths and conflicting demands for justice by all contenders."[47]

Asbell's own conclusion about politics after a year and a half of close observation of Muskie, his staff, and his colleagues is not the cynical one we have come to expect from journalists who pierce the veneer of principled public rhetoric in Congress to discover an underside of self-interest, power plays, and political deals, but rather the somewhat surprising one that "[t]he purpose of politics is to advance the public interest through mediation among conflicting contenders."[48]

PETE DOMENICI

Pete V. Domenici (R., New M᷍xico) was first elected to the U.S. Senate in 1972. He was reelected in 1978, 1984, and 1990. Between 1978 and 1984 Richard Fenno accompanied Domenici in both New Mexico and Washington, carrying out extensive interviews with the senator, his staff, and other observers of Domenici's electoral and governing activities. This resulted in a book-length study that focused particularly on Domenici's chairmanship of the Senate Budget Committee in the early 1980s.[49]

Given Fenno's previous interest in the nature and importance of the goals that structure the behavior of the members of Congress, it is not surprising that his study of Domenici has much to say about this subject. Upon his first election to the Senate, "Domenici brought with him . . . a strong desire to govern."[50] This desire took two related forms. First, "[h]e wanted to achieve a distinctive degree of influence within the organization—to 'be something' with respect to the governing activity of the Senate." Second, he wanted to have a beneficial impact on American public policy. His legislative activities exhibited nothing less than a "strenuous devotion to the production of good public policy."[51] "He came across not as someone rigidly ideological or slavishly partisan but as someone tenacious in pursuit of his view of good public policy."[52]

Domenici's elevation to the chairmanship of the Senate Budget Committee in 1981 gave him opportunities to govern that had not existed during his first eight years in the Senate. A strong believer in the importance of the new congressional budget procedures, he was committed to protecting the budget process from the centrifugal forces that threatened to destroy it and to using the process to pursue "his strongly held policy goals[:] . . . . reductions in federal spending, a balanced federal budget, and a growing economy."[53] These policy goals led him into occasional conflicts with fellow Republicans on his committee, frequent conflicts with committee Democrats and the Democrat controlled House of Representatives, and, by the later Reagan years, difficult disputes with the Republican administration. Throughout his chairmanship (which ended when the 1986 election returned the Democrats to majority status in the Senate) Domenici displayed a tenacity and forcefulness in pursuit of a balanced budget that was unequalled by the other prominent actors: "[h]is primary policy thrust was always to reduce excessive spending and to balance the budget."[54]

Domenici himself was but one of twenty-two members of the Budget Committee, and there was no guarantee that what the Budget Committee proposed would be endorsed by a majority of the full Senate. To achieve his governing goals, the New Mexico senator would require support from many others who did not necessarily share the same policy vision or who faced different constituency pressures. How did the committee chairman generate such support? One way was by earning the respect of his colleagues through hard work and the development of substantive expertise. To earn respect, he told Fenno, "you've got to specialize and become knowledgeable and get it out to your fellow man." [55] This was especially important within the Budget Committee. Committee members, according to Fenno, "respected his knowledge and hard work, credited his earnest desire to be constructive and responsible, and appreciated the difficulty of his task." [56]

Having established his credibility with his colleagues, Domenici sought to persuade them to his views through rational argument. "Chairman Domenici's strength [was] leadership by policy argument. . . . Pete Domenici is an educator; and he operates from a wealth of knowledge about his subject. As chairman, it was his style to design the best policy he could [and] explain it to whomever would listen." [57] As Domenici described his view of the importance of leading debate on the floor of the Senate: "I'm going to take as long as it takes to make an argument and persuade people that mine is the best way to do it." [58] Domenici was hardly naive about the ultimate sufficiency of persuasion through reason. He understood that at a certain point persuasion would not be enough and that he would have to "reach out to make accommodations [through bargaining and trade-offs] to build a majority." [59] But his budget efforts always began with a rational assessment of what ought to be done and then an effort to persuade others of the merits of his view: "His preference was to lead by economic argument and then to bargain incrementally, at the margins, over the budget numbers needed to attract majority support." [60] At times the bargaining in the final days of the budget process necessary to build a majority could result in substantial concessions:

> At this point [in May of 1982], the process of coalition building had brought the final out-year (fiscal 1985) deficit figure in the Domenici Plan from a projected surplus of $6 billion on May 3, to a projected deficit of $20 billion *early* on May 5, to a deficit of $40 billion as passed by the [budget] committee on May 6, to a deficit of $65 billion as presented to the Senate on May 19. [61]

Both the senator and his staff consciously viewed the Domenici approach as serious and responsible lawmaking in contrast to the kind of posturing and demagoguery often found in Congress. Reflecting on his sponsorship of legislation to set up a system of fees for the use of the nation's inland waterways, Domenici told Fenno that "I felt I was really accomplishing something—not bullshit and demagoguery"[62] He made a similar point in discussing his upcoming 1984 reelection contest:

> I want the people of New Mexico to know what I'm doing. I'm a player now. . . . I don't want any fru frus, any bullshit and demagoguery. I don't want to say, "I cosponsored such and such a bill" when I'm forty-sixth on the list . . . . No bragging, just straight.[63]

As one of his aides described his boss: "He's not a political guy. He's the least political senator around. He's a policy senator."[64] Fenno concurred with these characterizations: "He was not a prima donna. He was not a self-promoter."[65] "He is not a showboating, flamboyant, prima donna-type politician—anything but."[66]

One sign of Domenici's seriousness as a national policymaker was his willingness to incur political costs for the sake of good policy. For example, during his first term he supported an energy bill that phased out price controls on oil and gas much more slowly than desired by the energy industry in New Mexico:

> The oil and gas people of this state were mad at me. And they had been my strongest supporters. Up until the end, I voted with them; and the money was coming in. . . . The day after my vote, the money was shut off—just like that. . . . [T]hey'd rather have someone who committed himself beforehand to vote their way all the time than have a senator who is helping make policy.[67]

Some years later he tackled an even more controversial issue: the impending insolvency of the Social Security trust fund. In the fall of 1981, as the economy headed into recession and the budget outlook worsened, Domenici proposed to the administration cutbacks in Social Security. But after some initially encouraging words from the president, the administration sided with those opposed to any entitlement cuts. As Domenici told a New Mexico college audience, "We have to address entitlements in some way. . . . We need an $80–85 billion reduction in the next three years. . . . I may be dumb, but I'm ready to face Social Security now. But

Congress isn't. The President isn't. So we probably won't."[68] In the place of Social Security reductions, Domenici got his committee to agree to specifying that $40 billion would have to be found over three years in some combination of spending cuts and/or tax increases to keep the Social Security system solvent. Democrats immediately attacked this Republican proposal for $40 billion in "benefit cuts." Domenici defended his actions on the floor of the Senate:

> I take full credit for being responsible. I take full responsibility for producing a truthful budget. I take responsibility for putting in this budget the truth about Social Security. I take full responsibility for truth in budgeting. The truth is that Social Security will most probably be insolvent next year.[69]

In 1985 the Social Security controversy was revisited when Domenici's Budget Committee proposed a one-year freeze on cost-of-living adjustments. The full Senate endorsed the committee's proposal by a 50–49 vote. A week later, the House passed a budget resolution with no Social Security freeze. The conference committee to iron out the differences between the budget resolutions "opened with Domenici insisting on Social Security restraints." But "things reached an impasse." "At this point President Reagan . . . [u]nder pressure (as always) from House Republicans on Social Security . . . backed away from his agreement with Dole and the Senate Republicans on Social Security and cut a deal with the House Democrats . . . [promising] them full COLA adjustments." This left nearly the entire contingent of Senate Republicans "hanging in support of a highly unpopular position in favor of a COLA freeze."[70]

All of this is not to say that Domenici ignored reelection considerations while carrying out his governing responsibilities. His surprisingly slim reelection majority in 1978 (53 percent) had come as something of a shock and convinced the senator and his staff that he had to achieve a higher profile "both in Washington and at home." Over the next six years he ran through five different press secretaries: "They described his emphasis on the press in terms ranging from 'top priority' to 'insatiable' to 'paranoid.' "[71] To raise his profile back in New Mexico he engaged in the time-tested techniques of frequent trips home, extensive correspondence (doubling his letter output between 1980 and 1981),[72] and providing particularized benefits to his state. The last he accomplished by joining the Senate Appropriations Committee in 1983. Soon, according to one of his top aides, he had a "list of appropriations for the state . . . so long nobody can believe it." Domenici actively publicized his funding achievements, taking pride in the fact that "New Mexico is first in return from the government per tax dollar. . . . I didn't do all that; but I've been able to help."[73]

As noted in previous chapters, political scientists have little difficulty explaining why members of Congress engage in constituency service activities unrelated to broad national policymaking. The benefits in constituent goodwill are obvious, the costs minimal or nonexistent. But what Fenno shows about Domenici is that in addition to these activities the senator made every effort to derive electoral benefit from his substantive legislative accomplishments. The experience of Edmund Muskie, his predecessor as chairman of the Budget Committee, had convinced him that being a "good senator" could translate into electoral success.[74] Thus he consciously sought to fashion a national reputation as a dedicated and effective senator. He "displayed an eagerness for favorable media attention"; but in particular "he wanted media coverage that reflected his accomplishments."[75] In this he was eminently successful.

Throughout the early 1980s Domenici became a national figure on the decisive budget issues that dominated in Reagan's first term. His legislative activities and accomplishments were extensively and favorably covered by the national media. Once the *New York Times* even titled its lead editorial "President Domenici?" suggesting that the senator was acting more presidential on the budget than was the president himself. The national coverage was so positive that the New Mexico media were influenced by it and echoed Domenici's legislative accomplishments directly to his constituents. Typical was the view expressed by a reporter for the *Albuquerque Tribune:*

> His importance in the Senate . . . his role as a national leader . . . and the notoriety he has brought to his home state of New Mexico have combined to give him an unparalleled stature in the eyes of his fellow New Mexicans that crosses party lines, ethnic boundaries, and socioeconomic class barriers. People in New Mexico are just plain proud of Domenici.[76]

The favorable impression cast by the national and local media was supplemented by the direct efforts of Domenici's 1984 reelection campaign to advertise his substantive legislative accomplishments. This had not been done in 1978, when the campaign "emphasized the senator's personal characteristics and his local connections." But in 1984, "the campaigners . . . [paid] a lot of attention to the senator's extensive, influential, and highly publicized governing activity."[77] Although the campaign did not slight his constituency service, it was "structured and conducted . . . as a referendum on [Domenici's] performance as a senator."[78] In November of 1984 Domenici was reelected with 72 percent of the vote, winning every county in the state and setting an all-time record for a victory margin in a statewide contest in New Mexico. Six years later he topped his own record with 73 percent of the vote.

If Domenici's story demonstrates anything, it shows that there is no necessary incompatibility between serious lawmaking and electoral success. While serving in the Senate, Domenici was hardly indifferent to his prospects for reelection. There is no doubt that one of his goals as a member of the U.S. Senate was to return to that institution every six years. But this was not his only goal. It did not turn him away from substantive legislative responsibilities. It did not replace legislative work and deliberative activities with mere posturing and demagoguery, even when the political costs were obvious, as with Social Security. Domenici's self-interest in reelection did not, in a word, blind him to his governing duties.

Domenici believed not only that serious lawmaking and electoral success were compatible, but that they could even be mutually reinforcing. The evidence certainly seems persuasive that the development of Domenici's national reputation in the early 1980s—a reputation built on substantive achievement—contributed to his overwhelming success in the 1984 election (following the fairly close contest in 1978). This is not to say, however, that Domenici was unmindful of the tensions that can arise between substantive policymaking and electoral considerations. As he told Fenno:

> I suppose it's easy for me to say all this and take the positions
> I've taken because I'm not up for reelection, not now. I've
> come to the conclusion that it's not worth running—or win-
> ning—if you can't go ahead and do some of the things you
> really believe in. But I don't know how I would feel if I had to
> run for reelection this year and deal with Social Security and
> veterans and Medicare. Those are tough issues. It must be a
> bitch to run every two years. I couldn't stand it.[79]

Fenno himself concluded after his lengthy observations that Domenici's devotion to the responsibilities of his institutional position as Budget Committee chairman, though respected and admired by his Senate colleagues, carried with it some political costs:

> The budget chairmanship is an imposing as well as a liberating job. It pins its occupant to a perpetual grindstone, envelops him in procedural and numerical entanglements, associates him with economic woe, ties him to institutional frustration, and denies him fashionable legislative victories. It demands a responsible performance; it prohibits a popular performance.[80]

Evidence of this split between responsibility and popularity came in 1984 when Senate Republicans in April voted Domenici the most effective committee chairman and the second most respected member of the Senate but in November gave him only nine votes in the contest to select a new majority leader. Moreover, for all of Domenici's electoral success in New Mexico, he seems not to have translated his six years in the spotlight into the kind of national stature then or later enjoyed by such contemporary fellow Republicans as Robert Dole, Phil Gramm, Newt Gingrich, or Jack Kemp. It is one thing to develop a reputation among one's colleagues and the national media for serious and responsible fiscal management but quite another to fashion a national constituency in support of one's programs, policies, and ideas.

Why would any member of Congress choose substance over symbols, hard work over posturing, responsibility over popularity? Why take *any* political risks; why incur *any* political costs? How can we explain, for example, why nearly the entire contingent of Senate Republicans in 1985, led by Budget Chairman Domenici, publicly voted to freeze cost-of-living adjustments for Social Security when they knew that Democrats in the Senate and House would squeeze every possible drop of political advantage from this action?

Fenno's account suggests two reasons. One of these is institutional. The Senate and House Budget Committees were created to give each branch an institutional mechanism for fashioning responsible fiscal policy. And, more than anyone else on the committee, the chairman was vested with the special obligation to make the budget process work. As Domenici told Fenno, "I have a responsibility to the process."[81] Fenno called this "an institutional imperative" to keep the process moving and to assert Congress's proper authority over budget matters in disputes with the executive branch.[82] As chairman of the Budget Committee this was Domenici's "special responsibility."[83]

The other reason for choosing responsibility over popularity gets to the issue of character. "Pete Domenici's most distinctive personal quality," Fenno concluded, was "his sense of responsibility."[84] Throughout the budget battles of the Reagan years Domenici had displayed nothing less than an "extraordinary devotion to duty."[85] In concluding his book Fenno cites David Broder's assessment after the 1986 elections of the Senate Republican leaders Domenici, Robert Dole, and Richard Lugar. Broder praised all three for their "largemindedness, their ability to see beyond their personal ambitions . . . and beyond the parochial interests of their states." He praised Domenici in particular for "his tactical skill, sound judgment and political courage."[86]

To put it most simply, it was Domenici's character to be responsible. His deepest and most powerful political goal was to accomplish something "substantive and constructive." "Domenici wants, 'yearns,' to accomplish things."[87] His greatest satisfaction came from achieving this end. Fenno concluded: "As much as we value a responsible performance by our legislative leaders, for that much Pete Domenici was an exemplary leader of the United States Senate."[88]

☆

While we cannot say that Wilbur Mills, Edmund Muskie, and Pete Domenici are (or were) typical members of the U.S. Congress, other literature suggests that they were not so unusual that these three constituted a distinct breed or species of national legislator.

Consider, for example, Jeffrey Birnbaum and Alan Murray's description of Senator Bill Bradley (D., New Jersey) in their account of the passage of the Tax Reform Act of 1986.[89] Even while he was still playing professional basketball, Bradley "spent many off-court hours visiting local politicians and reading widely. He read Milton Friedman, the University of Chicago economist, and was fascinated to learn that a flat-tax system with a rate of just over 20 percent would raise as much money as the existing high-rate system."[90] As a result of this self-education, Bradley advocated a broad-based, low-rate income tax during his 1978 Senate campaign. Once in the Senate, Bradley "plowed ahead to devise a wholly restructured tax system."[91] His drive for tax reform in 1981 and 1982 reflected "discipline, painstaking analysis, and patience."[92]

> During this period, Bradley could be seen loping wide-eyed through the halls of Congress, laden with books and briefing papers. He would breeze through volumes of tax tracts and reach out to a brain trust of tax experts both inside and outside of government. While other senators left details to their staffs, Bradley remained intimately involved in the minutiae of his income-tax proposal. He demanded explanations and

would not relent until he understood. He wanted to know which tax breaks he was eliminating, how they got there to begin with, and why they should go. He took careful notes in spiral-bound notebooks. He sometimes spent eighteen-hour days at his task, studying and refining the proposal for a year and a half.[93]

A few years later, after President Reagan had decisively placed tax reform on the national agenda, Bradley worked hard to persuade his fellow legislators of the merits of reducing rates while eliminating deductions. And in a way unusual for a senator, he directed much of his persuasive effort to important members of the House: "He met with almost every Democratic member of the Ways and Means [Committee], and as well as many others not on the committee, including the liberal Democratic Study Group (DSG). He helped persuade DSG members to back the bill, despite their doubts about lowering tax rates at a time when budget deficits were pressing."[94]

Similarly, Elizabeth Drew's book on John Culver, Democratic senator from Iowa (1975–81), reveals a serious-minded legislator who doggedly pursued his view of the public interest in a few specific fields, using principally the weapons of facts and arguments. After just a few years in the Senate, Culver "had already established a reputation as one of the most effective members of the Senate . . . . a man with firm principles and beliefs . . . who gets in there and does the hard work of legislating."[95] Other senators told Drew that "he is not one of the posturers in the place, and not one of those who feel compelled, as so many do, to rush to the floor or to the television cameras with a statement on just about everything, . . . [T]his restraint adds to his effectiveness."[96] In the words of one Senator: "Culver has a towering intellect and an inquisitive mind and is intellectually enormously demanding of himself and of associates. When he gets hold of an issue, he studies it, he reads it, he thinks it, he absorbs it."[97]

Culver himself was quite aware that he could earn the respect of his colleagues through hard work, mastery of detail, and devotion to the substance of policy. "[H]e is aware," wrote Drew, "that when a senator makes a speech he is far more likely to command the attention and respect of his colleagues if he seems to actually know what he is talking about."[98] "Around here," he told Drew, "you admire someone who works from views and works hard and advocates effectively."[99] Accordingly, in advocating his positions Culver put a premium on persuading others through facts and arguments.

In charge of the fight for reauthorization of the Endangered Species Act and convinced of the need for some modifications of the law, he pressed his staff to "get the best substantive rebuttal to the argument [pressed by Senator Gaylord Nelson] that there is no need to change the law."[100] He wanted "the best answers to each argument, with specificity."[101] On the eve of the floor debate, Culver had his staff "list Nelson's best arguments on one side of the page and our best arguments on the other."[102] After some additional study of fact sheets, Culver was well prepared to lead the floor debate for the bill drafted by the Resource Protection Subcommittee, which he chaired. Referring only infrequently to notes as he defended the committee bill from "Nelson and the environmentalists," Culver "[was] doing what he prefers to do when he speaks, and what gives him his reputation as one of the most effective orators in the Senate—winging it, on the basis of having studied and thought through and organized the arguments he wants to make."[103]

Another area where Culver sought to develop expertise was arms control. He became part of a group of seventeen senators who met for lunch every two weeks in the office of Democratic Whip Alan Cranston. "The idea . . . was to organize a group that would become well informed and be in a position to conduct a strong debate on behalf of a SALT agreement and to help the Administration, whose competence to handle the issue was in doubt, prepare for a SALT fight."[104] At one meeting "the senators were assigned specific subjects in which they were to develop expertise so as to be able to handle them during the debate. Culver, along with four other senators, was given the largest subject: the United States-Soviet strategic balance."[105]

Although Culver relied primarily on the weaponry of facts and arguments in his legislative battles, he, like other legislators we have examined, recognized the limits of persuasion through reason. "We all want to know what the merits are," he told Drew, "and you want someone who will push public policy guided by that compass. But in the real cockpit of resolving these things you have to never lose sight of the need to compromise, and to know how to do it well, or even how to successfully effect a raw, naked deal."[106]

In his lengthy conversations with Drew, Culver articulated a thoughtful and sophisticated understanding of the representative function. He held little respect for the member of Congress who, despite high voter approval, "nervously puts his finger to the wind on each vote and is afraid to risk the slightest diminution of support by exerting leadership."

Although people in politics want the kind of public support that will help them keep their jobs, "obviously in public service there are additional requirements." Foremost among these "additional requirements" was "a core set of principles or beliefs" and a willingness to fight for these principles throughout the legislative process. But what Culver found "really disturbing and frustrating" was that some officeholders "make it the be-all and end-all to stay in office" even if it means weakening their commitment to "a core set of principles or beliefs."[107] Another force that can weaken this commitment is the pressure in Congress to simply go along with one's colleagues. When "[y]ou're working with peers, . . . it's easier to have everything be pleasant. . . . You could sit back and enjoy it and accept the perks and the psychic gratification, such as it is, but then no public purpose is served."[108]

Our constitutional system presumes that "we are a republic, where an elected official is given a franchise for a certain period of time—two, four, or six years—to represent as best he can the interests of his constituents as well as contribute his own best judgment. He has a dual responsibility: to constituency and conscience, and sometimes they're compatible and sometimes they're not." Culver even quoted from Edmund Burke to the effect that a British representative "is in Parliament to support his opinion of the public good, and does not form his opinion in order to get into Parliament, or to continue in it." But this basic understanding of democracy is now "under siege":

> Obviously, officials who consistently vote against the wishes of their constituents will not and should not be returned to office. But we should be expected to do more than simply mirror the momentary mood of the public. We hear so much today about people wanting strong leaders, but there's a certain contradiction in at the same time demanding leaders who do not lead but follow.[109]

Finally, Richard Fenno's book-length study of Dan Quayle's first term in the U.S. Senate elucidates some of the same themes of responsible lawmaking characteristic of these other legislative portraits.[110] Quayle (R., Indiana) viewed his defeat of Democratic incumbent Birch Bayh in 1980 as a triumph of his conservative philosophy. He had campaigned "primarily . . . as the agent of an orthodox conservative philosophy" and "as the agent of a political party that espoused conservative principles."[111] Like the many "new breed" politicians who entered the House of Representatives in the 1970s (Quayle had been elected to the House in 1976), he was an "issue-oriented activist . . . [who] wanted a piece of the congressional action."[112] His governing style, however, was not dogmatic or doctrinaire. In Fenno's assessment, Quayle displayed "an institutional independence—an openness to argument, a wariness of inflexibility, a pragmatism in the implementation of his ideas."[113] Thus, he was both conservative and open-minded, committed to the principles espoused by Ronald Reagan but willing to listen to arguments about public policy that did not fit into some neat conservative mold.

Quayle had jumped to the Senate after four rather indifferent years in the House: "[h]is lack of attentiveness to legislative work dominated his reputation in the House."[114] His own staff had worried that he would bring this same lackadaisical attitude to the Senate; they were pleasantly surprised. One of his aides told Fenno:

> Over in the House, when he saw the first ray of sunshine, he'd be out on the golf course. But he's not doing that [in the Senate]. He's had an incredible amount of information pushed at him and he's trying to absorb it. He's attending all his meetings. He hasn't missed a vote. . . . His mind is working and he's getting more interested in things than when he was in the House. . . . I think we're going to have us a senator.[115]

Instead of indifference to legislative matters, Quayle displayed "the ambition of a new young senator to make a mark for himself somehow in some part of the Senate's work."[116] Indeed, his ambition to serve in the Senate "seemed born of a desire to move to a place where he could get something done."[117] "What I like about this job," he told Fenno, "is being able to set the agenda, get my teeth into things, and have an impact. I want to affect the results."[118] Through substantive accomplishments he would seek recognition and respect both inside and outside the Senate: "I want to be known as an effective senator."[119]

As Fenno describes it, Quayle was quite conscious of the distinction between substantive legislative activities and reelection activities, and he planned to sort these out temporally. His first four years in the Senate would be devoted to substantive lawmaking; his next two to reelection: "the fourth year is the last chance I'll have to make a record since the last two years, I'll be a candidate again. Everything I do in those last two years will be posturing for reelection. But right now I don't have to do that."[120] Reflecting on his three election contests between 1976 and 1980, he told

Fenno that "[f]or the past five years, I've done nothing but run for election. . . . For the next three years I want to establish a solid legislative record."[121] "Some people," he noted, "campaign all the time. I would just burn out doing that. And I don't want to burn out."[122]

Much of Fenno's account focuses on Quayle's most significant legislative accomplishment: the passage of the Job Training Partnership Act (JTPA) of 1982. Circumstances had conspired to give Quayle an opportunity for governing unusual for a first-term senator. Because the Republicans became the majority party in the Senate after the 1980 election and because Quayle carefully chose committee assignments that would afford him opportunities for accomplishment, he found himself the chairman of the Employment Subcommittee of the Labor and Human Resources Committee at a time when the highly controversial and expensive Comprehensive Employment and Training Act (CETA) was about to expire. As Fenno relates, Quayle took full advantage of his position of institutional authority.

Quayle's statewide campaign for the Senate had "widened his horizons" beyond those of one congressional district. Now as a subcommittee chairman he developed a "national perspective," particularly through extensive hearings on employment problems, at which more than a hundred witnesses testified, and by relying heavily on substantive experts among the subcommittee staff.[123] Working closely with ranking minority member Edward Kennedy and with little encouragement (sometimes overt opposition) from the administration, he fashioned a replacement for CETA that, despite earlier intimations of a presidential veto, became one of the administration's proudest domestic accomplishments.

Fenno presents a variety of evidence that by 1985 Quayle's Senate work had impressed close observers of Congress. The editor of *Politics in America*, described by Fenno as "one of Washington's most knowledgeable and respected students of Congress," ranked Quayle among "the twelve most effective but underrated" members of Congress. In addition, "one of Washington's top congressional reporters wrote in *National Review* that 'Quayle has been a Senate success story.'" He ranked his legislative record as "among the most productive of the 1980 class," and said that Quayle had become "a force to be reckoned with" in the Senate. And around the same time the *Congressional Quarterly Weekly Report* wrote that Quayle had "built a reputation as a pragmatic, thoughtful senator."[124]

Despite his legislative achievements, Quayle was reluctant to seek public credit for his efforts. This was one of the things that most surprised Fenno:

> My own observation, throughout, had been that Quayle was less concerned about credit than I thought he would be or should be. He never mentioned it without prodding. I was around his staff a great deal and I never heard of any effort to garner publicity for his efforts. . . . The entire Quayle enterprise was remarkably unaggressive about credit claiming. In this respect, my experience ran totally counter to the proposition that senators are perpetually preoccupied with credit-taking publicity.[125]

For example, during a trip back to Indiana in August and September of 1982, with the job training bill in the conference stage, Quayle made virtually no mention of it, despite the obvious political benefits. Even after final passage, Quayle seemed reluctant to claim credit for his accomplishment.

By 1985, however, which Quayle judged as the beginning of his reelection fight, the reluctance was gone. The political appeal of JTPA in Indiana was obvious, especially among groups that were not part of Quayle's natural constituency. Indeed, his reelection campaign became nothing less than "a JTPA-centered campaign." The "central premise" of the campaign was "that a Washington accomplishment would anchor an election victory at home."[126] In the words of his campaign manager:

> JTPA is the whole campaign. It's everything. It's the first thing he talks about almost everywhere he goes. All our opinion polls tell us that jobs is still the number-one issue in this state. He can talk jobs like nobody else can, because he did something about it. When he goes someplace he can tell people how many jobs were created there and exactly how many dollars went into the area. . . . So it's pure gold. And it sews everything together. He brings home the bacon; he is a national leader.[127]

Quayle won reelection with 61 percent of the vote, setting a record for an Indiana Senate election. While admitting that he cannot prove it, Fenno argues that Quayle's "governing accomplishment with JTPA was indispensable and essential and necessary to this success at home." It can certainly be said that during 1985 and 1986 "Quayle exploited his JTPA achievement in every way imaginable. It overwhelmed every other aspect of his record and of a campaign conducted on his record."[128]

The High Art of Responsible Lawmaking

The political philosopher Leo Strauss once wrote: "It is safer to try to understand the low in the light of the high than the high in the light of the low. In doing the latter one necessarily distorts the high, whereas in doing the former one does not deprive the low of the freedom to reveal itself fully as what it is." [129] What these legislative portraits reveal is something of the high art of lawmaking in contrast to the low arts of mere self-seeking. To try to understand the legislative service of representatives like Wilbur Mills or senators like those portrayed here in the exclusive terms of reelection incentives would necessarily distort and obscure the essential nature of their activities. A theory of legislative behavior that posits only the low motive of reelection cannot even provide the vocabulary to describe and explain the serious lawmaking evident in the accounts summarized here. To repeat a question asked above, how can the reelection incentive explain why any legislator would choose substance over symbols, hard work over posturing, or responsibility over popularity? And, most incongruous of all, why would any legislator moved primarily by the reelection incentive ever take any political risks for the sake of substantive policy goals?

Conversely, a full understanding and appreciation of the high art of lawmaking allows the low arts of mere self-seeking to reveal themselves fully for what they are. Could it even be said that it is only some sense of what constitutes serious lawmaking that makes it possible to understand fully the nature of the lower self-seeking arts (what Hamilton called "the little arts of popularity")? Consider "posturing," for example, a term that came up in several of the portraits. Lawmakers and those who observe and study lawmakers have little difficulty identifying posturing when they see it; but surely this is because in the back of their minds they possess a rather clear picture or model of what posturing is not: reasoned argument and effort at genuine persuasion. Posturing can be understood fully only in contrast to this thing which it is not, in contrast to something higher than itself.

What, then, are the principal characteristics of those who engage in serious lawmaking in the United States Congress? Insofar as the accounts reviewed here are an accurate guide, the following stand out:

• Serious lawmakers are not satisfied simply to serve in Congress and enjoy its many perks. They want to make a difference, to accomplish something of importance, to make the nation (and perhaps the world) a better place through their governing activities. They believe that there is a public interest, that it is knowable, and that their efforts in Congress can help to achieve it.

- By virtue of their office (membership in the House or Senate, committee and subcommittee chairmanships, leadership positions, etc.) they feel a sense of responsibility to something beyond their personal advantage, a duty to larger ends. It is the accomplishment of these larger ends that is the source of their deepest political satisfaction.
- They seek to earn the respect of their colleagues and of those outside Congress through their deliberative efforts and their substantive achievements. They want to be known as effective legislators. The respect they so earn from their colleagues is a principal source of their power in Congress.
- They develop substantive expertise in the areas under their jurisdiction through careful and thorough analysis, engaging in the hard work necessary to master a subject. Open to facts and arguments, they are willing to learn from others.
- They seek to influence others on legislative matters principally through reasoned persuasion. Although they recognize that raw political bargaining may be necessary to build majorities, their decided preference is to influence through facts and arguments, not through bargains.
- They try to protect the opportunities for responsible lawmaking from the consequences of unrestrained publicity seeking. They have little respect for "legislators" who seek only popularity and reelection.
- Although they wish and seek reelection to Congress, they are, nonetheless, willing to take some political risks for the sake of good public policy.

It would be an understatement to say that these kinds of characteristics are not well accounted for by the reigning self-interest theories of Congress or of American government more generally. Moreover, the point here is not that the 535 members of the House and Senate fall neatly into two categories: the merely ambitious who pursue only narrow self-interest and the high-minded who strive for the public good. Rather these represent something like the extremes of a continuum, from the low to the high, between which the various members of Congress can be found. As this exercise has tried to demonstrate, some members of the U.S. Congress, perhaps especially the leaders within the institution, look more like the serious lawmaker described by these characteristics than like the mere self-seeker we have come to view as the norm. If, as those who created the U.S. Congress believed, the serious lawmaker is nothing less than essential to the success of American democracy,[130] then we ought to have a very great interest indeed in assessing the status and activities of such legislators in the contemporary Congress: How many members of the institution behave like serious lawmakers and has this changed over time? What electoral conditions promote the election of the serious-minded, public-spirited legislator as opposed to the mere self-seeking politician? How much influence do serious lawmakers have in the two branches? What are the forces that affect their lawmaking behavior? And what procedural or structural reforms, if any, would enhance the prospects of serious lawmaking in Congress? Although it is beyond the scope of this work to address systematically these various questions, a few additional points can be made.

A central issue is how many of our representatives and senators display the characteristics of the serious lawmaker described here—if not all of the time, then at least much of the time. That the serious lawmaker is not so rare as to be analytically uninteresting or irrelevant to the workings of Congress on major policy issues is amply demonstrated by the kinds of detailed portraits of legislators reviewed here, by the large body of evidence demonstrating the importance of the goal of promoting good public policy in attracting members of the House and Senate to many of the leading committees, and by such occasional episodes as the nearly united, and quite unpopular, stand by Senate Republicans in 1985 in favor of a COLA freeze on Social Security payments.

To this evidence we can add one of the more interesting and perceptive accounts of the modern Congress: Harry McPherson's description of the Senate of the late 1950s, a time when McPherson served as an aide to Majority Leader Lyndon Johnson. McPherson's memoir of life in the Senate includes individual portraits of some sixty-seven senators as well as more general reflections about the character of the institution and its members. What is revealing about McPherson's account is how many of his subjects possessed and acted upon deeply felt policy views that were in no apparent way derivative from, or fashioned to serve, their electoral interests. Some of his more interesting reflections follow.

> Joseph Clark of Pennsylvania: . . . . His mind was quick, and he cared passionately about arms control and the threat of nuclear war.[131]

> Paul Douglas of Illinois: a vivid man, full of apparent contradictions. Intellectual in the extreme, professorial, ...

Scrupulously honest, a liberal Saint George against the vested-interest dragon.[132]

Sam Ervin of North Carolina: . . . . [H]e was an ideologue, with a lawyer's devotion to the "truth" of rigid constitutional formulas. . . . [H]e had a sharp sense of civil liberties.[133]

Hubert Humphrey of Minnesota: . . . . He was interested in almost every legislative field, especially agriculture, foreign relations, arms control, and civil rights. . . . Humphrey's heart longed for a just and humane society. . . . [H]e had that indispensable element of a successful politician, tireless energy in pursuit of a political goal.[134]

Henry Jackson of Washington: . . . . "Scoop" Jackson was something of a loner, interested in arcane matters like national security policy machinery.[135]

Herbert Lehman of New York: . . . . [H]is deep compassion for the exploited poor represented Jewish liberalism at its best.[136]

Mike Mansfield of Montana: . . . . Asian policy . . . was one of Mansfield's passions; he thought the United States was obsessed by a missionary zeal to convert Asia, and that this would be our undoing and Asia's.[137]

Pat McNamara of Michigan: . . . . His opinions were deeply and unshakably liberal . . . . [H]e embodied the common sense and humanity of the old trade unionists.[138]

Mike Monroney of Oklahoma: . . . . He could feel strongly about issues . . . . A liberal, he was constantly tested by the divergence of his views from those of his state's. . . . [H]e was more interested in ideas than position.[139]

Richard Neuberger of Oregon: . . . . Neuberger was deeply concerned—in a private, as well as a senatorial way—about public issues that affected the quality of life. He was in politics because those issues were most exposed there.[140]

Richard Russell of Georgia: . . . . In foreign affairs he consistently voted against every statutory involvement of the United

States in international organizations, and against the more important treaties. The reason was that treaties and international responsibilities limited America's freedom of action, and hence its autonomy. . . . [H]e remained a great force; nothing could diminish his chairmanships, his cunning, or his integrity. Often I found myself offering counsel to him, seeking to forward his purposes, because his character and professionalism were magnetic to me.[141]

George Smathers of Florida: . . . . [H]e was . . . probably as progressive a senator as Florida would tolerate in the fifties and sixties. He moved left when he could, and he brought along several moderate-conservative senators by persuasion and example.[142]

John Stennis of Mississippi: . . . . Apart from Russell, he was the most impressive Southerner. . . . Other senators might argue the benefit-cost ratio of public works projects or the level of widow's pensions or the need for urban renewal; Stennis and Russell knew about, and looked after, the country's defense. . . . [T]hey cared deeply about preparing the country against bluff or attack, and this ultimate gut-concern gave them a standing in the Senate that far transcended that of more fashionable men. . . . [H]e was . . . a deeply responsible and important figure.[143]

Leverett Saltonstall of Massachusetts: . . . the classic exemplar of New England Republicanism. . . . He was simply true to what men of his heritage believed to be the national interest: a strong defense, an internationalist foreign policy, and a limited government role in the economy.[144]

Whether it is Clark's devotion to arms control, Humphrey's tireless pursuit of a more humane society, Lehman's compassion for the poor, Mansfield's passionate concern about Asian issues, or Russell's and Stennis's deep commitment to maintaining the nation's defense, what is evident in these descriptions is the importance of a personal belief in and commitment to the public interest, however variously defined by the Senate's members.

This is not to say, of course, that these politicians ignored electoral considerations. They were quite conscious of the demands placed upon them by their constituents. In those cases where "public opinion was rigidly fixed and overwhelming, they seldom resisted it." But where "it was more evenly balanced, or where it was inchoate and amorphous, their freedom to be independent was correspondingly enhanced."[145] If a senator "wanted both to do good and to be elected," he first had "to bow before the prevailing icons in his state." But "having made that obeisance," he could then "turn to more promising endeavors."[146] McPherson acknowledges that "[n]ot every man wanted to be independent of his constituency's views," but many did, at least insofar as their own policy views diverged from raw constituency opinion. To this end the Senate employed "many parliamentary devices—motions to recommit dangerous bills or amendments, points of order, and so on—that could be used to avoid an Armageddon of convictions."[147] Also helpful in creating the kind of good favor that fostered legislative independence was effective constituency service. Yet, as the epigraph to this chapter indicates, McPherson's judgment was that for most senators such service was not the core of their senatorial activities but merely "requirements" that had to be met so that they could pursue the higher purpose of lawmaking for the public good.

In addition to the evidence that serious lawmakers are more prevalent within Congress than modern theories acknowledge, there is also reason for believing that they have a greater impact on policymaking than their mere numbers (and relative proportion of the membership) might suggest. One reason is that because the serious lawmaker undertakes the kind of substantive legislative work that does not interest the mere self-seeker, he will *ipso facto* influence the details of policy in a way that the self-seeker rarely will. After all, the legislator dominated by the reelection incentive has "only a modest interest in what goes into bills or what their passage accomplishes." He knows that "in a large class of undertakings the electoral payment is for positions rather than for effects."[148] The second reason is that the serious lawmaker may be more prevalent among institutional leaders than among the membership generally. In part this is because the members of Congress may select as their leaders those with a reputation for legislative skill and seriousness of purpose. In addition, for formal leadership positions within committees and subcommittees, where selection is virtually automatic, the office itself may foster a sense of responsibility to ends larger than mere private advantage.

This latter point is one of the conclusions of Martha Derthick and Paul Quirk in their study of the deregulation movement of the Carter and Reagan years:

There is an unmistakable pattern in our leading cases: presidents, commission chairmen, and congressional committee and subcommittee leaders generally advocated reform. We infer that such leaders are especially induced or constrained to serve broad, encompassing, diffuse interests. Any officeholder faces conflicting pressures of personal conviction, desire for reputation, and political interest; some of these pressures will encourage service to broader, diffuse interests while others certainly will not. For leaders, the pressures that encourage such service are markedly enhanced by the very fact of leadership, which makes their actions visible to a wider public, exposes them to observation and comment among the political and governmental elite, and tends to elicit a more compelling sense of responsibility.[149]

And as they say about congressional leaders in particular:

To the extent that a congressman finds or places himself in [a position of leadership on an issue] . . . , two related conditions follow, both of them likely to affect his response: his actions will be more consequential to the outcome; and because they will be more consequential, they will also be more widely observed. Leaders on an issue will be more prone to act on their conception of the public interest, because it is more irresponsible for those in a position of power to do otherwise.[150]

It follows that even a handful of serious, responsible lawmakers in key positions within Congress may have a more consequential effect on the substance of public policy than a much larger number of mere self-seeking politicians who can pursue and achieve private advantage through nonlegislative means.

Deliberation and Self-Interest

The self-interest theories of Congress and its members force us to confront the issue of character. What goals do legislators seek? What matters to them personally and professionally? How do they understand their legislative responsibilities? What obligations do they feel they owe their constituents and the nation? The self-interest theorists are right, I believe, in arguing that a Congress filled exclusively with men and women who pursued only reelection would be a body virtually devoid of serious reasoning about the merits of public policy. (On this the framers of the Constitution would have fully agreed.) Deliberation will be an important force in a legislative body only if at least some legislators are moved by something more than mere private advantage, by a desire to accomplish some good for others through their lawmaking efforts. If there is to be sound deliberation, there must be legislators who feel a sense of duty or responsibility to the public good however they define it.

At one level, then, it can be said that the motive force behind deliberation is something different from mere self-seeking. Nonetheless, as noted above, it is safe to assume that all of the elected members of the House and Senate are also self-seekers in some sense. It is unlikely that any of them sought their office solely out of a solemn sense of obligation or duty and would prefer to be home engaging in private pursuits (unlike, for example, George Washington, who reluctantly agreed to stand for a second term as president and would apparently have preferred an earlier return to the enjoyments of private life). As all students of Congress willingly concede, the members demonstrably embrace a variety of self-interested goals, such as reelection to the same office or election to a higher one, power and prestige within the institution, and the development of national constituencies. How, then, does the pursuit of such goals affect deliberation within Congress? We will focus on the two self-interest goals identified as most important by Fenno—reelection and power and prestige within Congress.

To begin with the latter, the congressional literature, including but not limited to the legislative portraits reviewed above, suggests that on the whole there is a reasonably good fit between deliberation and the pursuit of power and prestige within Congress. Wilbur Mills, Edmund Muskie, and Pete Domenici were all more influential among, and more respected by, their colleagues because of their reputations for hard work, legislative craftsmanship, and seriousness of purpose. Insofar as they desired power within their institution and the prestige that their fellow legislators could confer, these goals were facilitated by years of serious deliberative efforts on the issues under their jurisdiction.[151]

More complex is the connection between deliberation and reelection. As we have noted, the self-interest theorists have argued persuasively that reelection can be more effectively and efficiently pursued through such nondeliberative activities as advertising, credit claiming, and position taking than by the kind of serious legislative work deliberation demands. Yet this is not the whole story.

Imagine, for example, a member of the House totally devoted to reelection who represents a district dominated by wheat farming. He knows that his reelection prospects will be considerably enhanced if he contributes to the formulation and passage of farm legislation that will benefit his constituents. Determining, however, what kind of legislation will actually accomplish this end will necessarily require some reasoned consideration of the problems that face his farmers and the impact that various legislative proposals will likely have. This will require assimilating information on the details of crop production, on the strengths and weaknesses of the wheat production economy, and on the principal complaints of his farmers. He will likely want to hear from the major farmers' groups and from the Department of Agriculture. And it would not be surprising if he met with other lawmakers from similar districts to discuss and evaluate their ideas about how best to promote the interests of wheat farmers. Whatever the motive, this kind of activity constitutes reasoning on the merits of public policy.

Then, once our legislator has settled upon a specific proposal, he may defend it before his colleagues—in subcommittee, committee, the full body, or informally—as generally beneficial for all wheat farmers, as productive of a healthy agricultural economy overall, or as serving the larger public interest in the availability of agricultural products at reasonable cost. If these arguments are taken seriously by others, then the congressman has contributed to a broader deliberation on the issue at hand.

This hypothetical example suggests that under certain circumstances the reelection incentive itself may promote genuine deliberation. Here there exists a constituency group that is capable of evaluating the direct consequences of legislative action. Attentive publics of this sort require more from their representatives than merely a pleasing public image. Whether it is by observing and experiencing the actual consequences of national policy or by directly monitoring the behavior of lawmakers within Congress, attentive publics, such as organizations with national lobbying activities, can reach informed judgments about the efforts and accomplishments of representatives and senators. They may then communicate such judgments to broader audiences.

At times the print and broadcast media serve a similar purpose. Local media, through reporting, editorials, and commentary, may convey to the voters substantive information on how well their representatives are serving their interests. Moreover, the national media will occasionally foster the image of a member of the House or Senate as a particularly effective legislator, an image that may prove electorally beneficial. Senator Pete Domenici, as noted above, discovered that serious and responsible lawmaking could result in the kind of positive press, both nationally and back home in New Mexico, that would enhance his reelection prospects. This was a lesson that he had learned from the experience of Senator Muskie, who preceded him as chairman of the Budget Committee. One need not, of course, wait for the press to advertise legislative achievements, as Dan Quayle demonstrated in his 1985–86 reelection campaign, which was centered on his sponsorship of the Jobs Training Partnership Act of 1982. This "governing accomplishment," Fenno concluded, "was indispensable and essential and necessary" to Quayle's landslide reelection victory.[152]

Similarly, when Derthick and Quirk explained why Senator Howard Cannon, chairman of the Senate Commerce Committee, became an advocate of airline and trucking deregulation, they noted both his desire "to build an impressive record of legislative achievement to mark his stewardship" and the way his committee chairmanship (which he assumed in 1978) "altered his electoral stakes." He told Derthick and Quirk that his role in deregulation "had helped him acquire an image as an opponent of unnecessary government regulation—an image very appealing, he noted, to voters in Nevada." Cannon's efforts were not mere position taking or credit claiming unrelated to real legislative effort. To get the credit, and therefore the praise, for bringing about deregulation Cannon "sponsored the bills, presided over their consideration in committee, and managed them on the Senate floor; they were, in a substantial and very visible way, a personal achievement."[153]

Another unlikely reformer who was pushed forward by electoral incentives was Oregon's Senator Robert Packwood during the battle over tax reform in 1985 and 1986. According to Birnbaum and Murray, Packwood and the Finance Committee which he chaired wanted nothing to do with tax reform. The committee had a well-earned reputation as a "bastion of pro-business sentiment"; it had no desire to eliminate the kinds of business write-offs that would make a flatter tax possible. Yet in the face of President Reagan's vocal support for reform and the passage of a reform bill by the House, Packwood and his committee were on the spot.

It was fortuitous for the cause of tax reform that Packwood faced reelection in 1986, including a tough primary election challenge. As Congress's leading recipient of money from political action committees (nearly $1 million during the eighteen months of the tax reform battle), he was under the watchful eye of the Oregon media for signs of caving in to the special interests. When it looked for a time as if the Senate Finance Committee would prove the pundits right and kill reform, Packwood came under attack in the Oregon newspapers. Quite conscious of the political stakes, the Finance Committee chairman salvaged reform in the Senate through intense personal effort: "he had turned a huge potential liability into an important political asset." By generating enthusiastic comment in the Oregon media, this substantive success in the Senate virtually guaranteed electoral success in the primary, which occurred just two weeks after Packwood got a unanimous committee vote for his plan.[154]

These examples suggest a major corrective to the view that the reelection incentive necessarily turns legislators away from substantive lawmaking and toward nonlegislative or merely symbolic activities. Nonetheless, these examples do not disprove the argument that a single-minded devotion to reelection will in general be more of a hindrance than a help to deliberation. Most representatives and senators most of the time do not win or lose reelection on the basis of a clear public understanding of their substantive legislative accomplishments in Congress. While this may be somewhat less true for the leaders within Congress, on whom public attention is focused during major legislative battles, it applies with special force to rank-and-file legislators in the two branches.

There is substantial evidence within the congressional literature that those who serve in the House and Senate are well aware of the tension between deliberation and electoral forces. Senator Domenici voiced this awareness in emphatic terms in his conversations with Fenno. Similarly, John Culver contrasted "leadership" based on "a core set of principles or beliefs" from "nervously put[ting] . . . [a] finger to the wind on each vote." And Dan Quayle made a conscious decision to devote his first four years in the Senate to serious lawmaking, since the last two "will be posturing for reelection."

Richard Fenno's study of how the members of the House of Representatives relate to their constituents affirms how aware and even troubled many representatives are by the ways in which reelection-oriented activities intrude upon the task of responsible lawmaking. One member who had served four years in the House complained that he had not "been a congressman yet," so preoccupied had he been establishing his electoral base. He looked forward to his fifth year when he could "be a congressman" for the first time. "By being 'a congressman,'" Fenno explained, "he means pursuing goals above and beyond that of reelection (i.e., power in the House and good public policy)."[155] Another congressman, this one in his fourth term, noted how his increasing interest in substantive governing activities had diminished his enthusiasm for constituency relations:

I'm not as enthused about tending my constituency relations as I used to be and I'm not paying them the attention I should be. There's a natural tension between being a good representative and taking an interest in government. I'm getting into some heady things in Washington, and I want to make an input into the government. . . . I'm beginning to feel that I could be defeated before long. And I'm not going to change. I don't want the status. I want to contribute to government.[156]

An even more senior member of the House had contemplated retirement rather than make the kind of electoral effort required after an adverse redistricting. Reelection would likely lead to a committee chairmanship, but an all-out effort would necessitate ignoring ongoing legislative responsibilities. He decided to run but not with "the same intensity" he had displayed earlier in his career.

I'm not going to neglect my duties. . . . If I do what is necessary to get reelected and thus become chairman of the committee, I will lose the respect and confidence of my fellow committee members because of being absent from the hearings and, occasionally, the votes.[157]

He won reelection but by his narrowest margin ever.

As these various examples show, the members of Congress make individual decisions about whether and how to meld reelection activities and substantive lawmaking into the same legislative career. The more responsible among them know that a total devotion to reelection interests would jeopardize the deliberation necessary for sound policymaking.

This awareness of the dangers to deliberation of unfettered self-seeking has led over the years to a variety of rules, practices, institutional features, and informal norms within Congress whose purpose it is to protect and promote responsible deliberative behavior. Leading examples from the past half century include the following:

• The norm of specialization, stronger in the House than in the Senate and stronger perhaps in the 1950s and 1960s than more recently, which holds that members should focus their legislative efforts on one or a few subjects (based principally on their committee memberships), do their homework, and speak only on matters they know well.

• The norm of institutional loyalty, again perhaps stronger in decades past than now, which holds that the well-being of the institution should take precedence over the personal interests of the members.

- The norm of committee deference, quite powerful before the 1970s but no longer, which held that non–committee members on most matters ought to defer to the expertise, substantive work, and deliberative judgment of the reporting committees.[158]
- The House practice of designating Appropriations, Ways and Means, and Rules as exclusive committees (whose members can serve on no other committees) so as to foster substantial expertise on the highly important matters under their jurisdiction.
- The practice of reserving membership on the tax-writing Ways and Means Committee to those from safe seats "as an insulating factor that . . . [would] allow a member to take an unpopular stand . . . without endangering his political career." Moreover, because committee members would feel somewhat less reelection pressure than would their colleagues from marginal districts, they would be able "to devote their energy and time to mastering the complex subject matter of the Committee."[159]
- The "custom," described by Mayhew in the mid-1970s but now apparently ended, "of arranging subcommittees [of the House Appropriations Committee] so that members do not handle programs they have a direct interest in financing."[160]
- The occasional use of the House Rules Committee to keep from the floor measures judged by the committee (and perhaps the House leadership) to be irresponsible, though popular.
- The use in the House of "closed rules" (traditionally quite common on tax legislation), "modified closed rules," or other restrictive rules to prevent the passage of popular but irresponsible amendments on the floor of the House.[161]
- The numerous formal constraints on publicity seeking, now mostly gone. Until recent decades markup sessions and conference committee meetings were generally held in secret; all hearings of the House Appropriations Committee were in closed session until 1971; radio and television coverage of House committee hearings were barred until 1970; and floor debates in the House were not televised until 1979 and in the Senate until 1986.
- The traditional practice in the House, which ended in 1970, of conducting all voting in the Committee of the Whole by methods (voice, division, or teller voting) that did not record how individual members voted. (Now, if twenty or more members request it in Committee of the Whole, members must cast a recorded vote.)[162]

• The practice, ended by the reforms of the 1970s, by which committee members could vote on provisions and amendments during markup sessions without a public record of individual votes.

This list suggests several generalizations. First, political scientists, journalists, and other observers of Congress have failed in the past to appreciate the extent to which the members of Congress themselves have consciously fashioned an institutional environment that would foster deliberation by protecting it from the kind of popularity seeking encouraged by democratic pressures. Second, such institutional constraints on self-seeking have been more characteristic of the House than the Senate. Finally, such constraints were much more common just a few decades ago than they are now; indeed, it is striking how many have been eliminated or weakened since the 1960s.

Two further conclusions would seem to follow from the second and third points. One is that the House of Representatives has been a more deliberative institution than the Senate over the past half century or so. This was certainly the view that a member of the House Ways and Means Committee expressed to John Manley in the late 1960s:

> With all due respect to the Senate, they don't know what the hell they're doing over there. They're so damn irresponsible you can get unanimous consent to an amendment that costs a *billion* dollars! And the Senate is supposed to be a safety check on the House. We really act as the stabling influence, the balance. Social security—they put over five hundred amendments on over there, and five hundred came out in conference. They don't know what they're doing. Some staff man writes up a section, they take it. Why, they can't stand up to Wilbur Mills. He knows every line.[163]

Moynihan's experience with the failure of Nixon's Family Assistance Plan led him to a similar conclusion. By the late 1960s, "the Senate had become less competent as a legislative body than the House . . . . The House had maintained discipline and protected its prerogatives. The Senate had allowed both to deteriorate. All the while presidential politics dissipated its energies and cohesion."[164] This institutional difference was particularly evident at the committee level; for the Senate Finance Committee, "unlike Ways and Means, had never acquired the individual and group discipline and work habits necessary to mastering a new and difficult subject."[165] Senators had become "individualists, and more than a normal quota were exhibitionists as well. At the expressive, symbolic level of politics they are hardly to be faulted, but there was lacking an eventual seriousness which is the mark of mature government."[166]

More recent evidence of the difference between the House and Senate came in November of 1991 just after President George Bush gave a speech complaining about high credit card interest rates. Just one day after the president's speech Senator Alfonse D'Amato (R., New York), facing a tough reelection fight in 1992, proposed a law to cap credit card interest rates at 14 percent, down from an average of 19.8 percent. D'Amato's proposal received overwhelming support on the Senate floor (passing 74–19) despite the absence of any real deliberation on the issue, including committee hearings where witnesses from the banking community could have been heard. But once the measure reached the House, the whole process was slowed down. At a press conference, House Speaker Thomas Foley (D., Washington), noting that there was "a lot of concern about the impact of credit-card legislation," complained that the "Senate acted very quickly." Foley didn't "see any reason why we should rush forward without considering all the ramifications."[167] The measure then died quietly in the House. Whatever one's position on the merits of a federal cap on credit card rates, it is clear that the House acted in a more deliberative fashion than its more prestigious counterpart.

Finally, the demise of so many Congressional constraints on mere self-seeking suggests that the Congress as a whole has become a less deliberative institution in recent decades. Less and less do the members of the House and Senate seem willing to sacrifice their private advantage for the sake of responsible lawmaking.[168] We shall turn in chapter 8 to the responsibility legislators bear for making Congress a more deliberative body.

☆ CHAPTER SIX

Deliberation and the Lawmaking Process

> [T]his House, in its Legislative capacity, must exercise its reason; it must deliberate; for deliberation is implied in legislation.
>
> James Madison, 1796[1]

> [O]bviously I bring a different view [to Congress]. That is what any congressman does. That is why we give speeches. That is why we are here.
>
> Representative Gary Franks, 1991[2]

As the last two chapters have demonstrated, any comprehensive account of the functioning of Congress must include both deliberation and nondeliberative activities or influences. Others have described these two ways of making policy decisions as "problem solving" and "persuasion" versus "bargaining" and "politics";[3] as "analytical policy making" versus "the play of power";[4] and as "discussion" versus "struggle."[5] If we adopt the term "political" to describe activities and considerations extraneous to the merits of an issue (which is consistent with common usage),[6] then we would say that political influences within Congress include such diverse activities as "wheeling and dealing," favor trading, exercising political muscle, pursuing private ambition, parliamentary maneuvering, bribery, etc. If we define bargaining broadly—so that exercising political pressure becomes making side payments—then bargaining and the pursuit of reelection probably constitute most of the political, or nondeliberative, activities and influences that affect policymaking in Congress. Writing about politics generally, Hanna Pitkin described well the combination of deliberation and nondeliberative activities and forces:

> Politics abounds with issues on which men are committed in a way that is not easily accessible to rational argument, that shapes the perception of arguments, that may be unchanged throughout a lifetime. It is a field where rationality is no guar-

antee of agreement. Yet, at the same time, rational arguments are sometimes relevant, and agreement can sometimes be reached. Political life is not merely the making of arbitrary choices, nor merely the resultant of bargaining between separate, private wants. It is always a combination of bargaining and compromise where there are irresolute and conflicting commitments, and common deliberation about public policy, to which facts and rational arguments are relevant.[7]

This suggests the utility of analyzing congressional behavior in terms of a deliberation-"politics" dichotomy. As table 3 illustrates, many of the most important features of the legislative process in Congress are subject to two distinct interpretations or explanations.

In addition to clarifying the differences between political and deliberative explanations, this sketch illustrates how far a deliberative interpretation may reach in explaining the structure and procedures of Congress. Such central features as the dominance of committees, the role of the leadership and of subgroups within Congress, and the influence of lobbyists and the executive branch may all contribute to the substantive consideration of public policy. The point is not that nondeliberative factors or forces are unimportant, but rather that policymaking within Congress is best understood as a complex mix of politics *and* deliberation, of the "play of power" and the reasoned effort to promote good policy. With this background we can turn to the key features of the lawmaking process in Congress.

The Locus of Deliberation in the Modern Congress

To the nonmember and casual observer, Congress presents its deliberative face most prominently in public debates on the floor of the House of Representatives and the Senate. This is where legislative proposals are advanced and defended, where the opposing sides present information and arguments to support their positions, and where, ostensibly, members are persuaded of the merits or deficiencies of legislative initiatives. In form at least, floor debate represents the most public and official expression of Congress's deliberative character, of its responsibility to reason about the merits of public policy.

In important respects, however, the substance does not match the form. Indeed, one of the frequent disappointments of tourists to the nation's capital is to sit in the gallery of the House or Senate chamber and observe a handful of representatives or senators reading speeches in

Table 3. A Comparison of "Political" and Deliberative Explanations of the Congressional Process

Issue or Characteristic	Political Explanation	Deliberative Explanation
Function of committee hearings	To publicize issues in order to mobilize support outside Congress	To elicit the information and arguments necessary to make informed judgments
Committee dominance in the legislative process (i.e., high success rate on the floor)	An implicit logroll across committees	Members defer to the judgment of those who have deliberated fully on the pending issue
Function of floor debate	Merely "pro forma"; or only tactically significant; or useful for enhancing standing with constitutents	Final opportunity to hear the strongest arguments pro and con; useful also as an information source regarding the contents of complex bills
Influence of committee and party leaders	Control over resources and/or parliamentary procedures enhances bargaining opportunities	Members of Congress defer to individuals of sound judgment; leaders persuade others through rational argument
Role of subgroups, such as state delegations or ideological groups	Tactically advantageous for coordinating the actions of like-minded legislators (e.g., maximizing attendance on key votes)	Facilitates collective reasoning about common concerns
Influence of lobbyists	Ability to influence voters; source of campaign funds; employment opportunities for retired legislators; bribery	Source of highly relevant information and arguments
Influence of the executive branch	Possesses vast resources with which to bargain for support within Congress	Uses its extensive information resources to persuade legislators of the merits of its proposals

a nearly empty room. In the Senate it is not uncommon for important bills to be "debated" with as few as three or four senators present. "We get in here working hot and heavy in debate," Senator Ernest Hollings of South Carolina complained, "and there is no one here to listen."[8] In the larger House, attendance is usually higher, but many of those who attend seem more interested in conversing with colleagues, reading the paper, or even napping than in attending or contributing to debate on the floor.

If Congress's deliberative character depended crucially on what happened on the floor of the House and Senate, one might be forced to conclude that serious deliberation plays only a tangential or episodic role in the business of fashioning the nation's laws. Yet given the number and variety of issues that confront the modern Congress together with the limited time available for floor debate, it is clear that most deliberation *must* occur elsewhere than on the floor. Consider, for example, the Nixon administration's Family Assistance Plan initiative, briefly discussed in chapter 4. This long and complex legislative proposal would have replaced the existing welfare program for families with dependent children (AFDC) with something like a guaranteed annual income. Assigned six hours for general debate on the House floor (in accordance with a rule issued by the House Rules Committee), it was debated on the afternoons of April 15 and 16, 1970. (Normally floor debate in the House and Senate takes place in the afternoon, with the mornings officially reserved for committee meetings.) It hardly needs arguing that a thorough examination of the issues involved in the Family Assistance Plan would require much more than six hours—which is already considerably longer than the House norm of one or two hours for floor debate on many bills. Indeed, by the time the bill had reached the House floor it had been the subject of thirty-five hours of public hearings before the House Committee on Ways and Means and of another seven weeks of executive sessions of the committee. Whatever deliberation took place on the floor of the House on the Family Assistance Plan on April 15 and 16, it was dwarfed by the months of deliberation that preceded it.

It is obvious that a few hours of general debate on the floor of the House or Senate cannot on most measures begin to provide the opportunity for the searching analysis of issues that a full-fledged deliberative process requires. The detailed analysis of information and arguments that constitutes the core of the deliberative process must be concentrated in earlier stages of the congressional policy process. A recent detailed analysis of floor politics in the House and Senate concludes that although floor discussion in the House and Senate does not "achieve the ideal form of either debate or deliberation," this does not mean "that little debate or deliberation takes place in Congress. To the contrary, debate and deliberation occur frequently and everywhere."[9]

Formulating and Introducing Policy Initiatives

Although the formal legislative process starts with the introduction of a bill in the House or Senate by a member of the respective body, the actual deliberative process may begin weeks and months before, as some combination of the members of Congress, their staff, executive branch officials, interest group representatives, and outside experts fashion a policy initiative. In some cases this formulation stage may occur entirely outside Congress. The historical extreme was reached during the famous "Hundred Days" of Franklin Roosevelt's first term, when eleven major bills were drafted in the executive branch "and sent to Congress in sequence." These received "less than forty hours of debate altogether in the House and all [were] enacted within sixty days of their submission. Only one major bill (a banking bill) originated within the Congress itself."[10] Three decades later, after Lyndon Johnson ascended to the presidency, Congress again exhibited an uncharacteristic willingness to accept policy direction from the executive branch. The landmark Economic Opportunity Act of 1964, for example, was

> "legislated" almost entirely within the executive branch and, indeed, virtually without prodding from congressional or other "outside" clienteles. The draft bill that President Johnson sent to Congress on March 16, 1964, was the product of almost a year of discussions and negotiations among high level administrators and economists. The process was culminated by a barnstorming five weeks of work by a special task force headed by [R. Sargent] Shriver.[11]

Such extreme deference by Congress on policy matters is, however, quite unusual. It is more common for the members of Congress to contribute directly to the formulation of policy proposals with the assistance of personal or committee staff and perhaps interested outside parties. This may involve a kind of mini-deliberative process: not a comprehensive canvass and assessment of diverse opinion on the matter at hand but instead a more narrowly focused effort by a small group of like-minded individuals to fashion a legislative remedy to some social, economic, or political problem. Such pre-introduction activity may constitute a major part of the total congressional deliberation on a bill. The Federal Aviation Act of 1958, for example (briefly discussed in chapter 4), was subject to the formal legislative process for a short three-month period from May 21, 1958, when it was introduced by Senator Mike Monroney, to the following August 23, when President Eisenhower signed it into law. Yet preceding the bill's formal introduction was an intensive three-month period of information gathering, studied analysis of air safety problems, and drafting and redrafting of legislative provisions by a team of technical and legal experts organized and guided by Senator Monroney. Thus, the deliberation responsible for the Federal Aviation Act occurred at least as much before the bill was introduced as after.[12]

Even bills drafted entirely outside the House and Senate may require some degree of congressional deliberation before formal introduction into the chambers. Only members of each body have the authority to introduce bills; and although members may perform this task as a courtesy to the executive branch, interest groups, or others, they may at times refuse to be so closely associated with a new proposal unless persuaded of its merits. Ranking committee members and party leaders, in particular, may be reluctant to lend their prestige to a bill until convinced of its basic soundness and value.

It is the importance of prominent sponsorship to a bill's prospects for success in Congress that leads administration officials to expend substantial effort in trying to convince committee and party leaders to introduce presidential proposals. For example, the Kennedy administration's successful persuasion of Congressman Kenneth Roberts of the need for federal enforcement authority in air pollution control (discussed in chapter 3) was part of an effort to convince Roberts to sponsor the administration's bill. Here an important part of the deliberative process in Congress involved simply the decision to sponsor the legislation. Roberts's switch was decisive for the subcommittee he chaired: "By changing his own mind he at once changed the minds of the subcommittee, the primary institution with which he was working."[13] It is possible, perhaps likely, that the Clean Air Act of 1963 would not have passed without the administration's successful persuasion of this key congressman. Such efforts at persuasion, however, are not always successful. President Nixon, for example, found that even a personal meeting in January of 1971 with Representative John Byrnes, ranking Republican on the House Committee on Ways and Means, could not convince Byrnes to be the major sponsor of the administration's revenue sharing plan.[14] This failure turned out not to be decisive, as the Revenue Sharing Act passed in 1972.

Deliberating within Committees

By design it is in committees and subcommittees that the most detailed and extensive policy deliberation occurs within Congress. The committee and subcommittee structure of the House and Senate is an institutional device intended to solve the fundamental deliberative problem that faces a finite legislative body entrusted with hundreds of complex domestic, foreign, and national security issues. Were the members of the House and Senate to meet only *en bloc* to consider legislative proposals, time limitations alone would render it impossible for the legislators to gather more than the most cursory understanding of the pertinent information and arguments bearing on each issue. When the number and complexity of issues outstrips the time available to each member to devote to legislative duties, some division of labor is necessarily called for. The committee system of the U.S. Congress, organized on the basis of subject matter, provides for one such division of labor.

It is within the committees and subcommittees of the House and Senate that true subject matter expertise can be developed. Although the full membership of the House and Senate cannot become expert on all the issues, smaller numbers of each branch can indeed develop expertise on a small set of issues, especially when members serve on the same committee (or subcommittee) for many years. Thus, the committees and subcommittees provide an opportunity for the kind of detailed examination of information and arguments that a genuine and serious deliberative process requires. In principle, these smaller decision-making units deliberate and exercise their judgment for the institutions they serve. As Senator Muskie explained in his conversations with Bernard Asbell, "In order to handle the volume of legislation, committees divide up the legislative work, the spadework as it were. So committee credibility is an awfully important thing." Indeed, "a reputation for good judgment" may be the most important factor in explaining why some committees are more influential than others in Congress.[15]

Public hearings are an essential element of committee deliberation. And although they often serve other purposes as well—such as generating public support for bills, embarrassing the administration, or promoting the visibility, and perhaps reelection prospects, of committee members—hearings are eminently suited for investigating the merits of pending proposals. Witnesses appear before the committee, make brief oral statements, present longer formal statements for the record, and respond to questions from committee members. Such witnesses often include the chief legislative sponsors of the bill, high-ranking administration officials, other interested members of Congress, state and/or local officials, representatives of interest groups (including public interest groups), and outside experts. In principle, hearings ought to provide for a wide range of views for and against the proposal under consideration; yet it is not unusual to hear charges that witness lists are "stacked" by the chairman and his staff to favor one side or the other. One scholar goes so far as to argue that congressional hearings on domestic spending programs have become, in effect, "rump hearings" where only the pro-spending side is presented, thus resulting in a "systematic departure from the parliamentary ideal."[16]

The vitality of discussion frequently manifested in committee hearings, especially on significant public issues, and the importance that politically sophisticated actors attach to the thorough and careful preparation of testimony indicate that the hearing process is not generally a pro forma exercise. Again, according to Senator Muskie, "committee hearings are supposed to make a contribution . . . . You try to shape the hearings so that there is dialogue, debate. Questions are raised so the committee understands the underlying complexities."[17] More so than is often recognized, committee members demonstrate an interest in, and openness to, what can be learned during hearings.

Not only do hearings serve the information needs of committee and subcommittee members entrusted with making the initial recommendation on a proposed bill, they may also shape the subsequent debate in Congress by surfacing the major arguments for and against the pending measure and by clarifying the strengths and weaknesses of each position. In his account of the passage of the Waterway User Charge Act of 1978 (reviewed in chapter 4), T. R. Reid relates how, even though the bill introduced by Senator Pete Domenici of New Mexico held little prospect of passage, "there was a host of people who considered the [Senate] subcommittee hearings crucially important."[18] These hearings in April of 1977 were "the first extended public debate by interested parties on the pros and cons of the idea [of a waterway user fee]. The arguments set forth at the hearing would shape Congress's debate over the issue for months . . . to come."[19] Through four days of hearings more than four dozen witnesses testified including several senators, an academic economist, representatives of the affected barge interests, conservation groups, and Secretary of Transportation Brock Adams. The participants in this initial public debate on the waterway user fee showed every indication of appreciating its importance to subsequent congressional deliberation on the issue.

If there is sufficient support to report a bill at the conclusion of the hearings, the committee (or subcommittee) will meet in a "markup" session, a line-by-line reading and (often) redrafting of the original proposal. It is in these sessions that the detailed substantive decisions are made in light of the testimony presented in the hearings. The character of these bill-writing sessions varies from committee to committee and from chairman to chairman; some markups are considerably more deliberative than others. Senator Muskie described his manner of running markups before the Senate Subcommittee on Environmental Pollution this way: "I don't come before them with a *fait accompli*. I don't begin markups saying, 'Now, this is what I think we need to do.' I let the thing evolve. But I make proposals as we go along . . . . I'll lay out issues one at a time, as something I think has merit, that I'm willing to discuss and debate, and listen to their reactions."[20] Here is how the lobbyist for the environmental group, Friends of the Earth, described the markups before Muskie's subcommittee:

> The whole operation is much more subtle than I thought. One of the surprises is that the orchestration of deals is not apparent, at least to me. What goes on is the working out of compromise. . . . I imagined, when they were behind closed doors, that the decisions would be much faster. You know, the chairman names the issue, everybody's already made up his mind or made his trades, and they vote. But it's not like that. There's a real *process*. . . .
>
> The best thing about markups, the reason I go to them religiously, is that you can pick up the nuances of each member's thinking. You don't get that from their public statements and public postures. You get to see who's articulate, who's respected, who isn't, how the dynamics work.[21]

This characterization is broadly consistent with an earlier description of markup sessions in one of the standard works on committees: "there tends to be informal give-and-take among the members that crosses party and seniority lines with considerable freedom. Perceptive staff members say that at this stage the 'gallery player' declines in importance and the member who has 'done his homework' takes the lead."[22]

This last description was written at a time when nearly all markup sessions were conducted behind closed doors. One reason why the "gallery player" was less important in markups than in hearings or on the floor was simply because there was no public gallery in markup sessions, no broader audience to which the member could appeal beyond the committee members and staff present. The markups put a premium on face-to-face discussions on the substantive details of legislative proposals, thereby enhancing the importance of the legislator who was more interested in drafting a sound bill than in promoting his personal popularity. This suggests that in some circumstances deliberation may benefit from restrictions on public scrutiny. It thus raises the question whether the reforms of the 1960s and 1970s in Congress designed to foster greater accountability of legislators and more "government in the sunshine"— including the opening of markup sessions—have been good for deliberation. (We shall return to this issue in chapter 8.)

The Committee Defense of Its Recommendations

As noted earlier, the committee system is a concession to the dictates of deliberation. To ensure that the merits of issues are adequately addressed, the full bodies delegate the central deliberative function to subunits of the institution. These subunits do not merely act, or will, for the parent body, but reason, or deli erate, for it. In an ideal legislature, ommittees will always decide exac y as the parent body would have i. the full body had considered with e same care and attention the information and arguments presented to the committee. In such a legislature, every committee would perfectly represent the full body across every dimension that might affect legislative decisions, such as party membership, ideology, geography, interest group support, responsiveness to public opinion, etc. In the real world, however, such perfect correspondence of committees with their parent institutions cannot be presumed; thus, the legislature cannot realistically expect that committee deliberations will invariably lead to the same decisions that would have resulted from full-fledged deliberation before the entire body.[23] It follows that the legislature must in some way judge the judgments of its committees. Although it lacks the time to duplicate committee deliberations, the full body must nonetheless assess the merits of committee recommendations. Consequently, it is not enough simply for the committees to make decisions; they must defend their decisions before the full body. In the modern House and Senate there are two principal mechanisms through which committees seek to persuade nonmembers of the merits of their decisions: in writing in a committee report and orally through floor debate.

The committee report is designed to communicate in a clear and efficient way the major provisions of a recommended bill and the arguments for and against (if there are dissenting views) its passage. More than a formal accounting of the committee's recommendation, it is written to persuade others of the wisdom of the committee's decision by providing "condensed, readily usable information."[24] The author of a major study of voting decisions in the House concluded that the committee report's "brevity and summary nature, its ready availability on the floor, and its usefulness as a kind of communication channel for members of the committee, make the report a particularly valuable source . . . . Of all the types of reading available, this one probably has more direct, immediate impact on specific votes than any other."[25] Similarly, the author of a standard work on congressional procedures writes that "[f]or many members, or their staff aides, the report is the only document they read before deciding how to vote on an issue."[26]

The final test of the committee's recommendation occurs on the floor of the House or Senate. Indeed, it is less accurate to think of the floor proceedings as open and general debate among the members of each body than as an opportunity for the committee to defend its recommendations. (A more general discussion of floor debate follows.) Those who manage the debate for and against the bill, by choosing the other speakers and controlling their time, are usually leading members of the reporting committee or subcommittee; and most of the principal debaters are usually members of the reporting committee. Throughout the debate the focus is on the committee's work and the committee's recommendations. Committee leaders seek to persuade the membership that the committee has carefully and fully deliberated on the bill at hand and reached a sound judgment of its merits.

Since floor debate offers relatively little time to demonstrate the merits of the bill under consideration, especially if it is a long and complicated proposal, one task of the bill's proponents is to convince noncommittee members to trust the judgment of the committee—in effect, to defer to the previous committee deliberations. For example, during the House debate on the Family Assistance Plan in April of 1970, Representative Hale Boggs, the ranking Democrat on the Ways and Means Committee, told the membership that more than a majority of the members of the Committee on Ways and Means at the beginning of the hearings approached the proposal with considerable misgivings. But after examining alternatives, and after looking hard, carefully, and critically at the existing welfare programs and how they have worked over the past 30 years—after that very intensive study and very intensive debate, the committee came, as I said, almost to a unanimous conclusion that this was the proper and right thing to do.[27]

A committee Republican, Jackson Betts, made a similar appeal:

The Ways and Means Committee has spent hours and days and weeks of deliberations and has, with refining amendments, approved this proposal overwhelmingly.

On the basis of this tremendous amount of work, honest and conscientious effort to answer the objections which have been made to the present welfare program over the years, I do not hesitate to ask the House to support this bill.[28]

At the conclusion of the debate, Carl Albert, the Majority Leader, spoke briefly in favor of the bill. He did not discuss its merits but simply noted that although "the bill before us may not be perfect, . . . an overwhelming number of those members who serve on the committee that has had the responsibility for this matter have reported it out and have recommended it to the House as being better than the existing system."[29]

In each of these cases, the bill's proponents were asking the members of the House to trust the judgment of the Ways and Means Committee. The proponents argued that the members of the committee were themselves initially skeptical of the administration's proposal. Yet, after seriously investigating the issue in great detail over many months and carefully reviewing the arguments for and against this major departure in welfare policy, they were persuaded of its merits. Non–committee members, who do not have the opportunity to duplicate this kind of detailed deliberation, ought to trust that the committee has done a serious and responsible job and has reached a sound judgment on the issue. Implicit in this appeal is the view that the committee reached the same conclusion that the full body would have reached if all the members of the House had engaged in the same "intensive study" and "intensive debate" and had devoted the same amount of "honest and conscientious effort" to this matter as had the committee. As noted in chapter 4, participant-observer Daniel Moynihan concluded that "the committee had done the work of the House, *for* the House. . . . This was deference to reasonable, moderate men."[30]

Thus, the very logic of the committee system in the House and Senate dictates some degree of deference by the full membership to the judgments of their committees; for there would be little point in having committees at all if the full bodies could thoroughly deliberate on committee recommendations afresh. It is not surprising, then, that on average the House and Senate endorse about 65–70 percent of committee recommendations without revision and pass another 15–20 percent of committee bills with amendments. In only about 10–20 percent of the cases do the full bodies simply reject committee proposals.[31] If observers such as Moynihan and participants such as former Senator Muskie are to be believed, a committee's "reputation for good judgment" is decisive to its success in the full body.

In addition to the importance of its collective reputation for sound deliberation and good judgment to its success on the floor, the committee also exerts influence through its individual members. When nonmembers of the committee are seeking guidance as to how to vote on the floor, they may look not only to the decision of the committee as a whole but also to the views and position of one or a few members whose judgment they trust. Every legislative committee in the House and Senate has both Democrats and Republicans; most also have some representation of the ideological range within the two parties; and most have members from diverse kinds of districts or states throughout the nation (urban or rural, industrial or agricultural, etc.). In many cases the nonmembers of the committee will be able to identify committee members who share their basic political orientation and whose judgment they can rely on as a guide to how they themselves would have decided if they had deliberated fully on the issue. According to one study of "cue-taking" in the House of Representatives: "When a member is confronted with the necessity of casting a roll-call vote on a complex issue about which he knows very little, he searches for cues provided by trusted colleagues who—because of their formal position in the legislature or policy specialization [i.e., usually members of the reporting committee]—have more information than he does and with whom he would probably agree if he had the time and information to make an independent decision."[32] This deliberative short-cut will be most effective when the "cue-giver's" policy views closely match those of the nonmember of the committee and when he has genuinely "done his homework" by closely reviewing the pertinent information and arguments and seriously thinking through the merits of the issue at hand. If either of these conditions is absent, then the nonmember's vote may not match what he would have decided if he had served on the committee and had personally reviewed the issue at length.[33]

Because the committee's success on the floor depends at least in part on convincing the full body that its members have reached a sound judgment on the bill under consideration, one way for opponents to undermine the committee's case is to challenge the sufficiency of its deliberations. An illustrative example is the Senate floor debate on a relatively obscure bill reported by the Government Operations Committee that would have disposed of several thousand acres of federal land in Illinois, the DesPlaines Public Hunting and Wildlife Refuge Area, by selling part of the land for industrial development, selling another part to the state of Illinois at fair market value, and transferring the final portion to Illinois at no cost for conservation and recreation purposes. The precise arrangement had been worked out by an ad hoc subcommittee of three, chaired by Senator Edmund Muskie. Senator Wayne Morse strongly opposed the bill because it violated the so-called "Morse formula," which was an understanding that had guided previous Senate decisions for several years that required that when federal land was transferred to public agencies for public purposes such agencies should pay one-half the fair market value. Muskie's bill had not actually applied this formula, although it may have approximated the result.

For three days Morse spoke out against the bill on the Senate floor. Throughout the debate he attacked the competence of the committee's work, especially its failure to investigate thoroughly the Army's claim that one of the tracts of land in the bill was needed for military purposes:

> I say most respectfully that the committee report does not satisfy me that the members of the committee went thoroughly into the matter of whether the Army in fact needs this property for Army purposes. I think the Senate is entitled to a much more thorough hearing, I say respectfully, than the one the committee gave this matter.[34]

Morse did not argue that the committee was wrong about the Army's claim, but only that the presumption in such a case should be in favor of the Army and that although "that presumption is subject to rebuttal . . . the committee should have presented in the report the evidence in rebuttal, in addition to the committee's conclusion."[35] The committee serves only "as an agent of the Senate as a whole," but on this matter "the committee has not fulfilled all its obligations of agency."[36] Morse concluded, "As the senior Senator from Oregon, I am entitled to evaluate the work of the committee. I think the committee did a poor job. I want the Record to show that evaluation."[37]

Muskie and subcommittee member Senator Ernest Gruening defended their work before the Senate. Gruening maintained that "the committee made a very thorough study. . . . [It] very patiently heard all sides again and again; and I doubt whether many investigations were any more thorough than this one."[38] Muskie was equally forceful in defending the committee's work:

> I submit, in behalf of the subcommittee, that we devoted long hours to this problem. We listened to a great deal of testimony in the hearings and talked with a great many persons outside the hearings. . . .
>
> I emphasize again that this action was not taken lightly. It was not done offhandedly. It was not done without long, serious, meticulous thought and care. . . .
>
> [W]e were not negligent in considering the bill; . . . we really probed for the facts which we considered important; and . . . we acted after deliberate consideration of those facts, and reached a judgment which we thought was fair.[39]

Although Morse was not successful in persuading the Senate membership to overturn its committee, the debate between him and the committee underlines the extent to which floor debate in Congress is dominated by the committee's deliberations and serves as a final testing of the soundness of the committee's judgment.

This debate also highlights an important House-Senate difference. In the House Morse's prolonged challenge to the committee would have been impossible, for it is unlikely that such a relatively minor bill would have been assigned more than one, at most two, hours of general debate. Morse, himself, would have been lucky to receive up to thirty minutes to make his case. Because the length of House floor debate, control over who speaks, and the kinds of amendments permitted on the floor are all determined by rules issued by the House Rules Committee and voted on by the membership, opponents to committee bills are forced to abide by procedural constraints and rigid time limitations beyond their control. In the Senate, on the other hand, where most debate is governed by "unanimous consent agreements," a single senator can refuse to abide by the proposed speaking limitations and can therefore can speak at length on a matter before the full body. This is perhaps the most important and consequential difference between House and Senate procedures. At times this privilege of speaking at length in the Senate, one of the most cherished traditions within the body, becomes a parliamentary device for actually preventing a vote on a bill. Such "filibusters" can be broken, under current rules, by a "cloture" vote requiring the support of a constitutional three-fifths of the membership (sixty senators). Even when "cloture" is invoked, however, it usually comes only after the opponents of a bill have had ample time to vent an issue fully.

It is the Senate's much smaller size than the House and its tradition of operating less by formal rule t an by "gentlemanly" agreement ar ong its members that make it pos le to have procedures that allow indi-vidual members to speak at len h on the floor (although this can wreak havoc with the scheduling prockss and give members numerous oppor-tunities at the end of the session to extort concessions from their col-leagues). This opportunity to engage in extended debate gives individual senators, especially nonmembers of the reporting committee (such as Senator Morse in the above example), a much greater chance than their House colleagues have to influence the full body's deliberations on a pending matter. Thus Senate deliberations on legislative issues are poten-tially much less constrained by prior committee deliberations. Senators need not defer to committees quite as much as their House colleagues do, because floor debate in the Senate affords much more opportunity for an independent review and assessment of the key issues involved in a committee recommendation.

It is only occasionally, however, that senators can take advantage of this opportunity; for over the course of a legislative session the Senate has only about as much time as the House to debate approximately the same number of issues and bills on the floor. The opportunity afforded individual senators to speak at length on the floor can neither increase the net time available for floor debate during a legislative session nor reduce the number and complexity of issues to be addressed. Thus, the basic pattern that applies in the House holds also in the Senate: most deliberation necessarily occurs within the committees, and floor debate serves as a final test of the committee's judgment.

Persuasion through Floor Debate

While it cannot be disputed that floor debate focuses attention on the information and arguments supporting a committee's policy recommendations, what is less clear is whether real persuasion occurs as a result of what is said on the floor. Such persuasion is most easily discerned when legislators actually change their minds after listening to or participating in floor debate. Although the conventional wisdom holds that floor debate does not change minds, case studies of the legislative process as well as the testimony of participants provide evidence to the contrary.

The authors of the studies of two modern landmark statutes, the Employment Act of 1946 and the Landrum-Griffin (Labor Reform) Act of 1959, report that speeches on the floor of the Senate were decisive to the success of the bills. During Senate floor debate on the former, Senator Joseph O'Mahoney, "an independent, middle-of-the-road Democrat . . . [with a reputation] of knowing more economics than anyone else on Capitol Hill," delivered a major speech in support of the Full Employment Bill.[40] In his comprehensive case study Stephen Bailey describes its effects:

> It is rare that a speech on the floor of the Senate actually changes stubborn Senate minds. O'Mahoney's presentation was an exception. It is generally conceded by friend and foe alike that the Wyoming Senator's dramatic, illustrated lecture on the economics of S. 380 had a marked effect on the final vote. With the use of charts and graphs placed in the well of the Senate floor and against the back wall of the chamber, O'Mahoney breathed economic respectability into the pending legislation. With the attitude of a patient professor he explained technical economic concepts to his colleagues.[41]

In the second case a speech by Senator John McClellan persuaded the Senate to adopt a tough labor reform bill. Here two independent investigators reported the persuasive effects of McClellan's speech:

> In a lengthy Senate speech . . . McClellan delivered an impassioned plea for a tough labor law, punctuated by references to the findings of his Select Committee. . . . The atmosphere in the Senate became one of marked deference and adulation for Senator McClellan, the proven, long-publicized fighter of labor corruption. As a result of his speech, the focus of the debate shifted suddenly to McClellan and away from [John] Kennedy. . . . McClellan now clearly had charge of the debate.[42]

Spectators could actually feel the Senate respond to the speech delivered in the grand manner reminiscent of the oratory of the century before. It was clear that senators had been moved.[43]

On these important bills, according to the case study authors, some senators were persuaded to vote contrary to their original inclinations by what they heard on the floor. How often this occurs is impossible to determine; nonetheless, no less seasoned an observer and legislative participant than former Speaker of the House Jim Wright of Texas has written that "some votes are always changed by debate."[44] As we have seen, however, genuine persuasion does not require an actual change of mind; for it also includes the process whereby the reasoned consideration of information and arguments moves a legislator from broad initial dispositions or preferences to specific decisions or actions. We should not conclude that because final positions are consistent with original inclinations the intervening debate was without effect. On the contrary, it may be the crucial link between inclinations and decisions.

Consider in this respect the House debate on the Elementary and Secondary Education Act of 1965. The following case study excerpts show the importance of a floor debate that in the end did not actually change congressional minds:

Carl Perkins then assumed the brunt of the leadership for the Democrats. He cited the need for federal aid legislation and offered broad supporting comments on the significance of the particular bill before the House. After he gave up the floor, the Republicans . . . , led by Goodell of New York, hit hard at what they thought were the weak spots in the legislation.

The Republican attacks on the formula and other aspects of the program began to have telling effect on the Democrats. Goodell had Perkins, Powell, and Hugh Carey disagreeing among themselves about what the bill was intended to accomplish and just how specific programs would work under the law. . . .

But even with all the research and preparation, the Democrats were reeling under the attacks of the Republicans. Perkins had been an effective subcommittee chairman by many accounts, but to several observers and participants he was not in control of the floor situation. It was precisely this kind of situation that the Democratic leadership wanted to avoid. They did not want the key sections of the bill to appear indefensible to that body of liberal Democrats unsure of what they were about to support. . . .

While all this was occurring, the Administration's education strategists were sitting in the gallery of the House, "scared to hell" as one of them put it.[45]

The Democrats eventually regrouped and carried the final vote. In the end, most liberals supported this liberal bill. But if this account is accurate, liberal support was not automatic, not a foregone conclusion independent of the debate on the floor. The proponents' early mishandling of the debate in the face of effective Republican opposition seriously jeopardized the bill's chances for passage because, for a while at least, key provisions "appear[ed] indefensible" to the body of liberal Democrats who were inclined to support federal aid to education.

In some cases a representative or senator may carry cross-cutting inclinations with him or her into floor debate. Senator Muskie recounts how he attended floor debate in the Senate one day in 1975 to decide how to vote on an appropriations bill amendment authored by Senator John Tunney that would have denied funds for an experimental demonstration of a breeder reactor. "On the face of it," Muskie reported, "that looked like an amendment I would naturally support, it being the environmentalist position." In this case, however, Muskie's inclination to support the "environmentalist position" was opposed by a five-page memo written by one of his staff recommending a vote against the Tunney amendment. Muskie's reaction: "What the hell gives? So I went there and sat and listened to the debate until I made up my mind. And I voted against the Tunney amendment. . . . That was a case where I decided to stay there long enough to hear Tunney explain his view, and [Senator John] Pastore explain his view, and that gave me a better perspective on the vote than the memo did."[46]

Whatever the actual impact of the arguments advanced on the floor of the House or Senate, there can be little dispute that most floor debates on important national issues involve some element of real, often vigorous, exchange between the opposing sides. The bill's sponsors (almost always from the reporting committee) begin by explaining and defending their proposal; opposing legislators attack weaknesses in the bill; the proponents respond to opposition charges. Generally, as in the case of the House debate on the Elementary and Secondary Education Act, a bill's defenders are not free to ignore the opposition. The two sides do not simply talk past one another but enter into a real exchange. Of course, the leaders in the debate do not try to persuade each other; rather their efforts are directed toward those listeners who remain undecided. Even if this is a small fraction of the whole, successful persuasion on the floor may be decisive on a closely divided issue. In fact, reports one investigator, "it is still a regular occurrence that a quarter or so of the House membership will spend hours in the chamber listening to the debate; if not to change their minds, then at least to gain more information, to listen for new arguments, or perchance to formulate an opinion when they do not hold a strong view."[47]

In addition to actually attending floor debate, there are other ways that members of the House and Senate can be informed and influenced by what is said on the floor. One is through staff. As an aide to Senator Domenici reported, a senator unable to attend floor debate personally may "send at least one staff guy to sit in the gallery and take notes, so you're debating for the staff and you hope they'll pass the good stuff on to their Senator."[48] Another mechanism for following floor debate without actually attending is through the *Congressional Record,* which is delivered to all House and Senate offices early in the morning following each day's debate. The legislator may scan the *Record* or have staff excerpt or highlight important sections. While this does not help with debate limited to a single day, it can be an effective way to track the information and arguments presented during a several-day debate. Indeed, it may be "a far more efficient way of following the proceedings than spending time on the floor."[49] Moreover, for some years now House and Senate offices have received live broadcast coverage (first just audio, then audio and video) of proceedings on the floor, allowing staff to track floor debate for legislators tied up with other activities. Finally, these mechanisms may be supplemented by informal word of mouth whereby important developments on the floor are communicated throughout informal networks of legislators and their aides.

It follows, then, that low attendance on the floor of the House or Senate does not mean that floor debate serves no deliberative purposes. A fascinating example of such a case reportedly occurred during Senate floor debate on the San Luis Reclamation Bill of 1960, during which the arguments advanced by Senators Paul Douglas and Wayne Morse over four days to a nearly empty chamber attacking a key provision of the committee bill successfully persuaded a majority of the body.

At issue was whether long-standing federal policy limiting to 160 acres the amount of a farmer's land (320 acres if married) that could be irrigated with water from a federal reclamation project ought to apply to the state portion of a proposed joint federal-state water project in California (called the San Luis reclamation project). The Senate Committee on Interior and Insular Affairs had unanimously reported to the full Senate a bill to authorize the joint project that specifically exempted the state portion from the restrictions of federal reclamation law. This exemption had not seemed particularly controversial since this issue had not been raised or debated by any of the parties during the one-day hearing before the Subcommittee on Irrigation and Reclamation. With its broad bipartisan support and unanimous committee endorsement, the bill seemed assured of passage by the full Senate. Nonetheless, after four full days of floor debate, during which Senators Douglas and Morse vigorously attacked the exemption provision in the face of the uncompromising opposition of the bill's sponsors, the exemption was defeated by the full membership. Douglas's explanation for why he and Morse were successful, presented on the floor just after the amended bill passed the Senate, is worth quoting at length:

> Mr. President, I think the result of this vote indicates the importance of discussion and debate, because when the bill was brought to the floor on last Tuesday everything was apparently primed for its speedy passage. The committee . . . had brought in a report advocating the bill with the inclusion of section 6(a) [the exemption provision]. This provision was supported by the two very amiable, popular, and able Senators from California. The great majority did not know a great deal about the bill, and therefore was ready to approve it.
>
> I must admit that the two Senators who primarily took the floor to oppose the measure, the senior Senator from Oregon and the senior Senator from Illinois, would probably never win any popularity contest among the members of this body.
>
> We had before us for consideration, therefore, a measure with everything in its favor.
>
> The Senator from Oregon and the Senator from Illinois in the debates of last week and yesterday tried to develop the facts in this case, and I think we demonstrated to the satisfaction of those who listened and read the Record that, with section 6(a) in it, it was a bad bill.
>
> There were only a few people who listened to the debates. At times it seemed to be a futile exercise. There were only a

few people on the floor as we talked against what seemed to
be overwhelming odds.

Yet the extraordinary thing is that as the facts were developed one could see the opinion of the Senate change. Senator
after Senator took the floor to say he believed section 6(a) was
a bad section and should be eliminated from the bill.

The analysis of the bill spread by a process of osmosis
through the Senate as a whole, so that those who did not hear
the debates nevertheless read the Record or colleagues upon
whom they relied relayed information to them.[50]

Normally a unanimous con 1ittee recommendation on a bill of primarily local interest would be (cisive. In this case senators who did not
serve on Interior and Insular Affairs knew little to nothing about the
details of the proposed reclamation project, had no reason to believe that
substantial controversial issues were at stake—especially given the committee's unanimous endorsement—and thus were inclined to defer to
the deliberations of the committee. Yet according to Douglas the arguments that he and Senator Morse advanced on the floor over four days
were decisive to the defeat of the exemption provision even though few
senators were actually present to hear their case. The "discussion and
debate" that occurred on the floor developed facts and issues that challenged the merits of the exemption provision of the committee bill. A
few senators "listened" to the arguments against the bill in person, some
"read the *Record*," and others were relayed information from "colleagues
upon whom they relied." In the end, the arguments made on the floor,
carried throughout the Senate largely through indirect means ("a process of osmosis"), persuaded a majority that the committee proposal "was
a bad bill."

A detailed examination of the four days of debate on the San Luis
reclamation project reveals additional features of the deliberative process
that led the Senate to reject the exemption provision. This episode about
a relatively obscure bill provides a useful window on the nature of deliberation in Congress.

First, in opposing the committee proposal Douglas and Morse emphasized that the committee had not really addressed the merits of exempt-
ing the state portion of the joint project from the restrictions of federal
reclamation law. Since the committee had not genuinely deliberated on
this issue, the usual deference to committee deliberations was not justified. Indeed, on the third day of debate, a member of the reporting com-

mittee, Senator John Carroll, took the floor to explain that the committee had not in fact considered the implications of the exemption provision and that the floor debate had convinced him to oppose this feature of the bill that he had previously endorsed. Thus, Douglas and Morse did not so much ask their colleagues to reject the judgment of the committee as to deliberate on issues largely overlooked by the committee; for the floor debate was the first time that these issues were fully addressed. As noted earlier, Senate procedures provide a greater opportunity than exists in the House of Representatives for challenging committee recommendations through extended debate on the floor.

Second, Douglas and Morse gave two kinds of reasons for insisting that the debate, after filling most of a Tuesday and Thursday, should carry over into the next week. One was to give senators not in attendance sufficient opportunity to study the record that had been made on the floor so that they could understand "the merits of this issue."[51] The other was to give the American people a chance to reflect on the controversy and to communicate their views to their senators. "We are confident," Morse explained, "that once the American people come to understand our position, they will be with us, as the American people always have been in all the other areas when land frauds and land steals—what I would call in this instance a water steal—finally come to be understood by them."[52] Even after debate resumed on the following Monday afternoon, Morse was still predicting an extended fight: "There will be some more afternoons of debate on this issue, if necessary, in order to make the public aware of what is involved."[53] Denying the charge that he and Morse were threatening to "filibuster," Douglas maintained that the vote had to be delayed "to develop the debate and the public understanding."[54]

At first glance these two reasons for extending debate might appear to reflect two distinct strategies for defeating the exemption provision: (1) a deliberative strategy, persuading senators through arguments on the merits, and (2) a political pressure strategy, generating constituency pressure by taking the case directly to the people. This second strategy helps to explain the heavy dose of high-flown rhetoric and impassioned declamation engaged in by Douglas and Morse. Characteristic was Douglas's vow "to fight on the beaches, in the fields, on the streets, and from house to house, in an effort to protect the people of the United States from one of the greatest land steals that has ever been attempted in the history of the Nation."[55] He accused the bill's proponents of "com[ing] into this chamber shackled with the chains of the Southern Pacific Land Co., the Boston Ranch Co., the Kern County Land Co., the Standard Oil Co., the other oil companies, and other large landowners in this area."[56] And he wondered why on this issue the bill's leading proponents, California Senators Thomas Kuchel and Clair Engle, should be "against the people."[57] In a similar vein Morse called on the Senate to "stand up . . . against powerful interests when they seek to execute such a diabolical scheme which would do such great damage to the public interest. There is no language I know of that could gloss it over. There it is, in all its ugly nakedness, in the pending bill."[58]

However effective rhetoric such as Douglas's vow "to fight on the beaches, in the fields, on the streets, and from house to house" might have been for Winston Churchill two decades earlier when Britain faced its greatest crisis, it is unlikely that Douglas and Morse truly expected such emotional and colorful language to carry the day with their colleagues on the matter of how federal reclamation policy ought to apply to a novel joint federal-state water project in central California. Rather, their intention seems to have been to reduce a fairly complex legal issue unlikely to have much impact on the general public to an easily understandable matter of simple right and wrong, of the "people" and the "public interest" against "powerful interests" with their "diabolical scheme." If the main issues in the debate over the exemption provision could be effectively communicated to the public in these terms, then it would become risky for senators to vote against Douglas and Morse, even if they were unpersuaded of their substantive case against the exemption.

While it is perfectly plausible that in a particular case political pressure could succeed in moving a majority of the Senate to vote in a certain way, irrespective of the merits of the issue, there is little evidence that popular pressure was a major factor in the disposition of the San Luis Reclamation Bill debate. Indeed, there seems not to have been much public interest at all in this controversy during the week the issue was before the Senate. For example, the few communications from the public opposing the exemption provision that Douglas inserted in the *Record* near the end of the debate were almost entirely from California. Moreover, neither the *New York Times* nor the *Washington Post* carried any stories at all on the San Luis controversy until after the amended bill passed the Senate. Even the *Congressional Quarterly Weekly Report* ignored the issue in its edition covering the week that included the first two days of Senate floor debate. Only after the bill passed the following week did *Congressional Quarterly* cover the story. Thus, there is little reason to believe that the debate on the Senate floor had aroused the public into pressuring their legislators to oppose the exemption provision in the San Luis bill.

Rather than viewing the public appeal of Douglas and Morse as a strategy distinct from their deliberative efforts, it is more accurate to see these two facets of their case as complementary or mutually reinforcing. Even while the San Luis bill was the subject of formal floor debate in the Senate, it was necessary for Douglas and Morse to compete for the attention of their busy colleagues. Committee business, paperwork, constituency service, meetings with interest groups and delegations from the state, staff guidance, raising campaign funds, and assorted other activities all compete with floor debate for a senator's time during the weekday afternoons when debate is usually scheduled. These pressures operate even when important legislation of national scope is before the Senate. When decidedly less important issues are at stake, such as a single water project affecting a single state, it becomes quite easy to ignore floor debate in favor of other business.

Faced with a decided lack of interest in the San Luis bill among their colleagues, it was necessary for Douglas and Morse to raise the stakes in the contest, to give senators good reasons to pay attention to the debate unfolding on the floor. One way they did this was by rhetorically converting the technical legal issues involved in the exemption controversy into a contest of broad principles with potentially widespread populist appeal. This alerted liberal senators in particular that significant principles might be at stake, not merely narrow legal ones, and that simply supporting the original committee bill might turn out to be politically unwise. After receiving positive soundings from a handful of Senate offices a few days into the debate, Douglas and Morse became increasingly confident that their arguments would prove persuasive if they could get the rest of their colleagues to pay attention. Thus, the political pressure strategy, not likely to be decisive on its own, was intended to serve the underlying deliberative appeal.

It is not uncommon in Congress for legislators to maximize the public appeal of their issues and positions in order to attract the attention of their colleagues. Committee hearings, in particular, are often staged, through the selection of witnesses and topics, to enhance the likelihood of media coverage and public interest. While publicity seeking often serves nondeliberative purposes—reelection, ambition for higher office, ego gratification, etc.—at times it is intended to foster deliberation by getting busy legislators to focus on the information and arguments that support policy innovations. For example, when Senator Pete Domenici led the fight in the 95th Congress to get the barge companies to pay for some of the upkeep of the nation's inland waterway system, he and his staff worked hard to generate favorable publicity on the bill in part just to get other senators to pay some attention to this fairly obscure issue. "One of the big problems with this user-charge business," Domenici explained, "was that nobody in Congress ever thought about the inland waterways—except the guys from the big barge states."[59] Domenici was delighted when the *Washington Post* picked his bill as the subject for a series of weekly articles on the legislative process in Congress: "If my bill was going to get on page one of the *Post* every week, that might make people around here start thinking, 'Hey, Pete's onto a pretty good idea,' and I'd have a better chance to win."[60] Because the *Post* was widely read by members of Congress, its continuing coverage of the progress of the user-charge bill greatly increased the prospects that other legislators would pay some attention to this issue and perhaps begin to think through the merits of this substantial policy innovation. This illustrates something of the complexity of the relationship of deliberation to such putatively nondeliberative activities as public appeals and publicity seeking.

In addition to the several ways described above in which floor debate may serve a deliberative purpose—changing or "making up the minds" of those in attendance, providing essential information and arguments that circulate throughout the chambers, and generating political forces that pressure legislators into making an independent assessment of the issues at stake—the nature of floor debate as a final, public testing of the rationale for a policy innovation may operate retrospectively to reinforce the deliberative process at earlier stages. Prior to passage virtually every important bill will be subjected to public attack on the floor of the House and Senate. Its opponents will attempt to expose weaknesses, highlight inconsistencies, and call into question underlying assumptions. Information will be disputed, arguments challenged, and conclusions denied. In anticipation of this public interrogation, the leading proponents of legislative proposals, those who will shoulder the burden of the public defense, will prepare themselves with the strongest arguments and most reliable information in support of their case. "I am trying to get at the basic facts," Ways and Means Committee Chairman Wilbur Mills explained during hearings on the Family Assistance Plan in 1970. "I can only make a decision and I can only propose something, so far as I am individually concerned, to the Members of the House when I have the facts, and I can substantiate it."[61] The proponents will pay particular attention to earlier attacks on the bill—during committee consideration, for example, or in the other branch, or perhaps from the executive branch—and they will fashion an appropriate rebuttal. Members of Congress who have built up a reputation for competence, seriousness, and effective leadership on the floor will be reluctant to jeopardize all this by defending a bill that can easily be made to appear foolish, ill conceived, or poorly drafted. In this respect the very prospect of floor debate may promote deliberation well before the actual debate has begun.

Deliberating outside Formal Channels

Committee consideration and floor debate constitute the basic formal elements of the deliberative process in Congress. These may be preceded, as discussed above, by informal deliberation in the formulation and sponsorship of legislation. Informal deliberation, however, need not cease after the formal process has begun; it may continue throughout congressional consideration and parallel the more structured process.

One of the principal mechanisms for deliberation in Congress outside the formal channels is the policy-oriented caucus, or "legislative service organization." This category includes broad-based ideological groups, such as the Democratic Study Group in the House, to which several hundred liberal Democrats belong; groups that focus on a specific policy area, such as the Environmental Study Conference with members from both the House and Senate; groups that promote the shared economic interests of districts or states, such as those focusing on steel production and tourism; and ethnically oriented groups, such as the Congressional Black Caucus and the Congressional Hispanic Caucus. Some policy-oriented caucuses do little more than sponsor occasional informal meetings; others, with full-time staff and office space, conduct a variety of activities meant to influence the legislative process. The Democratic Study Group, for example, conducts briefings for its members, sponsors task forces on specific topics, and produces several different kinds of reports analyzing bills and issues before Congress. It also has its own whip organization to maximize attendance on floor votes and to develop and communicate legislative strategy. What these caucuses have in common is that they are collections of legislators with shared policy interests who work together to promote common goals. Through briefings, discussions among members, and the preparation and communication of written materials, policy-oriented caucuses provide a channel and mechanism for deliberation distinct from committee meetings and floor debate.[62] In the 102d Congress (1991–92) there were 140 such caucuses in the House and Senate, organized around such issues or interests as animal welfare, aviation, beef, biotechnology, boating, clean water, copper, drug enforcement, energy, footware, forestry, health care, high technology, homelessness, insurance, mining, mushrooms, social security, soybeans, space, steel, textiles, tourism, and women's issues.

Less structured than these caucus activities but perhaps as important to the deliberative process in Congress are ad hoc private meetings among legislators and/or their staff. In chapter 5, for example, we saw how open Senator Muskie, Chairman of the Environmental Pollution Subcommittee, claimed to be to the arguments of his ideological opposite, Senator James Buckley, the subcommittee's ranking minority member. At a crucial stage in the formulation of the Clean Air Act amendments, Muskie and Buckley met to explore the possibility of a compromise on auto emission standards. To Asbell's surprise, the meeting seemed devoid of political conflict: "These two men aren't bargaining. They're not probing for each other's weaknesses and strengths. . . . [T]he air is free of tension." Although the author had expected a "meeting where, as they say around here, they 'cut the deal,'" instead he found something like genuine reasoning about the problem of controlling automobile exhaust emissions. Before the meeting ended, Muskie and Buckley agreed to a new set of auto emission standards that was a "retreat" from existing law but more stringent than what the industry was calling for. It was the expectation of the two men that having reached agreement between themselves "they [could] hold the Senate in line to pass the new standard."[63] Thus, Senate deliberations on this key public policy issue would be decisively affected by the informal and private deliberations of the two subcommittee leaders.

Another form that deliberation outside the structured process frequently takes is meetings between legislators and the representatives of interest groups. Organizations that represent the interests of commercial or industrial entities (such as banks or oil companies) or of discrete groups of individuals (such as farmers or veterans) or that promote certain broad "public interest" goals (such as "good government" or environmental protection) often make presentations in committee hearings to support or oppose policy innovations. Rarely, however, do interest groups limit their appeals to the formal legislative process, for they devote as much, if not more, of their persuasive efforts to private meetings with legislators and their staff. The legislative coordinator for the National Farmers Union gives the following description of how he and an ally tried to persuade senators to oppose the committee bill authorizing the San Luis reclamation project:

> George [Ballis] and I trudged up and down the Senate corridors, calling on one Senator after another. If the Senator was not in or could not see us, we talked to his administrative assistant. Our technique was first to set up a tripod for the maps [showing the high concentration of land ownership in the area to be irrigated by the San Luis project] and, while George's assistant hung them up, George and I talked.[64]

Occasionally, the lobbyists had to settle for brief exchanges in the Senate corridors:

> About a week before the San Luis debate started on the floor of the Senate, I ran into Senator [Richard] Neuberger as I was coming out of my cubbyhole in the Senate Office Building. . . .
>
> As we walked, I talked as fast as I could about how the San Luis bill would weaken reclamation law and the family farm in states other than California.
>
> "You've got a good point," the Senator said. "They told me the 160 acre limitation was protected. Otherwise, I wouldn't have voted for it in committee."
>
> When I told him I hoped that Senators Morse and Douglas were going to fight the bill on the floor, the Senator indicated that he could hardly sponsor and speak for an amendment of a bill he had previously voted for.
>
> "But I'll think about it. If what you say is true, this could be a dangerous precedent that might undermine reclamation law."[65]

In the course of the short walk from the Senate Office Building to the Capitol the lobbyists raised issues that Neuberger had not previously considered, even though he was a member of the reporting committee. As unstructured and ad hoc as this "meeting" was, it gave the lobbyist an opportunity to make his case in abbreviated form against the merits of the committee bill and thereby sow some doubt in Neuberger's mind, eventually leading to the senator's active opposition to the bill. Of course, to say that lobbyists make reasoned appeals to legislators in private meetings does not deny that other kinds of appeals may also be made, such as reminders about past financial or organizational support, intimations about the prospects for future support, and none-too-subtle references to "grass roots" interest in the issue back home (stimulated perhaps by interest group activities).

Finally, informal deliberation also includes private study and reflection by members of Congress. For example, when the House Ways and Means Committee decided to report out Nixon's Family Assistance Plan in February of 1970, committee chairman Wilbur Mills announced that he was "going into retreat" to think through his own position on the bill. He indicated that even though he would not lead the floor fight against the bill, he might vote against the measure on the floor. Yet, as we have seen, Mills soon decided not only to support the committee measure but also to sponsor it in the House. Thirty-five hours of public hearings and seven weeks of executive sessions had exposed Mills to a wealth of information and arguments in support of the administration's proposal. Yet, by his own account, he was not finally persuaded of the merits of the bill until he had spent another week privately thinking through the information and issues involved.

Such a clear-cut sequencing from the formal deliberative process to private study and reflection is not typical of lawmaking in Congress. More commonly, private deliberations will be brief periods squeezed out of a hectic daily schedule during which legislators review committee reports, clippings from the *Congressional Record,* or staff memos on legislative issues. Such private reflection may also extend to evenings at home away from the distractions of the Capitol.

Deliberation that occurs outside of the formal legislative channels, such as that described here, is by its nature more difficult to identify and analyze than that which occurs in the formal committee and floor stages. Moreover, it is more closely intertwined with the nondeliberative activities so common "behind the scenes" of the legislative process, such as vote trading, deal making, and pressure politics. It is almost second nature for journalists and political scientists to assume that whatever occurs behind closed doors in Congress must be something other than genuine deliberation about legislative issues. Yet there is nothing about the nature of reasoning on the merits of public policy that restricts it to public forums. The reasoned consideration of information and arguments can as well occur in a private meeting as in a public committee hearing or during floor debate. Indeed, as noted earlier, a shield of secrecy may actually foster deliberation by screening out political influences that might discourage free and frank discussion and exchange of views. (More on this last point in chapters 7 and 8.)

Deliberation over Time

The reasoned consideration of information and arguments that occurs within congressional forums, whether formal or informal, is part of a well-defined two-year lawmaking process that begins when Congress convenes in January after each national election and ends with final adjournment, usually a month or so before the next national election. Normally, a legislative proposal must pass the scrutiny of subcommittee, full committee, and floor debate in both the House and Senate within the two-year life of each Congress if it is to become law. If a bill fails to overcome all these hurdles by the time of final adjournment, it must start the process anew in the next Congress.

Yet, unlike the formal legislative process, the actual deliberative process in Congress is not confined to a rigid two-year cycle; for on some issues the full dimension of the deliberative process may extend over several, even many, Congresses. Consider, for example, the congressional deliberations that led to the passage of the War Powers Act of 1973. According to the Senate Foreign Relations Committee, "the immediate legislative history of the war powers bill can be dated to the controversial Gulf of Tonkin Resolution of 1964 and the subsequent conduct of hostilities in Vietnam, Laos and Cambodia without valid Congressional authorization."[66] By the late 1960s many in Congress had come to believe that the president had overstepped his proper constitutional authority in initiating military hostilities. This led first to the passage of the National Commitments Resolution by the Senate in 1969. Extensive hearings on this growing controversy were held in the Ninety-second Congress (1971–72) and resulted in the passage of separate House and Senate bills. These bills were reintroduced the following year in the Ninety-third Congress, where the differences were resolved and a law was passed over President Nixon's veto. Thus, the process of opinion formation on the war powers issue extended over the better part of a decade. Examining a single committee hearing or floor debate during this period would be like looking at one frame of a movie film. Movement of opinion would likely be indiscernible; the presentation of information and arguments would appear ineffective. Only a much wider temporal focus would reveal the true dynamics of the deliberative process in Congress.

On other important issues, as well, the deliberative process within Congress has extended over many years. It is not unusual for a policy innovation to take up to a decade or more to move from a novel proposal to the law of the land, as, for example, James Sundquist has shown in his account of the passage of key elements of President Johnson's Great Society program.[67] This is one reason why legislators are not reluctant to introduce proposals that have little chance for passage within the immediate two-year legislative cycle. The Senate, in particular, has been described as an incubator of public policies which makes a distinctive contribution by "gestating [new] ideas, by providing a forum for speeches, hearings, and the introduction of bills going nowhere for the moment." This "process of gestation" encourages policy advocates to "keep information up to date on . . . prospective benefits and technical feasibility. And it accustoms the uncommitted to a new idea."[68] Over time, what began as a controversial, or even radical, idea may gain adherents through increased familiarity with the underlying concepts, the persistence of the problem addressed by the proposal, and the persuasiveness of the supporting information and arguments.

Congress, in this respect, is not an isolated institution. It is necessarily influenced by the constellation of ideas that predominate in the larger social and political system. As these ideas change over time, so too does thinking within Congress. Although the correspondence is not perfect, changing congressional membership, staff turnover, and electoral considerations all ensure a degree of responsiveness to external opinion. "To a very great extent," writes Paul Quirk, "the direction of policy change depends on the state of opinion about the public interest. That opinion includes the values and attitudes of the mass public; the general ideologies of the attentive public and political elites; the more specific policy and program doctrines of practitioners in each area; and the pertinent theories and research findings of policy analysts and social scientists."[69] It follows that those forces that shape public and elite attitudes on social and political issues will have an impact on Congress and its deliberations about public policy.

☆ CHAPTER SEVEN

The President's Contribution to
Congressional Deliberations

> The law-making part of the government ought certainly
> to be very hospitable to the suggestions of the planning
> and acting part of it.
> Woodrow Wilson, 1908 [1]

The American presidency, as discussed in chapter 2, was designed to make three distinct contributions to deliberative
democracy in the United States. First, the consolidation of
administrative control under a constitutionally independent
chief executive would remove from congressional consideration the "details of execution," thus freeing the legislature to
focus its time and energy on broad policy matters. Second,
the president would influence congressional deliberations on
public policy (especially domestic policy) through the exercise
of his constitutional responsibility to recommend legislation
to Congress and through the actual or threatened use of his
qualified veto power. Finally, the president and his advisers
would engage in substantial independent deliberation to support executive decisions, especially in those areas where the
executive's constitutional mandate was firmest, such as the
formulation and execution of foreign and national security
policy (e.g., forming alliances, negotiating treaties, and directing the deployment and use of the military forces).

Because it would be impossible here to do justice to all
three ways in which the American presidency contributes to
deliberative democracy in the United States, the focus in this
chapter will be on the contribution that is most closely tied to
the major themes of this volume: the ways in which the president and those who work under him influence congressional
policy deliberations.

A Brief History

Although the Constitution places on the president the obligation "from time to time [to] give the Congress Information

of the State of the Union, and recommend to their Consideration such Measures as he shall judge necessary and expedient,"[2] it does not determine the vigor with which a president will approach this duty nor the scope of his legislative efforts. George Washington, the nation's first chief executive, took a very narrow view of his personal and official role in influencing Congress. "His messages," writes the administrative historian Leonard White, "went no further than to suggest subjects for consideration, and in no case did they contain any indication concerning the policy which he thought Congress should pursue."[3] Washington once wrote that he did not propose legislation to Congress, "lest it should be suspected that he wished to influence the question before it."[4] Despite a few mostly informal efforts to affect the course of lawmaking in Congress, Washington remained basically true to his rule not to influence policy deliberations within the House and Senate through direct, personal, and formal actions.[5]

Washington did not, however, extend this rule of official noninterference to his subordinates. Indeed, Secretary of the Treasury Alexander Hamilton exercised a legislative influence in the first Congresses that rivaled that of a prime minister in a parliamentary system. Within a week after Hamilton assumed his duties, toward the end of the first session of Congress, the House of Representatives discharged its Committee on Ways and Means and referred its business to Hamilton for a report. Hamilton's "great reports on public credit, on a national bank, and on manufactures," writes White, "laid the foundations of Federalist economic policy. . . . The Secretary of the Treasury became one of the most important forces in the first Congress and highly influential, although under attack, during the second Congress."[6] Those who opposed key elements of Hamilton's financial and economic program—such as paying off the existing national debt at full face value, assuming responsibility for the state debts incurred during the war, and establishing a national bank—complained not only that these policies were unwise but also that Hamilton's influence over legislation violated the constitutional independence of Congress and threatened the establishment of a monarchical system. Writing some years after these events, Thomas Jefferson, who had served as Washington's secretary of state, maintained that once the bill to assume the state debts had passed, "the whole action of the legislature was now under the direction of the Treasury."[7]

Even though Hamilton retained solid majority support in the House during Washington's first term, he was not able to persuade its members to allow him to report in person to the full membership, as ministers do in a parliamentary system. Although nothing in the Constitution prohibited such appearances, the members of the House drew the line here to define the proper limit of executive branch influence over the business of Congress. Personal appearances of department heads would be limited to committee meetings. This set the precedent, which continues to this day, that the chief formal modes of executive branch efforts to influence deliberations in the House and Senate would be written reports and personal appearances of administration officials before congressional committees.

The historical record demonstrates that Hamilton's success in influencing the deliberations of the first Congresses was not due solely to the cogency and persuasiveness of his written and oral arguments. With respect to at least one of his proposals, the assumption of the state debts, extraneous factors played a decisive role. Although Hamilton pushed the proposal on the grounds that such debt had been incurred to support the successful prosecution of the war, which benefited the entire nation, others, especially southerners, opposed the plan because it rewarded the less responsible states out of the common treasury. Hamilton's persuasive efforts proved insufficient, and his plan was voted down in the House. "So high were the feuds excited by this subject," Jefferson wrote, "that on its rejection business was suspended. Congress met and adjourned from day to day without doing anything, the parties being too much out of temper to do business together. The eastern members particularly . . . threatened a secession and dissolution."[8] Following entreaties from Hamilton to help resolve the impasse, Jefferson arranged a dinner at which the principal parties would seek "to form a compromise which was to save the Union."[9] To convince the southerners to change their votes on assumption, it was necessary, in Jefferson's words, "to sweeten it a little to them."[10] The sweetener was a promise to move the seat of government from New York City to the Potomac, at the border of Maryland and Virginia. Representatives from the northeastern and middle states would exchange their support for the move of the capital southward (after a temporary stay in Philadelphia) in exchange for southern support for the assumption of state debts. The deal was struck, the bargain was kept, and Congress subsequently passed both measures. Thus was transacted the first major logroll to influence lawmaking within the Congress.

However decisive this particular deal was to the passage of the assumption legislation, it would be a mistake to depreciate the importance of the administration's (i.e., Hamilton's) reasoned appeals to its success in influencing congressional deliberations. Most of those who traveled to New York City in 1789 to serve in the First Congress had learned first-hand the lessons of fiscal and economic mismanagement during the years since independence and shared with Hamilton a deep and abiding desire to establish the new government on a firm financial foundation. Public confidence in republican institutions had been severely under-mined by the effects of tender laws (allowing taxes or debts to be paid with products such as tobacco), paper money, restraints on trade, and the like. It was thus essential that Congress proceed in a careful and responsible manner. Hamilton's plans charted such a course and so proved persuasive on most points to the majority of those who possessed the formal lawmaking authority in the first years under the Constitution.

For over a century Hamilton's legislative efforts remained the high watermark of executive branch influence over congressional delibera-tions, matched perhaps only by the administration of Thomas Jefferson. As leader of the "anti-monarchical" Republican party that dominated national government after the "revolution of 1800," Jefferson scrupu-lously avoided any appearance of the president formally and directly influencing the legislative process, symbolized by his refusal to deliver the president's Annual Address (now called the State of the Union Ad-dress) in person before the House and Senate, as had Washington and John Adams. Notwithstanding such conspicuous demonstrations of presi-dential noninterference with Congress, Jefferson's administration exer-cised considerable influence over legislative policy in three distinct ways. First, Jefferson personally guided congressional activities quietly and be-hind the scenes through trusted lieutenants who occupied leadership po-sitions in the House and Senate, a method described by one historian as "achieving mastery through secret influence with Congress."[11] Second, his secretary of the treasury, Albert Gallatin, following Hamilton's pre-cedent, worked closely with Congress on financial and economic matters (by, among other means, attending committee meetings) and sought to steer the course of domestic policy by means of major reports on manu-factures, internal improvements, and the banking system. His writings have been described as "like lawyers' briefs, devoted to the question at hand, well reasoned, addressed persuasively to the intellect, exhaustively researched, and full of information."[12] However well argued, Gallatin's ambitious plans met with only partial success due to divisions within the Republican party. Finally, at the administration's direction Republicans embraced the Federalist invention of the party caucus to bring together members from the House, Senate, and the executive branch to formulate unified policy positions. Although no records exist of these meetings, "it is reasonable to presume that Gallatin played an important part, and it was alleged that Jefferson occasionally presided." [13]

Jefferson's immediate successors, who lacked his standing as undisputed leader of the controlling political party, were unable to sustain substantial executive influence over the course of congressional policy. Indeed, the party caucus, now centered in the House of Representatives, became the instrument of congressional control of the executive, abetted by the *de facto* election of the president through nomination by the Republican members of Congress (at a time when there was only one effective national party). It took the election of Andrew Jackson in 1828 to redefine the relationship of president to Congress and to introduce new modes of executive influence.

The extension of both universal white manhood suffrage and the election of presidential electors directly by the people (rather than by the state legislatures) in all states but two made the election of 1828 the first truly popular presidential election. As hero of the War of 1812 and spokesman for the agrarian forces, especially west of the Appalachians, the immensely popular Jackson was the easy victor in the electoral college, which simply ratified the popular choice. To the democratization of the presidential selection system Jackson added the theory that the president, as much as Congress, was "the direct representative of the American people." [14]

The greatest test of strength of the newly democratized presidency came in the battle over the rechartering of the Bank of the United States in 1832. Jackson's opponents in Congress, apparently trying to create an issue for the upcoming presidential election, had moved a bill through Congress in July rechartering the bank four years before its charter was due to expire. In response Jackson issued the most controversial veto in the forty-three-year history of the presidency, refusing his assent on both policy and constitutional grounds. In addition to rejecting the authority of the Supreme Court's decision in *McCulloch vs. Maryland* (1819) upholding the constitutionality of a national bank, Jackson attacked the bank in his Veto Message as threatening "great evils to our country and its institutions" from the "concentration of power in the hands of a few men irresponsible to the people." "It is to be regretted," Jackson wrote, "that the rich and powerful too often bend the acts of government to their selfish purposes," and when this happens "the humble members of society—the farmers, mechanics, and laborers . . . have a right to complain." Rich men who were not "content with equal protection and equal benefits, . . . have besought us to make them richer by act of Congress." It is up to the people and their president to "take a stand . . . against any prostitution of our Government to the advancement of the few at the expense of the many." [15]

Jackson's attack on the "rich and powerful" on behalf of the "humble members of society" was an overt appeal to the citizenry to support his veto of the bank bill. For the first time a president used a veto message to appeal to the people over the heads of their representatives in Congress. Indeed, it was the first time that any president had exploited the popular connection in a confrontation with Congress. It proved to be a resounding success. The Veto Message became a Democratic campaign document, and Jackson was reelected in November of 1832 with 55 percent of the popular vote and 219 of 286 electoral votes. Jackson interpreted his electoral success as an unambiguous endorsement of his efforts to dismantle the national bank. As he explained to his cabinet in September of 1833 in defending his decision to order the removal of the federal deposits from the bank, the election had effectively decided the issue:

> Can it now be said that the question of a recharter of the bank was not decided at the election which ensued? It was to compel the President to take his stand that the question was brought forward at that particular time. He met the challenge, willingly took the position into which his adversaries sought to force him, and frankly declared his unalterable opposition to the bank as being both unconstitutional and inexpedient. On that ground the case was argued to the people; and . . . the people have sustained the President . . . . Whatever may be the opinion of others, the President considers his reelection as a decision of the people against the Bank. [16]

As this brief historical sketch illustrates, Andrew Jackson's appeal to popular sentiment in the battle over the national bank added a wholly new dimension to presidential modes of influencing the legislative process. During the six administrations prior to Jackson, presidents had influenced congressional policy deliberations through (1) formal written reports to Congress, (2) personal appearances of cabinet officers before congressional committees, (3) informal and ad hoc efforts to guide Congress through trusted allies in the House or Senate, and (4) the use of the party caucus to bring together members of the executive and legislature outside of formal channels. Because these modes of executive influence, whether formal or informal, all involved direct communication between members of the two branches, they were suited for the kinds of reasoned appeals essential to inter-branch deliberation on public policy. Jackson's introduction of popular sentiment and the popular will into a policy dispute between the branches radically disrupted the historical pattern of executive-legislative communications.

In a way that would be unusual today, Jackson's Veto Message contained both a substantial constitutional and policy argument against the bank and elements of a popular polemic. It was clearly intended in part to tap deep-seated popular resentments against the rich and powerful. Moreover, the message itself virtually called on the people to use the congressional elections of 1832 (to occur four months later) as a means for "bear[ing] to the Capitol the verdict of public opinion" on this matter.[17] Indeed, Jackson interpreted his own election to a second term not merely as a broad statement of public confidence in his stewardship, but as a specific "decision of the people against the Bank."

However one assesses the merits of Jackson's position against the national bank in 1832, it must be acknowledged that he brought public opinion to bear on a specific policy dispute between the branches in a way that was not foreseen nor desired by the architects of the American separation of powers system. While it has become commonplace in the twentieth century for presidents to appeal to the people in a contest with Congress, the framers would have worried that such behavior would jeopardize the deliberations within Congress and between the legislature and executive. Why indeed should a popular president argue the merits of policy issues with those in the House and Senate if he can force compliance with his views by threatening electoral reprisals? While Jackson's actions as president re-energized the executive branch and helped to restore some of the constitutional balance lost after Jefferson's administration—Madison had written of "the irresistible force possessed by that branch of a free government, which has the people on its side"[18]—they also jeopardized some of the supports for institutional deliberation built into the original constitutional design. How could the representatives of the people "refine and enlarge the public views" through their greater knowledge and experience and their deliberations with their colleagues if important national issues were simply decided by contests for the public mind?

Yet it must be recognized that Jackson's appeal to public opinion was employed, contrary to more recent practice, in a restrained way for limited negative ends. As a firm proponent of the priority of the states on most policy matters, Jackson played the democratic card in a few highly controversial issues mainly to restrict the reach of the national power. He did not recur to the popular will for guidance on bold new policies or programs, nor did he use his widespread popularity to direct the legislative process. Although Jackson vastly expanded the reach of the executive power beyond then accepted norms—by, for example, using the veto for strictly policy purposes, maintaining that the president constitutionally controlled all discretion vested by statute in his subordinates, and threatening South Carolina with military action during the Nullification crisis—he did not become the "chief legislator" in the modern sense. Indeed, his administration was less active in directing the policy process in Congress than were those of Washington and Jefferson. Although he was like all his predecessors in avoiding personal and formal efforts to influence the legislative process, he failed to follow the Washington and Jefferson practice of fully exploiting the potential of the office for guiding legislative policy through strong department heads or trusted party allies in the Congress.

Because Jackson did not guide or direct the lawmaking process in Congress and because his successors did not enjoy his overwhelming popularity with the American people, his administration had little lasting impact on presidential-congressional relations for the balance of the nineteenth century. This was a time in American history when presidents deferred to Congress on the great domestic issues—issues such as slavery, commerce, and the westward expansion—and limited their energies mainly to administration and foreign relations. Indeed, even President Abraham Lincoln, who has never been accused of being a weak president, made little effort to guide the legislative process:

> Less than any other major American President did Lincoln control or even influence the Congress. . . . [He] had remarkably little connection with the legislation passed during the Civil War. He proposed few specific laws to Congress: his bill for compensated emancipation is notably exceptional. He exerted little influence in securing the adoption of bills that were introduced. In some of the most significant legislation enacted during his administration Lincoln showed little interest. The laws providing for the construction of a Pacific railroad, for

the creation of the Department of Agriculture, for the impor-
tation of "contract laborers" from Europe, for the tariff protection of American manufacturers, and for the establishment
of land-grant colleges had little connection with Lincoln aside
from his formal approval of them.[19]

As Jeffrey Tulis has shown, it was not until Theodore Roosevelt's administration that a president influenced Congress to undertake an important new policy initiative by mobilizing public opinion. Following his
substantial victory in the 1904 election (56 percent of the popular vote
and 336 of 476 electoral votes), Roosevelt engaged in an energetic campaign for the passage of legislation to grant the Interstate Commerce
Commission power to regulate railroad rates.[20] Not limiting himself to
formal appeals to Congress in his Annual Messages of 1904 and 1905,
Roosevelt took his case for railroad rate regulation directly to the people
throughout 1905:

> Roosevelt campaigned for a railroad bill on a "swing" through
> the middle west and southwest, en route to a Rough Riders
> reunion in Texas. Speeches in Dallas, San Antonio, Denver,
> and Chicago received extensive coverage in the press. A series
> of commencement speeches and other addresses later that
> summer continued that campaign. And in early fall, Roosevelt
> embarked upon another "swing" through the southeast en
> route to a visit to his mother's family in Georgia, speaking in
> Richmond, Raleigh, Charlotte, Atlanta, and Little Rock.[21]

In January of 1906 a bill embodying the principles of Roosevelt's proposal was introduced in the House. (It later became known as the Hepburn Act after its sponsor, Iowa Congressman Peter Hepburn.) It passed
the House in February and the Senate in May.

Roosevelt's public campaign was by no means the single decisive factor
in the passage of the Hepburn Act. There is evidence, for example, that
Roosevelt engaged in bargaining with some opponents of his proposal
by "feign[ing] interest in a bill to revise and reduce the tariff, in order to
trade that project for support for his most important objective, railroad
regulation."[22] Moreover, the House of Representatives had indicated a
willingness to move for reform even before Roosevelt took his case to the
people. Nonetheless, the president's rhetoric was extremely helpful in
fashioning a public sentiment in favor of this substantial expansion of
federal authority and in bringing that sentiment to bear upon Congress.
Yet contrary to more recent practice Roosevelt ceased his public cam-

paign once the legislative issue was formally before the Congress: "Roosevelt did not speak directly to the people on the eve of crucial votes, as is sometimes the case in our time, nor did he attack congressmen during the debate."[23] During this time he maintained private contact with congressmen and had his Bureau of Corporations "release its report on the Standard Oil Corporation, showing that it had benefited by secret railroad rates."[24] Tulis concludes that Roosevelt appealed "over the heads" of Congress "in a way that preserved, and did not preempt, Congress's deliberative capacities and responsibilities."[25]

Although Theodore Roosevelt was the first president to successfully mobilize public opinion for positive legislative purposes, it was Woodrow Wilson who provided a comprehensive theory of governance justifying and legitimating popular leadership for policy ends. In Wilson's view it was "natural that orators should be the leaders of a self-governing people."[26] Political oratory, or rhetoric, on major national issues and policies both focused public attention on the governmental process, with the result that public attitudes could be brought to bear on decisionmakers, and provided the principal means for leaders to educate and instruct the citizenry. Political rhetoric was the basis, then, for the link between leaders and led that is essential to true democracy. By 1908, twenty-three years after writing his famous critique of American government and politics, *Congressional Government,* Wilson had come to see the president as "the vital place of action in the system."[27] Unlike those who serve in Congress, the president "is the representative of no constituency, but of the whole people. . . . If he rightly interpret the national thought and boldly insist upon it, he is irresistible."[28] If, as a result, "Congress be overborne by him, it will be . . . only because the President has the nation behind him, and Congress has not. He has no means of compelling Congress except through public opinion."[29]

Wilson was not opposed to presidents trying to persuade Congress directly on legislative matters. Presidents and their department heads had occasionally, and with varying success, "tried to supply Congress with the leadership of suggestion, backed by argument."[30] Yet both the separation of powers system, which denied executive officials a central role in legislative decisionmaking, and historical precedent, which closed the floor of the House and Senate to direct access by presidents and cabinet officers, hindered the president from "exercising any direct influence upon [Congress's] deliberations."[31] It was particularly because of the structural constraints on direct persuasion that presidents who desired to move Congress were forced to do so by generating public pressure.

Thus, Wilson's theory effectively displaced direct presidential persuasion of Congress through reason and argument on policy matters with a popular leadership that operated outside of normal channels of presidential-congressional interaction and that would generate political pressure to bring Congress to heel. In this Wilson added a theoretical underpinning to the practice first employed by President Jackson of appealing directly to the people on policy matters. Yet Wilson's political prescription ranged well beyond the Jackson precedent by vesting in the president's hands the central responsibility for national legislative leadership.

That Wilson's prescription has been embraced by his successors— especially since Franklin D. Roosevelt—and by contemporary political scientists, historians, and journalists can hardly be doubted. It has become second nature to presidents to seek to mobilize mass opinion on pressing policy matters through televised addresses, speeches before groups and organizations throughout the nation, news conferences, and appearances by surrogates on news and talk shows. These appeals to the people over the heads of their representatives in the House and Senate coexist with the more traditional modes of presidential persuasion of Congress, such as testimony of administration officials before congressional committees and written reports to Congress.

To say, however, that direct public appeals by presidents on policy matters occur frequently in the twentieth century is not to say that such efforts are always, or even usually, successful. Perhaps the most famous failure of such an appeal was experienced by President Wilson himself. When in 1919 the U.S. Senate refused to ratify the Treaty of Versailles, which formally ended the First World War and established the League of Nations, without reservations and amendments he found unacceptable, Wilson set out in September on a three-week 9,500-mile speaking tour of the Midwest and West to take his case directly to the people. "He spoke with superb eloquence and passionate conviction," records one history, "but against the rising tide of isolationism and illiberalism he made little headway."[32] Wilson suffered a physical collapse at the end of the tour from which he never fully recovered. The full Senate defeated the treaty in November of 1919 and again four months later.

The most notable recent presidential success in focusing public pressure on Congress came in the first year of Ronald Reagan's administration. Faced with a Congress reluctant to embrace the tax and spending cuts essential to his domestic program, Reagan took his case directly to the people in several televised addresses on the eve of crucial congressional votes. David Stockman, Reagan's head of the Office of Management and Budget (OMB), describes the effect of the president's July 27, 1981, address to build support for a major cut in personal income tax rates:

> The President concluded his address with a summons to the public for support for this great boon: "I urge you again to write to your senators and congressmen—you will make the difference again. . . . Let us not stop now."
>
> We hadn't stopped, and now neither would the public. The letters and telegrams began arriving—bags of them descending upon congressional offices. And in the final two days before the vote, the tide began to shift our way.[33]

Stockman and other administration strategists, however, were not confident that the shifting popular tide alone would guarantee success on the floor of the House and Senate; consequently, they "rented" the Georgia delegation by ending administration efforts to abolish the peanut subsidy program.[34] Shortly thereafter, Congress passed the president's bill.

Two points should be noted regarding President Reagan's successful execution of the Wilsonian prescription. First, as noted here and elaborated below, Reagan's public appeals, though clearly helpful to his cause, had to be supplemented by private deals to secure the necessary congressional votes. Second, successful efforts by presidents to move Congress, or even some significant part of Congress, by generating public pressure are relatively rare phenomena in American political history and indeed are noteworthy precisely because of their rarity. (More on this below.)

Modes of Presidential Influence: The Not So Subtle Mix of Politics and Deliberation

As this historical sketch illustrates, presidents have employed a variety of different methods to influence the congressional policymaking process. These may be classified into three main types: bargaining, public appeals, and direct deliberative efforts to persuade lawmakers of the merits of administration proposals.

Executive branch *bargaining* with members of Congress began no later than Hamilton's deal in 1790 to agree to move the nation's capital south in exchange for congressional support for national assumption of the state debts. Other examples noted above include Theodore Roosevelt's implicit bargain with some of his opponents in the struggle to pass the

Hepburn Act, and the decision by Reagan administration officials to trade away their opposition to the peanut subsidy in exchange for votes for the 1981 tax cut. The use of *public appeals* to pressure Congress on policy matters has a less ancient history. Although President Jackson in the 1830s went to the people to justify his opposition to the rechartering of the national bank, even Jackson did not use his immense personal popularity to try to move Congress to adopt new policy initiatives. It was not until the twentieth century that American presidents embraced public appeals as an appropriate and even desirable means of compelling Congress to accede to presidential policy leadership. Direct *deliberative methods* of influencing Congress, which have changed little since the first administration, principally include (1) formal written reports and messages to Congress in the name of the president or cabinet officers, (2) testimony of administration officials before congressional committees, and (3) ad hoc efforts to persuade individual members of the merits of administration proposals. The differences between these three methods of influencing Congress have been obscured both by the frequent use of the single term "lobbying" to designate any executive branch efforts to guide the legislative process and by the use of the word "persuasion"—which, I maintain, is best understood as the result of a process of reasoning on the merits—to denote bargaining and other nondeliberative approaches.[35]

Case studies show that presidents and their aides are quite aware of the distinction between deliberative and bargaining strategies for influencing Congress and make conscious decisions about the appropriate mix of these two kinds of activities. In 1959, for example, the Eisenhower administration strongly opposed a major aid to airports bill introduced by Senator Mike Monroney and pushed instead for a more modest approach. The case study of this issue describes how General Elwood Quesada, the administration's chief spokesman on aviation matters, determined the best strategy for achieving legislative success:

> In approaching Congress Quesada favored the general strategy of stressing the merits of the arguments against the big bill [Monroney bill] and for the administration bill. The 1958 elections had produced an overwhelmingly Democratic Congress . . . and there was little use in trying to bargain for individual votes. . . . Thus it was essential to mobilize the Republican strength as a hard core and then appeal to conservative Democrats through reasoned arguments, supplemented with ridicule of past abuses of the program.[36]

Here the administration consciously rejected a bargaining strategy in favor of "reasoned arguments." Quesada's thinking seems to have been that too many individual bargains would have to be struck to build a majority for the president's bill, and that the sheer numbers involved made this either unlikely or too costly for the administration. In contrast to the "retail" operation of bargaining for individual votes, making reasoned arguments is a "wholesale" transaction in which dozens or even hundreds of legislators may be persuaded by the same argument. The Eisenhower administration believed that it was possible to mobilize large numbers of the Republican "hard core" as well as conservative Democrats to oppose the Democrats' aid to airports bill through a set of traditional arguments against expanding the federal role. Because most Republicans and conservative Democrats shared similar beliefs about the dangers of expanding federal power, it was not necessary to fashion a unique argument for each potential ally. Thus, deliberative strategies for influencing Congress may be more efficient than bargaining strategies.

At times the fate of an administration proposal may depend crucially on the support of one influential member of the House or Senate. (Several such examples have been described in previous chapters.) When this is the case, the administration may judge that bargaining with this one member will be a more effective way to secure support than trying to persuade him or her through arguments on the merits. For example, following the passage of the Juvenile Delinquency Act of 1961, Congresswoman Edith Green, the moving force behind the bill in Congress, became increasingly disenchanted with the direction given the program by the Kennedy administration, including what she perceived to be the political basis for project site selection. Wishing to extend the act in 1964, the administration made overtures to Green. In a meeting between Green and David Hackett, an assistant to the attorney general, the administration's representative virtually conceded the element of political favoritism in project selection, and as he "prepared to leave the meeting . . . he mentioned the Portland [Oregon] project [in Green's district], leaving the impression that it could be funded if Mrs. Green so desired. This gesture simply reinforced her belief that the administrators of the program were more concerned with politics than with juvenile delinquency."[37] When this approach backfired, the administration changed tactics and tried to persuade Congresswoman Green of the merits of the existing program and the value in extending it. She was encouraged to visit several projects to learn of their worth firsthand. After she personally examined projects in Boston, New York City, Washington, D.C., and Cleveland, she came around to support extension of the program.

Trading a project in Congresswoman Green's district in exchange for her support for the overall program had seemed to administration officials like an effective strategy. Green's reaction to this none-too-subtle ploy, however, demonstrated that the administration had seriously underestimated her commitment to the merits of the Juvenile Delinquency Act of 1961 and her concerns about the politicization of its administration. She had worked hard to pass the original bill and she had a personal stake in its effectiveness; thus, she was not inclined to push for an extension of the program without some demonstration of its merits to the communities it served.

As this example illustrates, efforts to "purchase" the support of a key member of Congress, like the original approach to Congresswoman Green, may prove to be both ineffective and counterproductive. Those committed to the merits of a government program or policy proposal will be genuinely interested in information and arguments on its purposes, consequences, and effectiveness. Such persons are likely to be unmoved, or even offended, by appeals for support that ignore the substantive merits of the issue at hand or that imply that the merits are irrelevant to the administration's position. In this respect, purchasing votes through bargains violates the decisionmaking norms that ought to characterize a deliberative policymaking process. In the same book, for example, in which Woodrow Wilson advocated presidential domination of the legislature through the political pressure generated by popular leadership, he denied the legitimacy of a president bargaining with Congress:

> There are illegitimate means by which the President may influence the action of Congress. He may bargain with members, not only with regard to appointments, but also with regard to legislative matters. . . . Such things are not only deeply immoral, they are destructive of the fundamental understandings of constitutional government and, therefore, of constitutional government itself.[38]

In Wilson's view, constitutional government provided a structure and arena for great contests of ideas and principles, not for secret deals or power plays. The content and direction of public policy should be determined by the stronger argument, not relative power positions or bargaining skills.

Reagan's Success in Moving Congress: Persuasion and Bargains

As noted earlier, the recent president who stands out as most successful in moving Congress to adopt his key domestic proposals is Ronald Reagan. Without doubt his most successful year was his first, 1981, when he moved major tax and spending reductions through a reluctant Congress. Although we touched upon Reagan's success above, it is worth examining his legislative tactics in more detail.

Some have attributed the Reagan administration's success in 1981 in both reducing taxes and restraining federal spending to the triumph in the national election of 1980 of "supply-side" and conservative ideology over welfare state politics as usual. Yet David Stockman, President Reagan's first budget director, argues that there was never an ideological majority in Congress in support of the president's program. Indeed, even with Reagan's enormously successful public appeals neither the administration's massive tax cut nor its spending plan would have garnered a majority of votes in the House and Senate without dozens of private deals.

As Director of OMB, Stockman was in charge of the administration's budget cutting plan, a mission he embraced with a revolutionary zeal. When an early assessment showed the administration "at least one hundred votes short of the House majority needed to implement every item on the budget reduction package," Stockman rejected the "major compromise" that circumstances seemed to call for: "revolutionaries do not compromise."[39] As reality set in during the coming weeks, however, the administration was compelled to make "accommodations." A group of thirty "Gypsy Moths," moderate to liberal northeastern Republicans whose votes were absolutely essential to a Reagan majority, "had a list a mile long of cuts they wanted restored."[40] In one meeting Stockman promised to restore several billion dollars of cuts in such programs as Conrail, Amtrak, low-income energy, elementary and special education, CETA youth and training, weatherization, Medicaid, and guaranteed student loans.

As the decisive congressional votes approached in late June, the pressure to deal became insurmountable:

> For victory on the House floor the magic number was 218. We needed that many votes, and not one less. With none to spare, each vote became all the more precious—and all the more expensive.

> All of a sudden the game of budget subtraction turned into
> something rather different: an open vote auction. Every con-
> cession we made quickly turned into a demand for more
> concessions.[41]

As word spread that the auction was on, new members lined up with
their demands even as those who had already been accommodated re-
negotiated their deals:

> Bill Green of New York wanted the Medicaid cap raised—
> first by 1 percent, then by 2 percent, then by 3 percent. Then
> he wanted its calculation base changed. I gave it all to him,
> thereby eliminating all but an insignificant portion of the sav-
> ings. Scratch another entitlement reform.
> Carl Pursell of Michigan wanted $30 million for nurses
> training. He got it.
> Jim Leach from Iowa wanted the $100 million family plan-
> ning program pulled out of the health block grant. He got it.
> Norm Lent of New York wanted still more money for Con-
> rail. He got it.
> On and on it went . . . . [42]

But this still was not enough. On the day of the crucial vote on the rule to
govern House debate on the budget resolution, Stockman got a call from
conservative Republican Congressman William Thomas of California:

> "We ain't gonna make it," he said. "Not unless you open up
> the soup kitchen."
> In the Congress, the "soup kitchen" is what you throw open
> in the last hours before a vote to get people off the fence. At
> this point, democracy becomes not a discussion of the ideals
> of Jefferson or the vision of Madison. It becomes a $200,000
> feasibility study of a water project; the appointment of a re-
> gional director of the Farmers' Home Administration in west-
> ern Montana.
> Bill Thomas had spent some time practicing this art in the
> California state legislature, and he was now the official cook
> of the GOP soup kitchen. And he was good at it. If someone
> came at him and started talking about the plight of the elderly
> or an end to hunger on the planet, Thomas would hold up his
> hand and say, "Don't give me all that bullshit."
> And of course it had nothing to do with the plight of the
> elderly or an end to hunger on planet Earth. It had to do with
> reelection. The deals that were dished out in the soup kitchen
> were the irreducible minimum, the quarks of politics.

Thomas ticked off half a dozen deals he had already made with various Boll Weevils and wobbly Republicans. "Give the word and they'll vote with us," he said. "But don't think about it too long. We've got about forty-five minutes before the vote." . . .

What deals they were. They ranged from things that turned my stomach to things that made me only faintly ill.[43]

One month later the bidding war expanded to Reagan's tax reduction package. Again the problem was insufficient votes to ensure a majority on the merits of the original plan and thus enormous pressures to make concessions. What resulted was a bill combining income tax cuts of 25 percent (Reagan's bottom line position), an accelerated depreciation schedule that greatly reduced corporate taxes (pushed by moderate Republicans on behalf of an industry coalition), and a variety of "politicians' tax ornaments." Standing alone, the income tax cut "never had a chance." It was only in combination with the depreciation liberalization bill and the "cornucopia of tax ornaments" that it was "legislatively viable."[44] By the time a majority was assembled in support of the administration's proposal, the accommodations necessary to secure its passage were projected to cost nearly as much in lost revenue as the 25 percent reduction itself.[45] In the end the payments necessary to build a majority for Reagan's taxing and spending policies "shattered the fiscal equation. They caused the budget reduction package to shrink and the tax cut package to expand. Winning any battle, perforce, meant losing the war."[46]

Stockman's account illustrates not only the complex mix of deliberation and bargaining in a major legislative battle, but also the uneasy alliance of these two kinds of approaches. Like oil and water, arguing the merits and bargaining do not well mix. They assume radically different bases for congressional behavior. Whereas the one rests on the premise that the people's representatives will vote according to their judgment of the merits of a pending issue, the other presumes that votes can, in effect, be "bought" by offering the members something of value in exchange for their vote. What is offered may be legislative in nature, as were the numerous deals described by Stockman, or nonlegislative, such as promises by a popular president not to campaign against a congressman of the other party in the next election (also reported at the time).

Because bargaining and deliberation rest on conflicting premises, any administration that seeks to pursue both approaches simultaneously will find itself in an awkward, if not untenable, position. A president and his emissaries can hardly insist that a proposal be judged strictly on its merits if it becomes widely known that the administration is willing to deal for some number of votes. Indeed, as Stockman argues, even those who generally support the president's position will want to "get theirs" once the trading begins. For example, during the negotiations on the tax reduction package the administration made what seemed like a minor concession to southern Democrats represented by Congressman Kent Hance from Texas: "a tiny, $2,500 per year tax credit for small oil royalty owners against the windfall profits oil tax." But as the administration soon learned, this small concession had "poisoned the political well." Republicans who supported the president "saw Hance's 'little gratuity' as blatant, parochial favoritism. . . . [I]f Hance 'got his' on oil, well, then there was no limit to what they were going to ask for. Hance's $2,500 tax credit had triggered a trillion-dollar bidding war."[47] At this point in the legislative process bargaining for votes simply overwhelmed and therefore displaced deliberative appeals.

Given every administration's objective to move its key policy proposals through Congress, what difference does it make whether a majority is built on judgments of a policy's merits or on numerous private deals? Do executive officials have any reason to prefer one "lobbying" strategy over the other? Case studies suggest four distinct reasons why presidents and their aides generally prefer deliberative appeals to bargaining.

First, it usually takes less time and energy to make the substantive case for a proposal than to engineer hundreds of separate deals. Second, majorities based on bargains must be rebuilt again and again either at each stage in the legislative process in the two branches or over the months or years that an issue is before Congress, whereas majorities committed to the merits of an issue ought to be sturdier and longer lasting. As Stockman noted, "all those votes we had either rented, bought, traded, or begged would never be there again for us."[48] But when most members of the House and Senate are genuinely committed to the merits of a course of action, it will not be necessary to start from scratch in building a majority each time the issue is revisited in the House or Senate. Third, bargains, unlike deliberative appeals, necessarily carry some direct costs for the administration. Every time a bargain is struck the administration gives up something it values; it pays a price. Deliberative appeals, by contrast, are virtually cost-free (except for the time and effort necessary to make the substantive case). Finally, the price paid in bargaining may be so costly as to undermine the very objectives of the policy or program for which the votes are sought.[49]

This last consequence can result either when a concession is made on a matter of principle that strikes to the heart of the administration's objectives or when the collective cost of the bargains is so high as to overwhelm the effects of the proposal itself. Consider, for example, the impact of the Reagan administration's decision to trade away its opposition to the peanut subsidy in exchange for the votes of Georgia congressmen for its tax reduction package. In Stockman's words:

> This was no nickel and dime program. It involved big money and a big principle: our free market farm policy.
> The peanut growers had, in effect, a government-subsidized producer's cartel. It was a close cousin to tobacco, and it was a pure corruption of state power.[50]

Conceding on the peanut subsidy in order to buy votes made it that much more difficult for the administration to argue persuasively the merits of a free market farm policy. Why, after all, should representatives whose constituents grew wheat or cotton agree to reduce or eliminate price supports or loan guarantees for these crops if the peanut subsidy was to remain untouched? And once the principle on the peanut subsidy had been bargained away, so many more deals had to be cut, so many new concessions made, that by the time the administration had its majorities, its policy objectives had been seriously compromised. In Stockman's view the administration's concessions on taxes and spending destroyed the fiscal equation and thus guaranteed huge deficits for the remainder of the decade. So high was the purchase price for the president's program that Stockman and fellow administration strategist Richard Darman seriously considered "sabotag[ing] . . . our President's most cherished initiative" just before a crucial congressional vote. After some debate the two decided that "winning now and fixing up the budget mess later" was better than "losing now and facing a political mess immediately."[51]

Public Appeals and Political Deliberation

As noted earlier, public appeals are the other principal means (in addition to reasoned persuasion and bargaining) by which modern presidents try to influence Congress on policy matters. In the context of deliberative democracy, such appeals would seem to serve both deliberative and nondeliberative purposes. At their best, presidential speeches inform and educate the citizenry, thereby promoting communitywide deliberation on important national issues. One thinks, for example, of such famous presidential speeches or addresses as Washington's Farewell Address, Jefferson's First Inaugural, Lincoln's First and Second Inaugurals and Gettysburg Address, and, more recently, Franklin Roosevelt's famous "fireside chats." Yet insofar as presidents use popular rhetoric not to inform and educate the Congress but rather to generate public pressures upon its members, such appeals would constitute a nondeliberative method for influencing Congress. Woodrow Wilson, it must be remembered, spoke of "compelling Congress" through public opinion. If a majority of the House and Senate cannot be persuaded of the merits of the president's proposal, then they must be given additional reasons to support it, such as the fear of losing their jobs if they oppose a popular president. The next chapter examines more fully the contribution of presidential rhetoric to communitywide deliberation; here we focus on popular rhetoric as a device for pressuring Congress.

On the surface, at least, public appeals would seem to avoid many of the disadvantages attributed above to bargaining strategies for moving Congress and to share some of the advantages of direct deliberative appeals. Like efforts to persuade Congress through arguments about the public good, public appeals are a "wholesale" transaction through which dozens of legislators may be influenced by one set of appeals, thus freeing the executive branch from the onerous task of "purchasing" each vote in Congress in a "retail" fashion. Thus, compelling Congress by generating public pressure may be more efficient than bargaining for individual votes. In addition, public appeals seem to avoid the problem of costs intrinsic to bargaining for votes. If a well-crafted and effectively delivered television address generates the kind of public response that shifts votes in Congress, the president can enjoy the satisfaction of knowing that he built his majority without paying the kind of price that bargaining requires.

When presidents, their aides, and department heads formulate and promote policies that they believe will benefit the nation, it matters less to them in the end whether they capture the hearts and minds of the members of Congress than whether they capture their votes. From the perspective of the White House, once a majority in Congress have formally endorsed a president's policy, it is largely irrelevant, at least for the time being, whether those who voted with the president did so because they believed that the proposal was good for the country or because they feared retribution at the polls. It is hardly surprising, then, that those in the executive branch who have sought to move Congress have wholeheartedly embraced the Wilsonian prescription to compel obedience through the force of public opinion.

At least since Woodrow Wilson's administration, pressuring Congress through the force of public appeals has seemed a more respectable way to garner votes in the House and Senate than the deal making and vote trading that, because of their somewhat unsavory nature, are nearly always carried out behind the scenes and are rarely admitted to by presidents or their aides. Wilson, himself, as we have seen, was simultaneously in favor of compelling Congress through political pressure but against bargaining with Congress as "deeply immoral" and "destructive of . . . constitutional government itself." Yet, at least at first glance, it is hard to see how pressuring Congress through public opinion is any less threatening to inter-branch deliberation than is bargaining.

Fundamentally, the use of public appeals to pressure Congress into doing something it otherwise would not presents the same stark contrast with deliberative appeals as does bargaining. Whenever a president takes his case on a specific policy matter directly to the people, he has, in effect, turned his back on the congressional deliberative process. Unable, apparently, to win majorities in the House and Senate through reasoned argument, he has moved the contest to an entirely different arena, that of public opinion and political pressure. There may be good reasons for doing so—he may otherwise face certain defeat on the issue or larger ends may be at stake than the fate of one bill—but what cannot be gainsaid is that such tactics violate the norms of inter-branch deliberation.

Whereas a deliberative process favors the Congress, with its unhurried opportunities to assimilate information and to reason through policy options, the arena of public opinion clearly favors the president. The very same institutional and procedural features that promote Congress's deliberative character—multiple points of access, dozens of semi-autonomous committees organized around subject matter, and weak central authority—place it at a decided disadvantage in a competition with the president for the ear of the nation. Because the president is the undisputed focus of the national media and of public attention, he can, at virtually any time, move a policy dispute onto the public stage. Such an action is likely to be greeted by resentment, if not anger, by the members of Congress; for a president can hardly expect the people's representatives to view with equanimity an overt effort to pressure them into doing something they oppose. Moreover, this kind of political move will likely contaminate the climate necessary for reasoned persuasion; it can, as Stockman said about bargaining, "poison the well." In trying to persuade Congress on the merits, the president is saying, "support my policies because they are good for the nation"; in trying to pressure Congress through public opinion, the president is saying, "support my policies because I have it in my power to jeopardize your standing with your constituents and perhaps your reelection." A president should not be surprised if the second message rings louder in the halls of Congress than the first.[52]

Here we must qualify Tulis's conclusion regarding Theodore Roosevelt's appeal "over the heads" of Congress on the Hepburn Act "in a way that preserved, and did not preempt, Congress's deliberative capacities and responsibilities." Although Roosevelt may have refrained from public appeals on the eve of crucial votes and avoided attacking the members of Congress during the debate on the act, it must be admitted that any large-scale effort by a president to generate public pressure on Congress to do his bidding necessarily violates the deliberative norm that decisions are to be made through reasoned argument about the public good. There is no avoiding the radically different bases of the two kinds of appeals: deliberative appeals presume that the members of Congress reach judgments about the merits of pending proposals; public appeals presume that legislators can be pressured to vote against their substantive judgments. Both presumptions may be true, but this does not dissolve the tension between them or mitigate the dangers to inter-branch deliberation when presidents resort to public opinion to move Congress.

As noted earlier, the enthusiasm with which so many have embraced the Wilsonian prescription to compel Congress through public opinion has not been matched by a historical record of marked success at such efforts. How often have presidents successfully "persuaded" Congress to do something it otherwise would not have done by generating public pressure upon the members of the institution? Wilson himself failed dramatically when he went to the people on the League of Nations. Franklin Roosevelt, who combined immense personal popularity with great legislative success, enjoyed on most matters a Congress that thought as he did, not one he browbeat into submission through the magic of his personal appeal. And on one key issue where Congress was reluctant to follow—increasing the size of the Supreme Court so that partisans of the New Deal could be added—Roosevelt found that his personal popularity and public appeals were not enough to bring Congress around. Ronald Reagan in 1981 seemed the perfect embodiment of Wilson's rhetorical president (in terms of means if not ends), but not even the "Great Communicator" at the height of his powers could build majorities in the

House and Senate with public rhetoric alone. Finally, as if to underscore the point, President George Bush, in one of his few efforts to move public opinion through a televised address, failed utterly in October of 1990 to generate public support for his budget compromise with congressional leaders. Indeed, there is reason for believing that the speech may even have had the opposite effect. Separation of powers and the concomitant independent election of legislators have proven far more resistant than Woodrow Wilson expected or desired to the kind of plebiscitary leadership he wished to see embodied in the government's one truly national officer.

Reagan and Tax Reform:
The Merits of Executive Branch Deliberations

Although a substantial treatment of deliberation within the executive branch is beyond the scope of this volume, most would agree that any deliberative process in support of sound presidential decisions ought to include at a minimum the following features:

• a wide range of opinions would be considered;
• the key proposals and decision options would be fleshed out in an organized and systematic way;
• the information and advice presented to the president would be fairly and objectively presented, distorted as little as possible by the personal preferences of the advisers; and
• on important matters the president would personally review the relevant issues in some depth and fully think through the various options.[53]

These requirements are analogous to what makes for sound deliberation within Congress: a variety of viewpoints, ample objective information, and sufficient opportunity to reason through arguments and options. In important respects these essential requisites of sound deliberation supersede the massive structural differences between Congress and the executive branch. That is to say, the hierarchically structured executive, less suited by nature to deliberation than the collegially organized Congress, must function in some ways like a legislature if it is to do a credible job of reasoning on the merits of public policy. Thus, the deliberative executive must aspire to embrace both the legislature's openness to a wide range of information and opinion and its formal norm that arguments are to be judged on their merits without regard to the organizational position of those who make them. Particularly in the formulation of domestic policy initiatives, where speed and secrecy are less essential than in national security or foreign policy matters, we would expect to find the greatest similarity between executive and legislative deliberation. Nonetheless, even here case studies demonstrate systemic differences between Congress and the executive branch in the way the deliberative process unfolds.

A telling example is the development in 1984 and 1985 of the Reagan administration's plan to reform the tax code in the direction of a modified flat income tax, the chief domestic policy initiative of Reagan's second term. The formal deliberative process within the executive branch was initiated by President Reagan in his January 1984 State of the Union Address in which he called for "an historic reform for fairness, simplicity and incentives for growth." Secretary of the Treasury Donald Regan was to prepare by December of that year "a plan for action to simplify the entire tax code, so all taxpayers, big and small, are treated more fairly." During the following months Secretary Regan met regularly with a group of ten advisers and high-level Treasury officials to fashion a detailed plan. This plan, to become known as Treasury I, was publicly unveiled in late November. Less than two months later Regan and White House Chief of Staff James Baker switched jobs. The Treasury I proposal was resubmitted to the Treasury Department for further deliberations under the direction of the new secretary. In late April a revised plan was submitted to the president. After several meetings involving the president, his staff, and Treasury officials the plan was finalized. In late May the president announced his initiative to the nation in a televised address.

Perhaps the most interesting and revealing stage in this sixteen-month process was the formulation of the Treasury I proposal. The authors of the leading case study of the passage of the Tax Reform Act of 1986 give the following description of the deliberative process that occurred throughout 1984 in the conference room that adjoined Secretary Regan's office:

> For months, [Regan] worked diligently with this small group of men, combing through complex tax law, section by section. He kept the group isolated from the political storms of the election campaign; indeed, he kept them isolated from all the pressures that usually play upon people in power. The meetings were supersecret; the secretary ordered members of the group not to talk about their work to anyone outside of the conference room. Papers presented at the gathering were

passed out just two days before each session, in sealed envel-
ops marked *Eyes Only*, with explicit instructions that the contents were to be viewed only by the ten policymakers, and not
by their deputies. After each session ended, the papers were
collected again. Week after week, the group debated proposals that promised to shake the financial foundations of virtually every American family and business.[54]

The secrecy insisted upon by Regan effectively screened out political influences on the deliberative process. Since the outside world had no idea
of what was occurring in Regan's conference room, it had no basis for
reacting to it. This was very much Regan's intention. He wanted to foster
a decision process that was not only thorough and systematic but also as
purely analytical as possible. The insulation from political considerations that secrecy promoted was reinforced by Regan's specific instructions to his subordinates "to ignore political concerns."[55] Regan also
practiced what he preached. Throughout the months of deliberations he
"listened carefully to the arguments and read the papers for each meeting from start to finish."[56] In the end he fully embraced fundamental
reforms which he well knew would cause a political firestorm among
long-standing supporters of the president and the party. One of the leading participants in these meetings, Ronald Pearlman, who served as assistant secretary for tax policy and who was one of the department's top
tax experts, described the process as "the most stimulating experience"
he had ever had: "It's the way government at some level should always
work."[57]

The president, however, did not endorse the Regan plan. In an unusual move, the Treasury bill was placed before Congress and the public as an independent proposal and then resubmitted to the Treasury,
now headed by Baker, for further deliberations. This reconsideration, it
turned out, bore little resemblance to the careful analytical process of the
Regan group, for, according to the case study authors, Baker saw it as
his job "to do what Regan had avoided; to bring politics fully into the
process." His goal was to restore "enough tax breaks to keep a coalition
of powerful special interests from killing the entire effort" while also
"repealing enough preferences to make meaningful tax reform possible."[58] Although the new tax-writing group within Treasury looked
much like the old one, the meetings themselves focused more on political
realities than analytical soundness: "Where Regan avoided all talk of
politics, Baker talked about little else. He had scant patience for . . .

theoretical presentations." Unlike Regan, Baker and his deputy, Richard Darman, met secretly with powerful members of Congress to gauge the political prospects of tax reform. Baker also met with dozens of representatives of the business community—"The leaders of corporate America streamed through his door"—who came to plea for preservation of their cherished tax breaks.[59]

Not surprisingly, this was a "demoralizing period" for the professional tax experts who had participated in both the Regan and Baker groups as "[a]ll the elaborate and elegant rationale for their original plan was simply ignored."[60] For the first time "gimmicks," such as hidden higher tax rates, were introduced for political reasons, however indefensible on analytical grounds: "If the top rate was going to be 35 percent, Pearlman and his staff thought, just make it 35 percent outright; don't use a bizarre scheme to hide the top rate."[61] The result was a much less "pure," or far-reaching, reform that retained many of the tax cuts eliminated by Treasury I.

If deliberation is best understood as reasoning on the merits of public policy and if this account of the development of the administration's tax reform proposal is essentially sound, then one must conclude that the Regan-directed effort was more deliberative than the later process guided by Secretary Baker. This is not to say that nondeliberative influences played no role in the development of Treasury I (such as Regan's personal ambition to make his mark in national affairs) but rather that the actual process of fashioning the tax reform package was dominated by information, arguments, and persuasion on the merits of radical reform. By contrast, what dominated in the revisions was not the substantive merits of revising the tax code but rather the political forces and prospects for passage. It is unusual to find such a clear-cut differentiation of the impact of deliberative and political forces in the policymaking process.[62]

Although the decision process that produced Treasury I may be atypical in its almost purely analytical nature, it nonetheless reveals much about how characteristics and capacities peculiar to the executive branch can initiate and sustain sound deliberation. Three points stand out. First is the importance of secrecy as an essential condition for the deliberation witnessed in this case. Closing the doors to the decision process screened out political forces that might well have undermined the entire effort to restructure the tax system along more rational lines. Indeed, it is hard to imagine how such a radical restructuring could have occurred if the process had been open to public and interest group scrutiny from the beginning. Not only was the process conducted behind closed doors, additional security measures successfully prevented leaks that might have generated insurmountable political opposition to what the reformers were about.

To the extent that secrecy may promote deliberation, the executive branch has a distinct advantage over the Congress, where the norm and the public expectation is an open decision process. In a free and pluralist political system, policymaking in public will of necessity generate a whirlwind of external forces and pressures upon decisionmakers. Such pressures may impair, indeed prevent, reasoned analysis. Note that even Secretary Baker, whose preoccupation was politics and not substantive analysis, conducted his meetings in secret. This gave policymakers some degree of insulation from forces they may not have been able to control and thus much more room to maneuver in deciding how to respond to political realities.

Second, when the deliberators who fashioned Treasury I entered the decision process, they were not beholden to powerful external interests in the ways that members of Congress often are. In the Senate, for example, most members of the Finance Committee began their deliberations on tax reform deeply committed to preserving certain existing tax breaks. For committee chairman Robert Packwood it was the tax-free status of fringe benefits (strongly endorsed by organized labor) and tax breaks for the timber industry (important to the economy of his home state of Oregon). For Steve Symms of Idaho it was mining, agriculture, and timber. For Charles Grassley of Iowa it was the state's Christmas tree industry. For George Mitchell of Maine it was solid waste disposal facilities. And so it went.[63] Such commitments to economic interests are usually of a long-standing nature and may be intimately tied to the legislator's electoral interests. Deliberation necessarily suffers when such commitments impair reasoned persuasion to a course of action adverse to the protected interests. The Treasury Department officials who met for months with Regan faced no such constraints. Owing their governmental positions to the presid t, the secretary of the treasury, o advancement through the caree civil service, they had much less of a personal stake, if any at all, in ollifying the powerful interests affected by their decisions. Thus, they were freer to respond to information and arguments on the merits of tax reform.[64]

Finally, the hierarchical structure of the executive branch allowed for a degree of organization and control in the Treasury I deliberations that is difficult, if not impossible, to achieve in the collegial Congress. There was no doubt that Secretary Regan was in charge throughout, that he controlled the direction and tempo of the discussions, that he was in a position to issue instructions to the others, and that in the end his judgment would determine the Treasury Department's position on tax reform. All the other participants were there at Regan's bidding and all, in effect, worked for him. Through his undisputed authority Regan was able to ensure that the issues at hand received a thorough and systematic treatment.

Contrast this hierarchical control with the situation that faces committee (or subcommittee) chairmen in the House and Senate. Though putatively in charge, they possess very little real authority over their colleagues, each of whom is an independent actor in ways that those who work for cabinet secretaries rarely are. Owing their jobs to their constituents rather than their superiors, committee members bring to the deliberative process commitments, interests, and views over which the chairman has little control. Consequently, they have little incentive to respond to direction from above on any matter inconsistent with their political interests. This situation necessarily impairs the chairman's ability to structure a thorough and systematic deliberative process within the committee or subcommittee. Indeed, even compelling attendance at hearings and markup sessions is problematic. This is not to say that every deliberative process necessarily requires hierarchical control, but rather that in some circumstances, particularly where issues are complex and the participants have their own private agendas, steady direction from the top may well result in a more comprehensive and better organized review of the key issues.

It appears, then, that the relationship of separation of powers to deliberation in American national government is more complex than originally outlined in chapter 2. While not incorrect, it is also not sufficient simply to describe the legislature as the more deliberative institution. When quick and decisive action is not required, when there is leisure to collect information, analyze alternatives, and fashion proposals, the executive branch can bring to bear capacities beneficial to deliberation not normally found in the legislature. These include (1) the greater insulation from political forces that secrecy can promote, (2) less of a commitment to the interests of powerful external groups, and (3) greater organization and control. Yet when the exigencies of modern government call for decisive executive action, it is energy, not deliberation, that predominates. And although such energy must be informed by deliberation, the two principles coexist only with a kind of uneasy tension.

According to the case study authors, the president and his subordinates were right on the merits of tax reform, whereas Congress, prior to Reagan's prodding, was committed to an unjust and inefficient system defended by a multitude of special interests. Reagan was simply "[t]he most important player in tax reform." Although he "seldom took an active role in the two-year tax debate . . . . the conservative president's support for an effort once considered the bastion of liberals carried tremendous symbolic significance. Without his backing, tax reform could never have happened. With it, it became a powerful political juggernaut."[65] Given the power of special interests in Congress on this issue, a fair assessment of the merits of reform had no chance without the popular president's involvement. Here it was not active public pressure that moved Congress—legislators noted how little public interest there seemed to be even after presidential speeches—but rather the fear on the part of the leading legislators that they would be publicly blamed by Reagan for killing reform. In contrast to the pattern in 1981 of delivering televised addresses on the eve of crucial votes in Congress, Reagan in 1984–86 used his popularity more to prod Congress into action than to dictate specific votes. This allowed his subordinates to continue to make the case for tax reform on the merits in the various formal and informal forums in the House and Senate.

Although Congress was designed to be the nation's premier deliberative institution, there is obviously no guarantee that it will function as it should. Madison and other leading framers, it will be remembered, had attributed the failures of the state legislatures and the national Congress during the 1780s at least in part to the strength of a "local spirit," or of "local prejudices [and] interests," in diverting state legislators from "the comprehensive and permanent interests of [their] state" and national legislators from "the great interests of the nation." Is this problem any different from Senator Packwood's commitment to preserving tax advantages for the timber interests in Oregon, from Senator Symms's efforts to protect timber, mining, and agriculture in Idaho, or from Senator Grassley's desire to help Iowa's Christmas tree industry? For those policy areas in which the national interest is not so easily viewed as the sum of the preferences of politically effective interests or of the parts of the whole, the presidency may well be better suited than Congress to reason about the common good. We shall return to the issue of separation of powers briefly in the next chapter.

CHAPTER EIGHT

Public Opinion and Democratic Statesmanship

> [I]t is the reason, alone, of the public, that ought to control and regulate the government.
>
> Publius, 1788[1]

Deliberative democracy is a system of popular government that fosters rule by the informed and reasoned judgments of the citizenry, by what Madison called "the cool and deliberate sense of the community."[2] The fundamental premise, or central proposition, of deliberative democracy, as sketched in chapter 2, is that there are two kinds of public voice in a democracy—one more immediate or spontaneous, less well informed, and less reflective; the other more deliberative, taking longer to develop, and resting on a fuller consideration of information and arguments—and that only the latter is fit to rule. Those who created the American constitutional system believed that on most issues, most of the time, deliberative majorities would not exist independently outside of government, but rather would be formed through the operation of the governmental institutions, as the representatives of the people reasoned about public policy for their constituents. These two points explain Madison's claim that in a well-designed republic "the public voice, pronounced by the representatives of the people" would often be "more consonant to the public good than if pronounced by the people themselves."[3] Because representatives have the time, information, and institutional environment to reason together on issues facing the nation, the public voice to which they give expression may better promote the public good than the immediate and direct voice of the people.

Madison's argument applied today would mean that public attitudes measured by an opinion poll are likely to be less deliberative and less conducive to the public good than public attitudes informed and deepened through the operation of representative institutions. The very term "public opinion" implies the existence of developed public attitudes. Yet when attitudes are measured by an opinion poll, they may represent little more than the aggregation of hundreds of off-hand, unreflective responses to a pollster's questions.

Consider, for example, how a national polling organization would measure "public opinion" on the desirability of initiating a comprehensive national health insurance program. It is likely that 500–1500 phone calls would be made to a nationally representative sample of homes. The respondents, interrupted from other activities and totally unprepared for the subject, would be asked one or more questions to gauge their support for a national program to ensure health care coverage for all Americans. It would be surprising if most respondents had read or thought much about the arguments on each side of this issue prior to the telephone call, or, if they had, if they could instantaneously recall the pertinent issues. Most respondents, consequently, would voice spontaneous reactions, unsupported by any serious reasoning about the arguments pro and con. Indeed, it could hardly be otherwise. Men and women who might be quite capable of reasoning about the merits of national health insurance if exposed to, and given ample time to reflect upon, the relevant information and arguments are not likely to produce a deliberative opinion instantaneously. Yet the results of 500–1500 of these instantaneous reactions will be aggregated to portray "public opinion" on national health insurance. Replace this issue with any other of at least moderate complexity—welfare reform, auto emission controls, the Strategic Defense Initiative, etc.—and the point is the same. We should not be surprised if instantaneous opinion bears little resemblance to what would result from serious reasoning on the merits.[4]

In his perceptive account of the role of public opinion in American politics in the late nineteenth century, the British analyst James Bryce describes unreflective public opinion this way:

> The simplest form in which public opinion presents itself is when a sentiment spontaneously rises in the mind and flows from the lips of the average man upon his seeing or hearing something done or said. Homer presents this with his usual vivid directness in the line which frequently recurs in the Iliad when the effect produced by a speech or event is to be conveyed: "And thus any one was saying as he looked at his

neighbour." This phrase describes what may be called the rudimentary stage of opinion. It is the prevalent impression of the moment. It is what any man (not every man) says, *i.e.*, it is the natural and the general thought or wish which an occurrence evokes[5]

At this rudimentary stage, public opinion is not the result of "conscious reasoning," but rather is little more than "impressions formed on the spur of the moment."[6] Later, by reading newspapers and talking with friends and acquaintances, individuals begin to move from first impressions to more settled views. If the issue is one of public policy, the opposing sides will vie for public support as the main lines of debate are formed and party allegiances take hold. In the end a majority of the people may endorse one side or the other. According to Bryce, however, the average man makes little independent contribution to this process of opinion formation. His beliefs have been largely influenced by "what he has heard and read," and the "element of pure personal conviction, based on individual thinking, is but small."[7]

To Bryce the chief and overriding impediment to the average citizen's deliberations on public matters was not lack of capacity but lack of time: "The citizen has little time to think about political problems. Engrossing all the working hours, his avocation leaves him only stray moments for this fundamental duty. . . . [H]e has not leisure to do [his thinking] for himself."[8] No matter how capable the average citizen might be of thinking through and reaching informed judgments on major policy matters, the reality is that the demands of earning a livelihood leave little time for independent analysis of public issues. This would be true even if the average citizen had a compelling interest in public matters; but, according to Bryce, this is hardly the case: "to the great mass of mankind in all places, public questions come in the third or fourth rank among the interests of life, and obtain less than a third or a fourth of the leisure available for thinking."[9] The problem is exacerbated when issues of substantial complexity are at stake; for some issues "require uninterrupted and what may be called scientific or professional study"[10] and others, such as financial matters, bankruptcy rules, and transportation policy, require substantial "constructive skill."[11] "Public opinion," Bryce writes, "is slow and clumsy in grappling with large practical problems."[12]

These three impediments to citizen deliberation on policy issues—severe time constraints, competing interests for leisure time, and the degree of complexity involved in many legislative and administrative matters—effectively undercut, in Bryce's view, the key premise of "orthodox democratic theory": that "every citizen has, or ought to have, . . . a definite view, defensible by arguments, of what the country needs."[13] What the people in a large and heterogeneous democracy can contribute to public policy is not detailed direction resulting from substantial independent deliberation but rather "a sentiment grounded on a few broad considerations and simple trains of reasoning." This sentiment is more likely to be influenced by broad considerations of "justice, honour, and peace" than by "any reasoning [the people] can apply to the sifting of the multifarious facts thrown before them, and to the drawing of the legitimate inferences therefrom."[14]

Obviously, much has changed in the United States since Bryce's account of the late nineteenth century. The work week has shortened, affording Americans greater leisure time. Educational attainment, measured by years of formal schooling, has risen substantially. Mass electronic communications have replaced newspapers as the principal information source on public issues. Compared to his counterpart of a century ago, the average American today has more leisure, more education, and more information about public affairs. Nonetheless, it would be a mistake to overstate the impact of these changes on the problem of citizen deliberation. The average American may now work an hour or two less per day (and perhaps one day less per week) than in Bryce's time, but once commuting time, meals, errands, and family time are factored in, the "leisure" available for the study of public policy is at most a few hours each weekday evening and a few more on weekends. Moreover, the same technological developments that have given us mass communication of information on current events have also resulted in the creation of an entertainment industry, especially television, that effectively competes for the attention of the citizenry. Indeed, accounts of the early nineteenth century suggest that Americans of the time, faced with fewer entertainment options, were exposed to more serious political discussions in the form of speeches, lectures, and debates than is the case today. In any event, it is likely that new competition for the attention of the citizenry has more than offset the net gain in leisure time from a century ago.

Finally, even if one concedes that Americans are now better educated and more informed about public affairs than ever before (not an unquestionable proposition), it must also be acknowledged that technological advancement, the rise of the United States as a world power, and the expansion of the domestic responsibilities of the national government (social welfare, health and safety, economic management, etc.) have vastly increased the number, breadth, and complexity of public policy issues. This presents a formidable impediment to public attention, understanding, and deliberation.

We have seen, for example, how in Congress itself most legislators faced with voting on hundreds of complex issues have limited opportunities to review in any sustained way the information and arguments that bear on issues outside of the committees on which they serve. If those whose full-time responsibility it is to monitor and review policy proposals face such impediments, we should not be surprised that the average citizen, with but a few hours a week to devote to public affairs, engages in little independent deliberation on complex national issues. On a complex matter like the Nixon administration's Family Assistance Plan, discussed in previous chapters, we should expect little more from the average citizen than a generalized sentiment on the need for welfare "reform," for a national income floor for all Americans, or for a larger federal role in promoting the welfare of the poor. Yet these sentiments, derived from a host of miscellaneous influences—radio and television coverage, newspaper reading, magazine stories, the views of "opinion makers," conversations with acquaintances, and personal experiences or prejudices, etc.—hardly constitute the kind of reasoning on the merits of public policy that ought to control governmental decisions. Again, the problem is not the intellectual capacity of the average American to reason about public policy, but rather time constraints, competition for leisure time, and the number and complexity of public policy issues.

It is important here to distinguish between deliberation about the details of complex national laws and deliberation on simpler issues or on matters closer to home and over which citizens exercise greater responsibility. Elihu Root, for example, who served for six years in the U.S. Senate after stints as Secretary of War and Secretary of State in the McKinley and Theodore Roosevelt administrations, argued against such democratic devices as the initiative and referendum but in favor of the people themselves deciding "certain great simple questions which are susceptible of a *yes* or *no* answer" such as "where a capital city or a county seat shall be located" or "whether the sale of intoxicating liquors shall be permitted." We might think now of such straightforward matters as whether to limit congressional terms or whether to legalize currently illicit drugs. Yet on normal legislative matters the problem is not determining "what ought to be accomplished" but "how to accomplish it." This necessarily involves the "study and investigation" of "the working of a great number and variety of motives incident to human nature" and "complicated and often obscure facts." Moreover, new laws impinge upon the existing body of laws in ways that are not obvious without detailed analysis. Thus, for Root, "the only method by which intelligent legislation can be reached is the method of full discussion, comparison of views, modification and amendment of proposed legislation in the light of discussion and the contribution and conflict of many minds." In a democracy such a process was much more likely to be found in representative legislative bodies than among the citizens directly.[15]

In addition to Root's "great simple questions" susceptible to simple yes or no answers, average citizens are obviously quite capable of deliberating on juries, where they are taken away from their normal pursuits to focus their attention for some hours or days on matters of great importance to criminal defendants or civil litigants. Jurors in criminal cases, for example, are made keenly aware of how profoundly their judgment can affect the life of the defendant. The vesting of such weighty matters in the hands of average citizens can hardly help but to concentrate the mind and promote serious deliberation.[16]

Similarly, local matters like public school policies or locating highways may have sufficient impact on the lives and interests of ordinary citizens as to create a powerful incentive to devote time and attention to the issue and to argue the merits of the opposing sides with family members, friends, and neighbors. Yet as the scope of the policy widens, from neighborhood to town (or city), to county, to state, and to nation, each individual's responsibility for the result diminishes to the infinitesimal (one in two hundred million or so), thus weakening the kind of incentive necessary to invest heavily in the reading and research to become well informed.

The point here is not to dispute the capacity of American citizens to reach sound judgments about their own interests, the public good, or justice, but rather to clarify the impediments to public deliberation about the details of national policies and thus the necessity for a large institutional role in determining and fashioning "the cool and deliberate sense of the community." Since the conflict between Federalists and Anti-Federalists over the ratification of the Constitution of 1787, Americans have vigorously, and at times passionately, debated the relative importance of direct citizen opinion versus the judgments of public officials in determining the course of national policy. The full contours of this debate must remain beyond the scope of this volume.[17]

Given the impediments to public deliberation on the details of national policies, and thus to the formation of a deliberative public opinion, what, then, must political leaders do to foster the rule of deliberative majorities in the United States?

The Responsibility of Legislators

In American representative democracy, national legislators serve, in effect, as surrogate deliberators for their constituents. Where the citizenry lack the time, the institutional environment, and perhaps the interest to deliberate in depth on public issues, legislators are expressly chosen to devote their full care and attention to public matters. They have the responsibility to review information and arguments on legislative proposals and to exercise their best judgment on behalf of those whom they serve. This deliberative imperative, this duty to deliberate, is an intrinsic element of the American constitutional order. It carries major implications for the behavior of the members of the House and Senate and especially for how they relate to public opinion while carrying out their representative responsibilities.

First, it bears directly on how legislators spend their time. If lawmakers are to meet their deliberative responsibilities, they must keep fundraising efforts, meetings with constituents, and frequent trips home from crowding out essential deliberative activities such as attending committee hearings and floor debates, studying key information and arguments on legislative proposals, and, generally, entering into reasoned exchange with their colleagues. Sound deliberation is uncompromising in the demands it places on the time and attention of lawmakers. Because the deliberative imperative dictates that legislators devote a substantial portion of their work time to serious reasoning about the merits of legislative proposals, a legislator who fails to do so forfeits an essential responsibility to his constituents. Thus, it is a mistake to view constituency service as legislators' only responsibility to those they represent. Legislators who properly understand their duty to their constituents will not allow the ombudsman role to squeeze out the activities necessary for sound deliberation.

Second, legislators must not delegate excessive deliberative responsibilities to staff. It can hardly be doubted that representatives and senators need policy information and advice from staff. Not only do too many issues come to the floor for each member to monitor and analyze in advance, but most legislators would find it impossible without staff support even to stay abreast of the issues that come before the committees and subcommittees on which they serve. In such a situation the temptation can be strong to delegate the essential deliberative function to staff, with the member reserving to himself or herself only a final review, through a staff briefing, prior to voting in committee or on the floor.

Yet legislators are not elected merely to cast votes based on staff recommendations. Rather, their responsibility is to exercise their own reason and judgment on behalf of their constituents. There is no assurance, after all, that a decision arrived at primarily through staff deliberation and recommendations will be identical to one that the legislator would have reached on his or her own by personally engaging in the deliberative process. Although most high-level staff likely share the basic policy dispositions of their principals, some may in fact have personal policy agendas at variance with the elected official or beliefs that are more ideological or doctrinaire and thus less amenable to compromise. Since congressional staff are not elected by or accountable to the citizenry, excessive delegation to staff raises questions about democratic control of governmental decisions. At the very least such delegation adds another stage between the public and policy; at worst it severs the link between governmental deliberations and public interests and sentiments by handing over the deliberative process to a publicly unaccountable body.

Thus, the vast expansion of staff in Congress in recent decades poses serious issues for the linkage between democracy and deliberation in the American political system. Moreover, as Michael Malbin has argued, even if staff aides faithfully represent the political views and interests of those for whom they work, their sheer number and importance in Congress have replaced direct face-to-face discussion and deliberation among representatives and senators, rather common not so long ago, with staff negotiations "in which each party is trying to achieve the best deal for his own side."[18] Rather than experienced elected officials from throughout the country coming together to articulate the interests of their constituents, share their experiences and judgments with one another, and reason toward common goals, "we see members relying on staff technocrats . . . whose knowledge of the world is limited to what they learned in school or from other participants in the specialized Washington issue networks." In turn, "we see politicians taking general positions, leaving the details to staff, claiming credit, and learning about the impact from their constituents. . . . . Instead of thrashing it all out before the fact, the members too often do not know enough of the details they would need to deliberate until after a program is implemented."[19] Concomitant with, and at least partly the result of, staff growth has been a "weakening of deliberation" in an institution "that works best when it responds to constituents' needs and interests in a setting that encourages the members to think more broadly."[20]

The role of staff in policy deliberations within the national government nicely highlights the potential tension between democracy and deliberation. Few would dispute that if the elected members of the House and Senate delegated all deliberative functions to their aides and simply rubber-stamped staff recommendations, the American Congress would per force be a less democratic institution. Yet in some circumstances decisionmaking by staff may more closely approximate the deliberative ideal of reasoning on the merits than decisionmaking by elected officials. Indeed, we have seen how well the staff that was assembled under Secretary of the Treasury Donald Regan deliberated on the fashioning of the administration's proposal for income tax reform in 1985. Not one member of the group, including Regan himself, was an elected official. Had this proposal originated with the elected members of Congress, rather than in the executive branch, it is unlikely that this issue, which affected so many powerful interests, would have been as thoroughly and as fairly analyzed with a view to serving the national interest in tax reform. It may be wondered, then, why deliberation within Congress would not be well served by a similar staff-dominated decision process.

The issue here is how far one can go in the direction of rule by professionals or experts, wherever located in the federal government, without undermining the regime's fundamental democratic character. It is one thing for the president, an elected official, to delegate the formulation of a detailed proposal to his aides and quite another for the members of the House and Senate, elected to make the nation's laws, to delegate the decisive decisionmaking power to those they appoint to their personal and committee staff. What emerge as proposals from the executive branch, which must after all be cleared by the Office of Management and Budget or, on important matters, by the president himself, are merely recommendations to the Congress. No matter how many professionals or experts contributed to their formulation, the lawmakers in the Congress retain complete formal authority to enact the proposals virtually as is, to amend them, or to reject them. It is at this stage that the interests and desires of the American people must be brought to bear through their elected officials, where deliberation and democracy must be conjoined. There is some point, however hard to define, beyond which the growth of staff influence in Congress necessarily undermines this conjunction of deliberation and democracy.

The third implication for the behavior of legislators is that they must be open to what they can learn from their colleagues and others and thus must be willing to reach conclusions that deviate from, and perhaps contradict, their original dispositions. When the deliberative process commences, legislators cannot know where it will lead. Reasoning through the information and arguments brought to their attention may solidify original dispositions, modify them, or in some cases show them to be inconsistent with good public policy. Since legislators' initial policy positions are likely to mirror those of their constituents, their deliberations may result in policy positions at variance not only with their initial opinions but also with the views of those they represent. This is a fundamental and recurring issue for deliberative democracy. It is why, for example, members of the House and Senate are not, under the U.S. Constitution, recallable between elections, as were the delegates to the national Congress under the Articles of Confederation. A fixed term of office assures legislators that they will not be immediately disciplined by their constituents for responsibly carrying out their duties. It also gives them some time to explain the soundness of their views to constituents, potentially fostering a more informed and deliberative public opinion (more on political rhetoric and public opinion below).

Fourth, the duty to deliberate well may often be inconsistent with attempts to conduct policy deliber tions on the plane of public opinion. Formal legislative deliberations in le contemporary Congress—committee hearings, markup sessions, anc loor debates—are, with few exceptions, now conducted in public. This necessarily creates multiple audiences for every question, comment, or speech delivered in a committee room or on the floor. These audiences include the legislators in attendance, other members of the full body, interest groups, the media, the members' own constituents, and the American public more generally. Although sound deliberation demands that legislators address each other with reasoned appeals, the openness of the legislative process creates incentives to curry favor with interest groups or to posture before outside audiences. This can take the form of what David Mayhew calls "position taking"—making "pleasing judgmental statements."[21]

Posturing, or position taking, is hardly a new phenomenon in the U.S. Congress. "In all assemblies," wrote James Bryce a century ago, "one must expect abundance of unreality and pretence, many speeches obviously addressed to the gallery."[22] Indeed, according to Bryce, the House of Representatives was more prone to this kind of behavior than any comparable legislative body: "it talks and votes . . . as if every section of American opinion was present in the room."[23] As a result, "a set speech upon any subject of importance tends to become not an exposition or an argument but a piece of elaborate and high-flown declamation."[24] This was less common in the smaller Senate, where the members were better known to each other and possessed a keener sense of the connection between their personal behavior and the actions of the full body. Yet even in the Senate there were "show days":

> . . . a series of set discourses are delivered on some prominent question. Each senator brings down and fires off in the air, a carefully prepared oration, which may have little bearing on what has gone before. In fact the speeches are made not to convince the assembly,—no one dreams of that,—but to keep a man's opinions before the public and sustain his fame. . . . [T]hese long and sonorous harangues are mere rhetorical thunder addressed to the nation outside.[25]

Such posturing, so common in Bryce's time and in our own, undermines deliberation in several distinct ways. First, it deflects the time, attention, and energy of legislators away from productive deliberative activities. Second, it can make genuine reasoned exchange virtually impossible within formally deliberative forums such as committee meetings. How, for example, can some members coolly and rationally exchange information and debate issues if others are playing to the cameras or trying to make headlines? And third, it degrades the deliberative process by reducing argument and persuasion to the plane of unreflective public opinion, often resulting in oversimplifications, distortions, and, at times, outright appeals to passion and prejudice.

This points to the broader issue of the relationship of secrecy and its opposite, accountability, to sound deliberation, a matter that was touched upon in the discussion of markup sessions in chapter 6 and in the treatment of the deliberative capacities of the executive branch at the end of chapter 7. Next to the desire to democratize power in the House and Senate, the most powerful idea driving the massive institutional reforms of the 1960s and 1970s in Congress was the demand for "government in the sunshine." Secret meetings, such as markup sessions and conference committees, should be ended; public meetings of committees or the full bodies ought to be open to electronic broadcast so that the widest possible audience could observe Congress in action; and votes in committee and on the floor should be recorded so that constituents could hold their representatives accountable for their actions. All this was accomplished. But while these changes were being made, few either inside the institution or out asked how they would affect Congress's core responsibility to deliberate well for the nation. The drive for accountability—and therefore less secrecy, more recorded voting, and more publicity—rests on one or both of two premises. One stems from democratic theory: If the people are to control their elected officials, they must know what their representatives and senators are doing on their behalf. Because it is the job of legislators to carry out the wishes of their constituents, they have no basis for making important decisions insulated from public view. The second premise, though related to the first, is less principled and more cynical: Legislators cannot be trusted to do what is right for their constituents or the nation on their own. Behind the closed doors of a markup session or during the effectively anonymous voting in Committee of the Whole in the House, they will "sell out" their constituents or the broader public in order to curry favor with some powerful interest group for some narrowly self-interested reason: campaign funds, organizational support for upcoming campaigns, future employment possibilities, etc.

If, however, we take seriously the deliberative responsibilities of national legislators, particularly in light of the tension between democracy and deliberation, we may come to view the issue of secrecy and accountability somewhat differently. For example, if we begin not with the democratic premise that the people have a right to monitor every official act of their representatives or with its cynical variant that legislators are not to be trusted, but rather with the view that most lawmakers who serve in Congress genuinely desire to promote the public good, then the question becomes whether the glare of public scrutiny and formal accountability for every vote in committee and most votes on the floor contributes to or hinders deliberation in service of the public good. Indeed, we can identify in principle a variety of ways in which maximizing accountability and publicity can harm deliberation or, conversely, ways in which insulating legislators to some degree from public scrutiny can support and enhance deliberation within Congress.

First, maximizing publicity can, as we have seen, promote posturing at the expense of genuine reasoning about the public good. To put it differently, when meetings are not held in public—like markup sessions and conference committee meetings for most of the history of Congress—or when the audience of open meetings is limited to those in attendance—like committee hearings and floor debates until radio and television were allowed in a few decades ago—the serious substantive lawmaker who has "done his homework" takes precedence over his less studious colleague with a knack for publicity. This can only be good for sound deliberation on public policy.

Second, the opening up of the legislative process can make lawmakers much more directly accountable to interest groups whose support they may need for reelection. Lobbyists, after all, now actually sit in on committee markup sessions. This may constrain the policymaking efforts of lawmakers to actions that serve the interests of narrow groups at the expense of the broader public good. It must be recognized that there is no way to open up the legislative process to the people without also opening it up to lobbyists and interest groups.

Third and similarly, by making lawmakers more directly answerable to their specific geographic constitutents, greater accountability and publicity may make it more difficult for these putatively "national" legislators to reason together and work toward policies in the broad national interest. If national policy ought to be merely the aggregation of the perceived interests of the geographic parts of the nation, then there is no problem. But if there is such a thing as a national interest in areas like defense policy, international trade, domestic economic policy, responsible budgeting, or social welfare that cannot be reduced to the perceived interests of the geographical parts of the nation, then it is the responsibility of those we send to the House and Senate to reason together about how to achieve it. Such collective deliberation will be rendered impossible if the members of the House and Senate are, like ambassadors from sovereign states, bound down in their day-to-day policymaking efforts to what is acceptable to their geographic constituencies.

What was absent in the 1960s and 1970s in Congress as the old ways were swept aside was an understanding of the tension between democracy and deliberation and therefore a recognition that "reforms" that make the American governmental system more democratic may not enhance the deliberation that is necessary for democracy to be successful. We are now living with the consequences of this shortsightedness, as a growing body of evidence is demonstrating.

One study, for example, argues that making the markup sessions of the House Appropriations Committee public has exacerbated budget problems by decreasing "committee members' willingness to reject spending requests." In addition, requiring recorded voting in Committee of the Whole has led to "more votes by those lacking knowledge about and interest in the issues before them" both because of the dramatic increase in the number of recorded votes and because members fear the electoral consequences of being recorded absent.[26] Several other studies have documented how "government in the sunshine" has significantly increased the access and influence of lobbyists, and therefore interest groups: "The idea was to make the process more 'democratic,' but in practice, sunshine measures intensified the access of lobbyists."[27] "We now know," concludes another author, "that open meetings filled with lobbyists, and recorded votes on scores of particularistic amendments, serve to increase the powers of special interests, not to diminish them." He adds that "the increased reliance on recorded votes has actually made it easier for narrow groups to hold legislators accountable because most of these votes are on particularistic amendments."[28] A study of tax policy in Congress showed how "the sunlight of open meetings" meant that the members of the Ways and Means Committee in the House "could now be held accountable for their positions on every provision that made up a tax package. In short the . . . Committee was easier to penetrate, particularly by organized interests, and much less autonomous. In turn, the committee could no longer provide cover for House members."[29]

The opening up to public scrutiny of the markup sessions of the House Ways and Means Committee is especially interesting because this is one of the few reforms in Congress that has subsequently been rolled back: in 1983, after a decade of open markups, the committee returned to closed sessions. Since then, "all major tax legislation has been drafted in closed session."[30] Why this change against the grain of openness and accountability that so dominated the reform period? To put it most simply, the committee, wishing to act responsibly on tax matters, had learned how enhanced accountability to interest groups and constituents had undermined collective deliberations about national tax policy. As reported to the author of the most recent book-length study of the Ways and Means Committee, the members found it difficult in open sessions "to support measures that might impose costs on their own constituencies or groups that had provided support in past elections." Complex tax issues that involved competing interests could not be solved "in front of an audience." In closed sessions, on the other hand, the members could "avoid some of the direct responsibility for imposing costs on constituency interests or group allies." As one committee member related about closed sessions: "A member can enter a mild protest about the defeat of an amendment he might otherwise feel compelled to support . . . . Then, when the markup is over, the member can go out into the hall and say to the lobbyist, 'I worked to get your amendment adopted but I just got outvoted.'" In a word, closed markups allowed the members "to take a broader view of the issues" and to think less "about the posturing, about satisfying someone sitting there watching you." Committee members were convinced that returning to closed markups reduced constituency and interest group pressures, enhanced deliberations about the national interest in tax policy, and resulted in better policy outputs.[31]

Contrary to this general line of argument, however, it could be maintained that reducing secrecy in Congress promotes deliberation by reducing the opportunities for logrolling, making side payments, or other kinds of "wheeling and dealing." It is rare, after all, for such deal making to be conducted in the open, which is testimony to the force of the public norm that legislation should be decided on its merits. If bargaining can be forced out of the formal legislative channels through the disinfectant of publicity, then perhaps congressional deliberation will benefit.

There are two problems with this argument. First, there is no reason to believe that if bargains cannot be made in committee meetings, for example, they will not be made somewhere else. Phone calls and private meetings in congressional offices provide plenty of insulation from public scrutiny and thus ample opportunity to strike deals. Second, as Woodrow Wilson argued in his famous critique of the late-nineteenth-century Congress, it is principally *public* deliberation—"the instruction and elevation of public opinion"—that benefits when Congress operates openly, rather than internal congressional deliberation.[32] Consider, for example, the question period in the British Parliament. This public opportunity for the opposition to question the prime minister and the cabinet, now even televised, serves not so much to improve the quality of reasoning about policy within Parliament as to inform the broader community about the government's policies and plans.

It must be emphasized that the point here is not that one cannot have at the same time both democratic accountability and sound reasoning about public policy. Indeed, the American constitutional system was consciously designed to accommodate both principles or goals. Rather, the issue is what kind and degree of popular control, of public accountability, is appropriate in a democracy whose governing institutions must retain the capacity to reason well about laws and their administration. As noted earlier, the proper test of legislative responsiveness in a deliberative democracy is whether the results of the deliberations of the lawmakers approximate what the majority of citizens would have decided if they had engaged in the same reasoning process. Yet if lawmakers are properly to carry out their deliberative responsibilities for the citizenry, they must to some extent be protected against the intrusions of unreflective public opinion. The institutional environment in which they work must allow, and even encourage, legislators to proceed wherever reasoning on the merits leads, even if this is some distance from initial public sentiments. The results, though at times inconsistent with unreflective public attitudes, may be the best approximation that can be achieved of deliberative public opinion, of the "cool and deliberate sense of the community."

If we are not used to thinking about the positive benefits of secrecy for deliberation in Congress, we are more willing to accept the connection between secrecy and deliberation in other contexts. The secret ballot in democratic elections, after all, was intended to free voters from pressures that might distort their decisions from judgments on the merits of candidates for public office. Similarly, within Congress itself leadership contests are usually decided by a secret ballot of the members of each party within each branch. Yet, i' could be argued, such secret voting renders the rank-and-file membe   unaccountable to their constituer s in their choice of party leaders. . lowing secret ballots sacrifices account-ability in favor of protecting .e individual's private judgment of the merits of candidates for leadership positions. Indeed, the U.S. Constitution itself was written in secret, and although a journal was kept (not published until 1819), votes were recorded only by state, with no indication of individual votes. Delegate George Mason's reasons for opposing the recording of individual votes is instructive: "such a record of the opinions of members would be an obstacle to a change of them on conviction."[33] Maximizing public accountability could impair sound deliberation. The point of these examples is not that Congress would function more deliberatively if it simply closed the doors and stopped recording votes, but rather that the drive for maximum openness and accountability is not an unmixed blessing. Those responsible for making Congress more accountable over the past several decades have thought too little about also making Congress more deliberative and about the ways in which accountability can threaten deliberation.

The relationship of secrecy and accountability to sound deliberation within Congress is but one example, though perhaps the most important, of how the structure, procedures, and rules of the House and Senate affect the capacity of these institutions to deliberate well for the nation they serve. Another is the proliferation of subcommittees in Congress in the decades after the legislative reorganization of 1946 substantially reduced the number of full committees. This proliferation has spread legislators so thin, especially in the Senate, that it is impossible for the members to keep up even with the business before their own committees and subcommittees. Between the mid-1950s and the early 1990s the average number of committee and subcommittee assignments per House member more than doubled, from 3.0 to 6.8, and per senator increased about 40 percent, from 7.9 to 11.0.[34] As a result, attendance at committee hearings is often notoriously low (it can be difficult even to get a quorum at markup sessions) and lawmakers defer more and more to staff for information and direction. As noted earlier, deliberation is uncompromising in the time demands it places on lawmakers. If they spend half as much time at twice as many hearings and markups, they will of necessity be less well informed about more matters for which they bear a formal responsibility and on which they vote at the crucial stages in the legislative process. In this way, the empowerment of the members may undermine the deliberativeness of the lawmaking process.

One could make a similar argument about the practice of legislating through those "omnibus" bills in which a myriad of distinct measures are brought together into one legislative package of such length and complexity that few who vote for it understand its contents. Granted that in a body like Congress some deference must be shown by rank-and-file members to the recommendations of committees (or else the committee system would collapse), if a legislative proposal gets too large and complex and contains too many distinct provisions, it will become virtually impossible for the reporting committee to inform the members adequately through the committee report and floor debate of the contents of the bill and the reasons supporting its passage. At this point the kind of reasoned judgment that the full membership can make about committee recommendations in a deliberative body becomes nothing more than blind deference.

As the catalogue of institutional features near the end of chapter 5 suggests, until recent decades the members and leaders of Congress understood well how important it was to structure the legislative environment to foster responsible lawmaking and a national outlook. But as power has been democraticized and public scrutiny enhanced, there has been too little attention both within Congress and without to the institutional requisites of sound deliberation.

The Political Executive and the Bureaucracy

The question of how political leaders ought to promote the rule of deliberative majorities, and therefore how they ought to relate to public opinion, is not restricted to the legislative arena. Those in the executive branch confront the same issue, although in a different form, and make their own distinctive contribution.

By the very nature of the executive branch, the deliberations that occur within it are less closely tied to public sentiments or to the views of external groups than the deliberations within Congress. This is largely because the electoral principle does not extend as deeply into the executive branch as it does into the legislature. With the exception of the president and vice president, the principal players in the executive branch—White House staff, high-ranking political appointees in the departments and agencies, and senior careerists—owe their positions to appointment or to advancement in the career service.[35] Thus, high-level political executives and senior careerists are not individually accountable to the electorate. Their career interests are less affected by what those outside the governing institutions think of them than is the case for elected representatives. Consequently, they do not face the same pressures as those in Congress to embrace, or at least to mollify, either generalized popular sentiments or the views of specific external groups. Moreover, as noted previously, the secrecy of most executive branch deliberations insulates the decision process from public attention and influence in a way that is uncharacteristic of deliberations in Congress. This relative insulation of executive branch deliberations from public scrutiny presents special challenges to executive branch decisionmakers.

Because there is less public posturing and less deference to unreflective public opinion within the White House and the administrative agencies than within Congress, officials of the executive branch have greater freedom and opportunity to promote the kind of expertise, systematic analysis, and long-range view of the public good that is essential to sound political deliberation. To a substantial degree this is done through the permanent bureaucracy, which, at its best, is a repository for practical wisdom about problems of governance derived from years of firsthand experience. As the late Herbert J. Storing has argued, "the civil service is one of the few institutions we have for bringing the accumulated wisdom of the past to bear upon political decisions."[36] In carrying out its deliberative function the bureaucracy is benefited by a "degree of insulation from shifting political breezes." The thoughts and actions of civil servants, who have a *de facto* life tenure, are "not governed so strictly as [are] that of the political executive by periodic elections. Their position enables them to mitigate the partisanship of party politics, and it gives them some protection from the powerful temptation, to which the party politician is always subject, to serve the people's inclinations rather than their interests."[37]

If, however, some insulation from public opinion can be beneficial to deliberation, it can also create problems for democratic control. There remains the danger that the deliberations of career civil servants will bear little relationship to public sentiments and desires. Storing's response is that the civil service in the United States does not represent a distinct will or spirit independent of the broader political community. On the contrary, "the American civil service . . . represent[s] the American society with a fair degree of faithfulness." Indeed, "the interests, opinions, and values of civil servants are intimately bound up with those of the community as a whole."[38] It must be admitted, nonetheless, that the same degree of insulation from public sentiments that promotes decision-making through expertise and systematic analysis creates a potential for narrowness of view, rigidity of approach, and ideological commitment inconsistent with fundamental public desires.

Thus, the issue of the conjunction of deliberation and democracy takes opposing forms in Congress and the bureaucracy. In Congress the predominantly democratic character of the decisionmaking process creates environmental influences and personal incentives not always congenial to serious-minded deliberation. In the bureaucracy, on the other hand, the same institutional features that promote sound deliberation create conditions that may impair democratic control.

Political executives, like legislators, have a responsibility to foster the rule of deliberative majorities. In so doing, they must understand both the contribution that the bureaucracy makes to this end and the corresponding danger that it poses. Their task is to promote an atmosphere of genuine deliberation within the bureaucracy by encouraging and supporting the development of substantive expertise, the rational analysis of information and arguments, and decisionmaking through reasoned persuasion. This requires protecting the deliberations of career civil servants from political forces and pressures that might undermine reasoning on the merits, much like the way Treasury Secretary Donald Regan protected his small band of deliberators, which included both political appointees and careerists, in the development of the Treasury I tax reform proposal. On the other hand, because career civil servants are not directly accountable to the community, the political executive must be especially alert to signs that a civil servant's attachment to external interests or personal ideology have intruded upon and distorted the deliberative process. The deliberations of the men and women who constitute the career service, like the deliberations of congressional staff, will not necessarily result in conclusions consistent with what a deliberative majority would have decided.

Presidential Actions

Although the White House staff, department and agency heads, other high-level political appointees, and civil servants all contribute to executive branch deliberation, the president alone possesses the constitutional authority to take binding executive actions. The Constitution vests the chief executive with authority to enforce the laws, make nominations to high office, pardon offenses, recommend measures to Congress, receive ambassadors, and command the Armed Forces. In carrying out these tasks presidents exercise their personal judgment, informed by the facts and arguments brought to their attention through the presidential advisory process. What relationship is there, then, between the judgment and actions of presidents and deliberative majorities? What is, and what ought to be, the connection between presidential decisions and public opinion?

When the framers vested the executive power in an office with indefinite reeligibility, a term longer than any state governor's, substantial independent powers, a salary that could not be changed by Congress during any one term, and a mode of election independent of the legislature, they sought to ensure that presidents would act on the basis of their independent judgment and will. Freed from the "unbounded complaisance" [39] to the legislature so common among state governors and somewhat insulated from direct popular control, presidents were to function as constitutional officers, responsibly and independently carrying out their duties. However respectful presidents might be of widespread public sentiments or of strongly held congressional opinion, for actions properly within the executive sphere they were to be guided by their own best understanding of what the national interest required. As Hamilton put it, "the executive should be in a situation to dare to act his own opinion with vigor and decision." [40] At times such actions might take the form of temporary resistance to popular, if unwise, measures or actions pushed by the people or Congress to allow time for "more cool and sedate reflection." [41] In other cases the discordance between presidential judgment and public or congressional desires might endure throughout the president's term, creating an issue for the next election, especially if the incumbent was running again.

As elaborated in chapter 2, the capacity of constitutional officers to resist public desires, at least for a time, was intended not to create a governing will independent of the people themselves but rather to promote rule by deliberative majorities by protecting them against the follies of unreflective public opinion. The president's four-year term and indefinite reeligibility were intended to foster the kind of long-range view of the public good that ought to guide the citizenry itself but is often overcome by more immediate, or transient, impulses and desires. In this respect the president was to be like the Senate, and both were to serve as a counterbalance to the most popular branch, the House of Representatives.

DELIBERATION, REPRESENTATION, AND SEPARATION OF POWERS

In one respect, however, the president is unique, even by comparison with the Senate; for he alone represents the entire nation, something to which no single representative or senator can lay claim. For Jefferson it was especially the president who "command[ed] a view of the whole ground."[42] The president's representational uniqueness, his identity with the nation as a whole, fits him, more than any other single political figure, to articulate and promote the deep-seated values and goals of the American citizenry—values and goals that may be overmatched or overshadowed by more tangible and immediate political or economic interests within a congressional district or state.

This representational difference can be the source of significant conflict between Congress and the presidency. President Jimmy Carter discovered this when he sought to subject congressional decisions on water projects of great interest to local communities—projects such as building dams, dredging rivers, and improving harbors—to a rational assessment of national water policy needs. Intense congressional opposition thwarted any serious change in existing practice. In this and like controversies both of the political institutions seem to reflect public opinion, but in two different ways. During the water policy controversy, Congress, it is reasonable to argue, effectively gave voice to the millions of citizens who wanted better flood control, cheap hydroelectric power, improved irrigation of farmlands, more efficient water transportation, and expanded outdoor recreational activities. The presidency, on the other hand, articulated the generalized public sentiment for economy in government and for rational and coherent national policies, a sentiment likely shared even by those who favored the water projects.

This dichotomy in public sentiments—institutionally manifested in separation of powers conflicts—is not limited to issues such as water policy. Indeed, some maintain that it is a pervasive feature of the modern American social welfare state and even that it helps to explain why the electorate has opted for divided party government more often than not in recent decades. The voters, it is argued, send large majorities of Democrats to Congress to provide services and goods while they elevate more conservative Republicans to the White House to promote economy in government and restraints on taxation. (It is impossible at this time to know whether Bill Clinton's election to the presidency in 1992 is like Jimmy Carter's election in 197(an aberration from the current nor n of divided government or a retu: to the more usual historical pattern of one-party control.)

Thus, conflict between Congress and the presidency may represent a clash among competing values, interests, or goals of the citizenry itself, reflecting such dichotomies in public opinion as (1) the interests of the parts versus the whole, (2) considerations of short-term versus long-term benefits, and (3) the desire for goods and services versus a recognition of costs and limits. In this respect the kind of deliberation fostered by American separation of powers is not unlike the deliberation that occurs within an individual who is forced to assess and balance competing issues or benefits at stake in some decision or course of action. In so far as this balancing is essential to sound deliberation, separation of powers conflicts may actually promote the formation of deliberative majorities.

LINCOLN AND THE CIVIL WAR: PRESIDENTIAL ACTIONS AND DELIBERATIVE MAJORITIES

The framers' distinction between surface public opinion and deeper deliberative opinion was at the core of their understanding of government and politics and, accordingly, central to their institutional design. As we have seen, it was hoped that the relatively lengthy terms of office for the president and senators together with their indirect modes of election would give these officials the institutional capacity to resist nondeliberative impulses or demands of the people, thereby allowing time for reason and justice to prevail. As wielders of the executive power, presidents would be enabled to resist unreflective surface opinion as they sought to promote the deeper and more reasoned goals and values of the American people.

This is, for example, precisely how Abraham Lincoln's biographer, Lord Charnwood, described his actions during the critical Civil War year, 1864.[43] Three long years of war and very heavy casualties in Grant's campaign against Lee in Virginia had sapped public confidence in the war effort and weakened the North's resolve to press on to complete victory. Responding to this public dissatisfaction in the spring and early summer of 1864, Republican party leaders seriously considered replacing Lincoln as the party nominee for president for the November election. The Democrats, who nominated General George McClellan for the presidency in August, sought to gain political advantage by adopting a platform that decried "four years of failure to restore the Union by the experiment of war" and called for an immediate "cessation of hostilities." About the same time Lincoln, who had received the Republican nomination the month before, was advised by leaders of his party that his election was hopeless. The chairman of the central Republican Committee even recommended to Lincoln that he make overtures for peace.

Throughout this troubling time Lincoln remained steadfast. He absolutely refused to initiate any overtures to the South for a negotiated settlement or to enter into any discussions initiated by the other side that did not concede the inviolability of the Union and the abolition of slavery. Moreover, fearful that McClellan would succeed him in March of 1865 and negotiate an end to the war on terms that would ultimately undermine the Union or preserve slavery, Lincoln moved vigorously to end the war militarily before March.

We have no systematic public opinion data from 1864. If we had, it might well show that by the summer of that year a majority of the people had lost confidence in Lincoln's handling of the war (a "failed presidency"?) and were willing to reach an accommodation of some sort with the South. The president, however, refused to conform his actions to the shifting public sentiment and resolutely pursued a firm and unambiguous course of action. If Lincoln was right in insisting upon the end of slavery and the indestructibility of the Union, this might appear to be simply the case of a wise leader acting on the basis of his personal understanding of the common good contrary to less wise public desires. Yet Charnwood's interpretation suggests a more complex view:

> And to those Americans of all classes and in all districts of the North, who had set their hearts and were giving all they had to give to preserve the life of the nation, the political crisis of 1864 would seem to have been the most anxious moment of the war. It is impossible—it must be repeated—to guess how great the danger really was that their popular government might in the result betray the true and underlying will of the people; for in any country (and in America perhaps more than most) the average of politicians, whose voices are

most loudly heard, can only in a rough and approximate fashion be representative.[44]

Here Lincoln, by refusing to follow the shifting public attitudes, was a more authentic representative of "the true and underlying will of the people" than those with their fingers on the pulse of the citizenry. In Charnwood's view, Lincoln was

the embodiment, in a degree and manner which are alike rare, of the more constant and the higher judgment of his people. It is plainer still that he embodied the resolute purpose which underlay the fluctuations upon the surface of their political life.[45]

In a narrow sense Lincoln's insistence on pursuing total victory throughout 1864 in the face of growing public opposition might appear undemocratic. If, however, one accepts the central principle of deliberative democracy—that surface opinion may bear little semblance to deliberative judgments and that only deliberative opinion ought to rule—then Lincoln's actions appear in a very different light. Indeed, if Charnwood's interpretation is sound, then Lincoln's behavior stands as a quintessential example of political leadership in a deliberative democracy. Despite "the fluctuations upon the surface" of the political life of the nation, the "true and underlying will" and the "resolute purpose" of the people remained unchanged. Unswayed by the change in the surface views, Lincoln remained true to the "higher judgment," the more deliberative opinion, of the citizenry.

Lincoln's actions of 1864 were ultimately vindicated, not only by the judgment of history but also in a very tangible way by his overwhelming reelection in November (55 percent of the popular vote and 212 of 233 electoral votes). What explains this apparently massive shift of public opinion between August of 1864, when Lincoln seemed a sure loser, and November, when he became a big winner? While some part of this shift was certainly due to Northern success on the battlefield (Atlanta fell to General Sherman in September), another may have been the result of the public deliberation that the approach of the election and the campaign itself fostered. Elections, like hangings, concentrate the mind. They force the electorate to review an incumbent president's record, to reflect upon his policies and character, and to make considered judgments about whether he or his opponent will better serve the nation. The result is likely to be a more deliberative assessment of a leader's performance than one normally finds between elections. This public deliberation is fostered by the rhetorical activity that accompanies a presidential campaign. And although in Lincoln's time it was not yet acceptable for presidential candidates to campaign personally for office, others did so on their behalf: "men of high character conducted a vigorous campaign of speeches for Lincoln."[46] Lecturing at Yale in 1907, Secretary of State Elihu Root described presidential election campaigns as the "greatest, most useful educational process ever known in the world . . . [during which millions of voters] are engaged for months in reading and hearing about great and difficult questions of government, in studying them, in considering, and discussing, and forming matured opinions about them." This educational process lays "the solid foundation of sound judgment, sober self-restraint, and familiarity with political questions among the governing mass."[47]

The events of 1864 recall not only the framers' desire for leaders to resist unsound public desires until "reason, justice, and truth [could] regain their authority over the public mind,"[48] but also Hamilton's defense of a substantial term of office for the president. "Between the commencement and termination of [a four-year term]," Hamilton wrote, "there would always be a considerable interval in which . . . [a president] might reasonably promise himself that there would be time enough . . . to make the community sensible of the propriety of the measures he might incline to pursue." The president, like Lincoln in 1864, would convince the citizenry of the rightness of his actions not through rhetorical persuasion, but rather by "establishing himself in the esteem and good-will of his constituents" through "the proofs he had given of his wisdom and integrity."[49] Four years ought to be enough time for the people to recognize the fruits of wise leadership. It is through performance, not persuasion, that the president would merit reelection.

Political Rhetoric and the Formation of Deliberative Majorities

Hamilton's failure to promote rhetorical leadership in his systematic defense of a strong presidency in the *Federalist Papers* was not through inadvertence; for the framers believed that political rhetoric was more of a threat than an aid to the formation of deliberative majorities. This view may seem odd to the contemporary student of politics; for upon first consideration, it might appear that political rhetoric is at least beneficial, if not essential, to the functioning of deliberative democracy. Insofar as political rhetoric takes the form of instruction or reasoned persuasion, it would seem to be productive of public deliberation and thus of reasoned and informed public judgments. Indeed, reflecting the sentiments that led Theodore Roosevelt to describe the nation's highest office as a "bully pulpit," modern Americans particularly expect their presidents to be rhetorical leaders—guiding, instructing, and inspiring the citizenry. As the focus of public and media attention, presidents, it is believed, are in a unique position to address the citizens on public affairs, to appeal to their better natures, and to seek their support for farsighted policies to promote the commonweal. By acting as a kind of national schoolmaster, the president can promote the formation of deliberative majorities.

In contrast to this modern expectation that presidents and other public officials ought to promote public deliberation through rhetoric, most of those who wrote the American Constitution neither intended nor desired that the nation's leaders engage in frequent direct rhetorical contact with the citizenry. Cognizant that the public at large lacked the time and information necessary for sound deliberation on the specifics of national policy and that average citizens were much more subject to misinformation, deception, prejudice, passion, and demagogic appeals than were their representatives, they believed that the best sort of political deliberation would occur mainly *within* their carefully crafted institutions. The lessons of the history of popular governments and the experiences of the "critical period" had confirmed the dangers of conducting public policy on the plane of public opinion. As noted in chapter 2, in the newly independent American states men with "talents for low intrigue, and the little arts of popularity" had risen to public office by appealing to public disenchantment over taxes and debts and by promising simplistic cures for economic ills. In some states they managed to gain control over public policy and to push through measures that reflected the unwise and short-sighted sentiments they had helped to incite.

In the framers' view this experience amply demonstrated that a too direct linkage between public sentiments and public policy was a danger to governments "wholly and purely republican." In providing that linkage, popular rhetoric lay about as a ready but dangerous instrument by which ambitious men with little to commend themselves to their fellow citizens but their skill at inflaming popular prejudices and passions could rise to power and direct public policy. Moreover, if rhetoric bound the people and their officials together into a close union of sentiment and opinion, this would undermine the leader's ability to withstand public desires on those occasions when the people's inclinations and interests did not coincide. Because of these kinds of dangers, the framers rejected popular rhetoric as a normal or regular means of "refin[ing] and enlarg[ing] the public views." Rather, they put their stock in representation and in institutional design for moderating and elevating public attitudes and desires and thus achieving just and effective republican government.

Although framers like Madison and Hamilton did not deny the possibility of a popular rhetoric of reasoned persuasion, they feared that if popular oratory were encouraged, deliberative rhetoric would not hold its own against irresponsible passionate appeals. The great threat to popular government was that the *"passions, . . .* not the *reason,* of the public would sit in judgment. But it is the reason, alone, of the public, that ought to control and regulate the government."[50] Rhetoric was dangerous precisely because it was the principal means of inflaming passions, of appealing to envy and prejudice. "In the ancient republics," Hamilton wrote, "where the whole body of the people assembled in person, a single orator, or an artful statesman, was generally seen to rule with as complete a sway as if a scepter had been placed in his single hand." But these ancient orators neither gained nor maintained their rule because they excelled at public instruction and reasoned persuasion. On the contrary, because of "infirmities incident to collective meetings of the people . . . . [i]gnorance [is] . . . the dupe of cunning, and passion the slave of sophistry and declamation."[51] When orators rule, it is because they are masters not of reason and argument, but of cunning, sophistry, and declamation.

It must be acknowledged that the kind of "hard" demagoguery feared by the framers is not now the problem in the United States it once was.[52] Few modern American politicians, at the national, state, or local level, seem to harbor the truly dangerous ambitions of the demagogue and, accordingly, few engage in rhetorical efforts to foment envy of the propertied classes or to incite racial or ethnic hatred or prejudice. Certainly the growth of a large middle class, whose members appreciate the importance of property rights and of sound economic and financial policies, has had a moderating effect on American politics and has softened popular rhetoric.[53] In addition, the universalistic character of the American creed—"All men are created equal"—has helped to foster a sense of what it means to be a citizen of the United States in a way that has resisted, albeit not always successfully, a politics of divisiveness.

To say, however, that there is little genuine demagogic rhetoric in contemporary American politics is not to say that deliberative rhetoric is the norm. Indeed, the framers' concerns about the nature and quality of popular rhetoric are perfectly analogous to the frequently voiced complaint that modern campaign rhetoric in the United States ignores the "real issues" in favor of personalities, unrealistic promises, manipulation of symbols, charges of unethical behavior, and distortions of opponents' records. This charge is leveled against both paid campaign comme cials and face-to-face debates. In fac campaign debates bear so little the har- acter of reasoned argument th   reporters and commentators frequently make light of the label itself, p   ferring to describe these events as "joint appearances" or "joint press conferences."

Several major contemporary studies of the popular rhetoric of those elected to Congress and the presidency tend to confirm the relative in- frequency of deliberative rhetoric. Between 1970 and 1977, Richard Fenno traveled with eighteen members of the House of Representatives to their districts to observe how the legislators interacted with their con- stituents. About two-thirds of the visits took place during the fall elec- tion period. Although Fenno did see "a few instances" of education, or reasoned persuasion, by legislators, "the only generalization supportable by the evidence," he wrote, "is the apparent paucity of educational ef- fort."[54] Similarly, in his study of presidential campaign rhetoric that fo- cused on the elections of 1960 through 1976, Benjamin Page reached conclusions consistent with the view that genuine reasoned persuasion is not common:

> the most striking feature of candidates' rhetoric about policy is its extreme vagueness. The typical campaign speech says vir- tually nothing specific about policy alternatives; discussions of the issues are hidden away in little-publicized statements and position papers. Even the most extended discussions leave many questions unanswered. In short, policy stands are infre- quent, inconspicuous, and unspecific. Presidential candidates are skilled at appearing to say much while actually saying little.
>
> In most campaign speeches, much of the verbiage consists of descriptions of problems, promises to attain general goals, criticism of the opponents' past performance, and lavish praise for the past performance of the candidate's own party.[55]

Perhaps the most interesting study in this respect is Jeffrey Tulis's analysis of the character of presidential speeches in the nineteenth and twentieth centuries. Tulis categorized speeches according to whether they manifested a "developed argument" that "moved logically from begin- ning to end," a "series of arguments" but no overall argument, or were simply a "list of points" strung together.[56] In his sample of 336 presiden- tial speeches from the twentieth century, Tulis found that not a single one could be classified as a "developed argument" and only 11 percent of the speeches were a "series of arguments." By contrast, 55 percent of the speeches were a "list of points" and 34 percent were a combination of a series of arguments and a list. When all inaugural addresses and State of the Union messages were analyzed separately, 9 percent of those delivered in the twentieth century were judged to be "developed arguments" and 18 percent a "series of arguments." In the nineteenth century the corresponding figures were much higher: 21 percent and 74 percent respectively.[57] Although we should be careful not to infer too much from the mere classifying of speeches in this manner, the conclusion would seem to follow that relatively few speeches and addresses of modern presidents bear a formally deliberative character (whether or not well argued or persuasive).

If, as the evidence here suggests, popular deliberative rhetoric by national legislators and presidents is a relatively rare phenomenon in the United States, this would seem to confirm the views of Madison, Hamilton, and other leading framers that civic instruction by political leaders through reasoned persuasion is not a necessary day-to-day activity in a deliberative democracy. Does it follow, then, that because popular deliberative rhetoric is relatively rare in the United States that it is entirely incidental to the success of American democracy?

Contrary to the principles of the leading framers, according to which popular deliberative rhetoric would play no formal role in the governing of the new nation, American statesmen from the beginning have demonstrated by their actions a belief in the utility, and perhaps necessity, of at least occasional efforts to guide and instruct the citizenry through rhetoric. The most famous early example is President Washington's "Farewell Address," which was issued as a written message on the ninth anniversary of the signing of the Constitution by the delegates to the Philadelphia Convention and was disseminated throughout the nation. In what he described as the "counsels of an old and affectionate friend," Washington sought to instruct his fellow citizens in the principles and actions necessary to preserve the blessings of liberty achieved through years of war, civil strife, constitutional change, and the beginnings of effective self-government for the new nation. He appealed to his countrymen to preserve the union, "the palladium of your political safety and prosperity"; to reject alterations in the government that would "impair the energy of the system"; to guard against the spirit of faction and party; to recognize that religion and morality are "indispensable supports" to "political prosperity"; to promote "institutions for the general diffusion of knowledge" so that "public opinion should be enlightened"; to preserve sound public credit; and to "observe good faith and justice to all nations."[58]

This major effort of civic instruction, issued on the very eve of Washington's departure from public life—indeed, in the very address announcing his decision not to run for a third term—stands virtually alone among Washington's presidential speeches and addresses. Only his First Inaugural Address, which provided a natural opportunity for the incoming president to address the nation on the virtues of union and the new constitutional order, provides a comparable example from the first president of public instruction through rhetoric. It is revealing that when the occasion for such a speech was repeated after his reelection in 1792, Washington delivered what still stands as the briefest Inaugural Address in the history of the presidency—a mere four sentences, totalling 133 words. It is virtually unthinkable that a modern president would shrink from any such opportunity to speak to the people.

Nonetheless, however reluctant Washington was to engage in popular rhetoric of any sort throughout his service in the executive office, the drafting and issuance of the Farewell Address evidences a belief that some public benefit might well result from efforts at civic instruction through rhetoric. Washington himself had rather modest expectations of the impact of his words. Not likely to make a "strong and lasting impression," or to "control the usual current of the passions," at best they might produce "some partial benefit, some occasional good" as the arguments of the address "now and then recur to moderate the fury of party spirit, to warn against the mischiefs of foreign intrigue, [and] to guard against the impostures of pretended patriotism."[59]

Washington's successors also tended to engage in popular deliberative rhetoric sparingly, limiting such occasions principally to inaugural addresses. One of the most noteworthy examples occurred just four years after Washington left office when Thomas Jefferson and his supporters, seeking to reverse "monarchic" trends in the administration of the national government, engineered what Jefferson called the "revolution of 1800"—a kind of refounding of the regime on Jeffersonian-republican principles. Upon taking office after his party had won this "contest of opinion" by capturing the House, Senate, and presidency from the Federalists, Jefferson sought in his Inaugural Address to heal partisan wounds by emphasizing common beliefs and principles: "[E]very difference of opinion is not a difference of principle. We have called by different names brethren of the same principle. We are all Republicans, we are all Federalists." He went on to detail the "essential principles of our Government," which would shape the new administration. These included, among others: "equal and exact justice to all men"; no "entangling alliances" with foreign nations; "the support of the State governments in all their rights"; "the preservation of the General Government in its whole constitutional vigor"; "absolute acquiescence in the decisions of the majority, the vital principle of republics"; "economy in the public expense"; "encouragement of agriculture, and of commerce as its handmaid"; "the diffusion of information"; and freedom of religion and of the press. These principles, according to Jefferson:

> form the bright constellation which has gone before us and guided our steps through an age of revolution and reformation. The wisdom of our sages and blood of our heroes have been devoted to their attainment. They should be the creed of our political faith, the text of civic instruction.[60]

The other inaugural address that rivals in importance the first of Jefferson's was delivered by Abraham Lincoln on the eve of the nation's greatest crisis. Between Lincoln's election to the presidency in November of 1860 and his inauguration on March 4, 1861, seven southern states had formally "seceded" from the union. This was one month before the fall of Fort Sumter, the secession of four more states, and the beginning of full-scale hostilities. After reassuring the southern states that he had no intention of interfering with slavery where it already existed, Lincoln used his First Inaugural to present a masterful case against secession. After refuting the argument that secession had a constitutional or legal basis, Lincoln got to the heart of the matter:

> Plainly the central idea of secession is the essence of anarchy. A majority held in restraint by constitutional checks and limitations, and always changing easily with deliberate changes of popular opinions and sentiments, is the only true sovereign of a free people. Whoever rejects it does of necessity fly to anarchy or to despotism. Unanimity is impossible. The rule of a minority, as a permanent arrangement, is wholly inadmissable; so that, rejecting the majority principle, anarchy or despotism in some form is all that is left.[61]

Secession, then, was nothing less than a contradiction of the bedrock principle of republican government: majority rule. Anarchy was its certain result as disaffected minorities would continually break away from majorities with which they disagreed. Although Lincoln's rhetoric failed to persuade southerners of the evils of secession, it may have been helpful in convincing northerners why a portion of the country, desiring to sever its bonds with the rest, ought not simply to be allowed to go its own way.

The most notable early examples of popular deliberative rhetoric by presidents other than through inaugural addresses occurred during Andrew Jackson's administration. As we saw in chapter 7, Jackson's message to Congress in 1832 announcing his veto of the bill rechartering the Bank of the United States was addressed to the people over the heads of their representatives. (Its popular character is amply demonstrated by the fact that it became a Democratic campaign document in the 1832 election.) And although this lengthy document ended with a passionate attack on the rich and powerful, most of the message was a substantial, detailed critique of the Bank on constitutional and policy grounds. Thus, as a rhetorical appeal it was both popular and deliberative, at least in large part. On other occasions, also, Jackson utilized formal addresses to make deliberative appeals to the citizenry. Such addresses included his annual messages to Congress, his proclamation on the attempt by South Carolina to "nullify" federal law, and his "protest" to the Senate contesting its authority to censure him for ordering the secretary of the treasury to remove the public funds from the Bank of the United States three years before its charter was to expire.[62]

Presidents, of course, are not the only public officials who engage in popular rhetoric. This was as true in the republic's first century as it is now. Moreover, although the governing norms at the beginning discouraged popular rhetoric for all national officials, this injunction applied less severely to members of the House and Senate than to presidents. Thus, candidates for the House and Senate were personally campaigning for office through speeches and debates in the early nineteenth century, more than a half century before this became acceptable for those aspiring to the presidency. Indeed, it can be argued that the most consequential popular deliberative rhetoric of nineteenth-century America came not from a president, but from a private citizen and former Whig congressman from Illinois. This refers, of course, to the speeches of Abraham Lincoln in the 1850s on slavery, which culminated in his famous seven debates in the 1858 Senate campaign with Stephen Douglas, the incumbent senator in Illinois and a national leader of the Democratic party.[63]

Just a year before the Illinois Senate campaign, the U.S. Supreme Court's *Dred Scott* decision had created a political crisis for the nation by ruling that Congress had no authority to prohibit slavery in the territories, thus overturning the famous Missouri Compromise of 1820. Douglas responded to this controversy by basing his campaign for reelection to the Senate on "the great fundamental principle" of "self-government" or "popular sovereignty": "that the people of each State and each territory of this Union have the right . . . of regulating their own domestic concerns in their own way, subject to no other limitation or restriction than that which the Constitution of the United States imposes upon them."[64] The strength of Douglas's position was that it seemed to provide the basis for reconciling the views of North and South and thus defusing the controversy over the extension of slavery. Lincoln believed strongly otherwise. Throughout the campaign he sought to persuade the people of Illinois that the nation was at a critical turning point on the issue of slavery. The founders, he maintained, had recognized the fundamental injustice of slavery and had looked toward its ultimate extinction. Slavery violated the deepest principle of the American nation—the equality of all men—and it ought not to be extended to any territory or state where it did not then exist. "[T]here is no reason in the world," Lincoln insisted, "why the negro is not entitled to all the natural rights enumerated in the Declaration of Independence, the right to life, liberty, and the pursuit of happiness."[65] In frequently quoting his antagonist's declaration that he "cares not whether slavery is voted down or voted up," Lincoln insisted that Douglas's position, at bottom, was one of moral indifference to slavery. Should Douglas's views be embraced by the American people, Lincoln maintained, this would amount to a repudiation of the principles of the Declaration of Independence, thus undermining the cornerstone of the freedoms enjoyed by Americans and eventually leading to the extension of slavery throughout the country.

In Lincoln's view what was at stake in his rhetorical clash with Douglas was much more than a seat in the U.S. Senate. (The actual election was by state legislators, who in their own campaigns were pledged to one candidate or the other.) This was nothing less than a grand contest to shape "the public mind" on matters of the deepest importance to American democracy. At the time of the founding the public mind recognized the injustice of slavery, was committed to restricting its spread, and "rest[ed] in the belief that it was in the course of ultimate extinction."[66] But that old view of the founding generation had been progressively undermined by the relentless pressure of the slave interest to extend its domain, by the promulgation of a school of thought that slavery was a positive good, and by views of prominent political leaders like Douglas who professed a moral indifference to the extension of slavery. Lincoln's challenge, as he saw it, was to limit the "influence [Douglas] is exerting on public sentiment":

> In this and like communities, public sentiment is everything. With public sentiment, nothing can fail; without it nothing can succeed. Consequently he who moulds public sentiment, goes deeper than he who enacts statutes or pronounces decisions. He makes statutes and decisions possible or impossible to be executed.[67]

Or, as Lincoln had put it two years before: "Our government rests in public opinion. Whoever can change public opinion, can change the government, practically just so much."[68]

Although Lincoln lost the Senate race, the campaign achieved two large purposes. First, by getting Douglas to affirm that the people of a territory could prevent slavery by denying it the protection of positive law—contrary to the rights of slave holders as enunciated in the *Dred Scott* decision—Lincoln was able to drive a wedge between Douglas and southern Democrats, thereby undermining Douglas's prospects for national leadership on the slavery issue and later election to the presidency. Second, Lincoln's forceful defense of the anti-slavery position earned him fame outside of Illinois and greatly assisted in his nomination and election to the presidency in 1860.

Conclusion:
Democratic Statesmanship and Deliberative Democracy

The first seven decades of national life under the Constitution of 1787 had witnessed periodic popular struggles over the fundamental principles of American democracy. These "contest[s] of opinion," to use Jefferson's term, did not stop with the ratification of the Constitution, as many of the leading framers had expected and indeed wished, but went on to include the Jeffersonian and Jacksonian "revolutions" of the early nineteenth century and the struggle over the slavery issue in the 1850s. Later, such contests of opinion recurred during the Progressive era of the late nineteenth and early twentieth centuries, Roosevelt's New Deal of the 1930s, the civil rights struggles of the 1950s and 1960s, and the Reagan "revolution" of the 1980s. However well the framers' institutional design, with its focus on deliberation within and between the branches of government and its injunction against popular rhetoric, may have worked during the "normal" times between these contests, these struggles over the public mind have called forth a type of popular leadership for which the architects of the Constitution did not plan.

The kind of communitywide deliberation involved in these periodic renewals, or even re-foundings, of the American polity unavoidably places rhetorical demands on national leaders. Unless one posits that all political development in a democracy is necessarily beneficent, then one must accept the possibility that over time a once democratic people could lose their commitment to the twin pillars of freedom and equality of rights that sustain republican government. At those decisive historical moments when the very character of deliberative public opinion is at issue, it is not enough for political leaders simply to reflect and articulate the underlying will or judgment of the people. Certainly Lincoln's great fear in the 1850s was that even deliberative public opinion would embrace a position of moral neutrality toward slavery, in direct contradition of the deepest principles of the nation. *Molding* the "cool and deliberate sense of the community," not merely responding to it, became at this critical juncture the highest task and the most profound responsibility of democratic statesmanship.

When fundamental regime principles are at stake in a democracy, public interest in and attention to the business of government increase dramatically, and national elections become contests for the public mind. The functioning of the institutions necessarily becomes a secondary matter as the basic direction of national policy is decided by the election returns. Whether the decision is for good or for ill cannot be known in advance, for in the end there is nothing in human nature or in how deliberative democracy is structured that can guarantee the wisdom of popular deliberations. We are led to conclude that deliberative democracy must be guided by a body of thought—an understanding of individual rights, of the duties of citizenship, and of the means and ends of self-government—that is external to itself and that is the basis, at least occasionally, of popular statesmanship of the highest order.

Case Studies of Congress

Domestic Legislation, 1946–1970

The selection criteria for these studies are described at the beginning of chapter 4 (p. 67).

Employment Act of 1946
Bailey, Stephen K. *Congress Makes a Law.* New York: Columbia University Press, 1950.

Selective Service Act of 1948
Jacobs, Clyde E., and John F. Gallagher. *The Selective Service Act.* New York: Dodd, Mead and Company, 1968.

Reciprocal Trade Act of 1955
Bauer, Raymond, Ithiel deSola Pool, and Lewis A. Dexter. *American Business and Public Policy.* New York: Atherton, 1963.

Federal Minimum Wage Increase of 1955
Tyler, Gus. *A Legislative Campaign for a Federal Minimum Wage (1955).* Eagleton Case Studies in Practical Politics No. 4. New York: McGraw-Hill, 1960.

Natural Gas (Harris-Fulbright) Bill of 1956 (Vetoed)
Carper, Edith T. *Lobbying and the Natural Gas Bill.* Inter-University Case Program No. 72. University, Alabama.: University of Alabama Press, 1962.

Civil Rights Bill of 1956 (Rejected)
Anderson, J. W. *Eisenhower, Brownell, and the Congress.* Inter-University Case Program No. 80. University, Alabama: University of Alabama Press, 1964.

Water Pollution Control Acts of 1956 and 1961
Jennings, M. Kent. "Legislative Politics and Water Pollution Control, 1956–61." In *Congress and Urban Problems,* edited by Frederic N. Cleaveland, pp. 72–109. Washington, D.C.: Brookings Institution, 1969.

Federal Aviation Act of 1958
Redford, Emmette S. *Congress Passes the Federal Aviation Act of 1958.* Inter-University Case Program No. 62. University, Alabama: University of Alabama Press, 1961.

National Aeronautics and Space Act of 1958
Griffith, Alison. *The National Aeronautics and Space Act.* Washington, D.C.: Public Affairs Press, 1962.

Housing Act of 1959
Gordon, Glen. *The Legislative Process and Divided Government*. Amherst, Mass.:
Bureau of Government Research, 1966.

Federal Airport Act of 1959
Ripley, Randall B. "Congress Champions Aid to Airports, 1958–59." In Cleaveland, *Congress and Urban Problems*, pp. 20–71.

Landrum-Griffin Act of 1959
McAdams, Alan. *Power and Politics in Labor Legislation*. New York: Columbia
University Press, 1964.
Patterson, Samuel C. *Labor Lobbying and Labor Reform*. Inter-University Case
Program No. 99. Indianapolis: Bobbs-Merrill, 1966.

Civil Rights Act of 1960
Berman, Daniel M. *A Bill Becomes a Law*. 2d ed. New York: Macmillan, 1966.

San Luis Reclamation Bill of 1960
McDonald, Angus. *The San Luis Reclamation Bill*. Eagleton Cases in Practical
Politics No. 28. New York: McGraw-Hill, 1962.

A Bill Disposing of the DesPlaines Public Hunting and Wildlife
Carper, Edith T. *Illinois Goes to Congress for Army Land*. Inter-University Case
Program No. 71. University, Alabama: University of Alabama Press, 1962.

Area Redevelopment Act of 1961
Davidson, Roger H. *Coalition Building for Depressed Area Bills, 1955–1965*. Inter-
University Case Program No. 103. Indianapolis: Bobbs-Merrill, 1966.

Public School Assistance Act of 1961
Price, H. Douglas. "Race, Religion, and the Rules Committee: The Kennedy
Aid-to-Education Bills." In *The Uses of Power*, edited by Alan F. Westin, pp. 2–
71. New York: Harcourt, 1962.

Juvenile Delinquency and Youth Offenses Control Act of 1961 and 1964 Extension
Moore, John E. "Controlling Delinquency: Executive, Congressional and Juvenile, 1961–64." In Cleaveland, *Congress and Urban Problems*, pp. 110–172.

Mass Transit Assistance: Housing Act of 1961 and Urban Mass Transportation Act of 1964
Hanson, Royce. "Congress Copes with Mass Transit, 1960–64." In Cleaveland,
Congress and Urban Problems, pp. 311–49.

Department of Housing and Urban Development (Rejected in 1961–62, passed in 1965)
Parris, Judith Heimlich. "Congress Rejects the President's Urban Department,
1961–62." In Cleaveland, *Congress and Urban Problems*, pp. 173–223.

Clean Air Act of 1963
Ripley, Randall B. "Congress and Clean Air." In Cleaveland, *Congress and Urban Problems,* pp. 224–78.

Food Stamp Act of 1964
Ripley, Randall B. "Legislative Bargaining and the Food Stamp Act, 1964." In Cleaveland, *Congress and Urban Problems,* pp. 279–310.

Economic Opportunity Act of 1964
Bibby, John, and Roger Davidson. "The Executive as Legislator." In *On Capitol Hill,* pp. 219–51. New York: Holt, Rinehart and Winston, 1967.

Elementary and Secondary Education Act of 1965
Eidenberg, Eugene, and Roy D. Morrey. *An Act of Congress.* New York: W. W. Norton, 1969.

Medicare Act of 1965
Marmor, Theodore. *The Politics of Medicare.* Chicago: Aldine, 1970.

Family Assistance Plan, 1969–70 (Rejected)
Moynihan, Daniel P. *The Politics of a Guaranteed Income.* New York: Vintage Books, 1973.

Employment and Manpower Act of 1970 (Vetoed) and Emergency Employment Act of 1971
Davidson, Roger H. *The Politics of Comprehensive Manpower Legislation.* Baltimore: Johns Hopkins, 1972.

Political Broadcast Act of 1970 (Vetoed)
Peabody, Robert L., Jeffrey M. Berry, William G. Frasure, and Jerry Goldman. *To Enact a Law: Congress and Campaign Financing.* New York: Praeger, 1972.

NOTES

Preface

1. Joseph M. Bessette, "Deliberation in Congress: A Preliminary Investigation," Ph.D. dissertation, University of Chicago, June 1978, p. 5.

2. Michael Malbin, *Unelected Representatives: Congressional Staff and the Future of Representative Government* (New York: Basic Books, 1980), esp. pp. 239–51; Arthur Maass, *Congress and the Common Good* (New York: Basic Books, 1983), esp. pp. 3–31; Randall Strahan, *New Ways and Means: Reform and Change in a Congressional Committee* (Chapel Hill: University of North Carolina Press, 1990), esp. pp. 5–10, 83–90, and 171–75; Steven S. Smith, *Call to Order: Floor Politics in the House and Senate* (Washington, D.C.: Brookings Institution, 1989), esp. pp. 233–52; James L. Payne, *The Culture of Spending: Why Congress Lives beyond Our Means* (San Francisco: ICS Press, 1991), esp. pp. 1–4, 7–11, 87–92, 123, 132–33, 141–47, 163–74, and 181; and David J. Vogler and Sidney R. Waldman, *Congress and Democracy* (Washington, D.C.: Congressional Quarterly Press, 1985), esp. pp. 1–19, 49–50, 88–91, 115–18, and 159–66.

3. William K. Muir, Jr., *Legislature: California's School for Politics* (Chicago: University of Chicago Press, 1982), esp. pp. 1–8, 179–86, and 189–202.

4. Steven Kelman, *Making Public Policy: A Hopeful View of American Government* (New York: Basic Books, 1987), esp. pp. 13–66 and 207–70; and Giandomenico Majone, *Evidence, Arguments, and Persuasion in the Policy Process* (New Haven: Yale University Press, 1989), esp. pp. 1–20 and 37–41.

5. Martha Derthick and Paul J. Quirk, *The Politics of Deregulation* (Washington, D.C.: Brookings Institution, 1985), esp. pp. 96–146 and 237–58.

6. Robert B. Reich, ed., *The Power of Public Ideas* (Cambridge, Mass.: Ballinger, 1988), esp. pp. 1–53, 157–78, and 205–27.

7. James S. Fishkin, *Democracy and Deliberation: New Directions for Democratic Reform* (New Haven: Yale University Press, 1991); Benjamin I. Page and Robert Y. Shapiro, *The Rational Public: Fifty Years of Trends in Americans' Policy Preferences* (Chicago: University of Chicago Press, 1992), esp. pp. 1–17, 31–34, 37–42, 362–66, and 381–98.

8. Jeffrey K. Tulis, *The Rhetorical Presidency* (Princeton: Princeton University Press, 1987).

9. Steven E. Rhoads, *The Economist's View of the World: Government, Markets, and Public Policy* (Cambridge: Cambridge University Press, 1985), esp. pp. 199–212.

10. Jane J. Mansbridge, *Beyond Adversary Democracy* (Chicago: University of Chicago Press, 1983), esp. pp. 3–35, 275–302; *Why We Lost the ERA* (Chicago: University of Chicago Press, 1986), esp. pp. 1–7, 118–64, and 187–99; and Jane J. Mansbridge, ed., *Beyond Self-Interest* (Chicago: University of Chicago Press, 1990), esp. pp. 3–22, 183–206, and 209–23.

Article-length treatments of deliberation include Mansbridge, "Motivating Deliberation in Congress," in *E Pluribus Unum: Constitutional Principles and the Institutions of Government*, ed. Sarah Baumgartner Thurow (Lanham, Md.: University Press of America, 1988), pp. 59–86; Mansbridge, "A Deliberative Theory of Interest Representation," in *The Politics of Interests,* ed. Mark P. Petracca (Boulder, Colo.: Westview Press, 1992), pp. 32–57; Joshua Cohen, "The Economic Basis of Deliberative Democracy," *Social Philosophy and Policy* 6 (1989): 25–50; Joshua Cohen, "Deliberation and Democratic Legitimacy," in *The Good Polity,* ed. Alan Hamlin and Philip Petit (New York: Blackwell, 1989), pp. 17–34; Bernard Manin, "On Legitimacy and Political Deliberation," *Political Theory* 15, no. 3 (August 1987): 338–68; Michael J. Malbin, "Delegation, Deliberation, and the New Role of Congressional Staff," in *The New Congress,* ed. Thomas E. Mann and Norman J. Ornstein (Washington, D.C.: American Enterprise Institute for Public Policy Research, 1981), pp. 134–77; and George E. Connor and Bruce I. Oppenheimer, "Deliberation: An Untimed Value in a Timed Game," in *Congress Reconsidered,* 5th ed., ed. Lawrence C. Dodd and Bruce I. Oppenheimer (Washington, D.C.: Congressional Quarterly Press, 1993), pp. 315–30.

11. James Q. Wilson, "Interests and Deliberation in the American Republic, or, Why James Madison Would Never Have Received the James Madison Award," in *PS: Political Science and Politics* 23, no. 4 (December 1990): 561. For an analysis of the contrast between the political science that informed the fashioning of the American Constitution and the modern emphasis on public choice, or rational actor, theories, see both the Wilson essay and Harvey C. Mansfield, Jr., "Social Science and the Constitution," in *Confronting the Constitution,* ed. Allan Bloom (Washington, D.C.: AEI Press, 1990), pp. 411–36. For a discussion of the relative importance of "self-interest" and "public spirit" in theories of government and politics, see Steven Kelman, *Making Public Policy,* pp. 231–47 and 250–70, and "'Public Choice' and Public Spirit," *The Public Interest,* no. 87 (Spring 1987): 80–94. See also Reich, ed., *The Power of Public Ideas,* pp. 1–53, and Mansbridge, ed., *Beyond Self-Interest,* pp. 3–22.

12. Woodrow Wilson, *Constitutional Government in the United States* (New York: Columbia University Press, 1961, originally published in 1908), pp. 104–5.

13. See, for example, Joseph M. Bessette, "Is Congress a Deliberative Body?" in Dennis Hale, ed., *The United States Congress: Proceedings of the Thomas P. O'Neill, Jr., Symposium on the U.S. Congress* (Chestnut Hill, Ma.: Boston College, 1982), pp. 3–11. For a discussion of "the play of power" see Charles Lindblom, *The Policy-Making Process* (Englewood Cliffs, N.J.: Prentice-Hall, 1968), p. 29.

14. Consider, for example, the contrast between David Mayhew's "vision of United States congressmen as single-minded seekers of reelection" in *Congress: The Electoral Connection* (New Haven: Yale University Press, 1974), p. 5, and his description of the two congressmen in whose offices he served as a Congressional Fellow as "two members who truly serve in the public interest," p. vii. Mayhew is discussed at some length in chapter 3.

Chapter One

1. Alexis de Tocqueville, *Democracy in America,* ed. J. P. Mayer (Garden City, N.Y.: Anchor Books, Doubleday and Company, 1969), p. 395.

2. The term "deliberative democracy" has gained some currency in the literature on American government and politics during the past decade or so. See, for example, my essay, "Deliberative Democracy: The Majority Principle in Repub-

lican Government," in *How Democratic Is the Constitution?* ed. Robert A. Goldwin and William A. Schambra (Washington: American Enterprise Institute, 1980), pp. 102–16; Michael J. Malbin, "Congress during the Convention and Ratification," in *The Framing and Ratification of the Constitution*, ed. Leonard W. Levy and Dennis J. Mahoney (New York: Macmillan Company, 1987), pp. 189–96; Joshua Cohen, "The Economic Basis of Deliberative Democracy," *Social Philosophy and Policy* 6 (1989): 25–50; Cass R. Sunstein, *After the Rights Revolution: Reconceiving the Regulatory State* (Cambridge: Harvard University Press, 1990), pp. 12, 15, 57, and 164; Bruce Ackerman, *We the People* (Cambridge, Mass.: Belknap Press of Harvard University Press, 1991), pp. 197–99; Terry Eastland, *Energy in the Executive: The Case for the Strong Presidency* (New York: Free Press, 1992), pp. 20, 27, 30, 35, and passim; and George Will, "Most of Our Presidents Have Been Mediocre," May 28, 1992, Washington Post Writers Group, and *Restoration: Congress, Term Limits and the Recovery of Deliberative Democracy* (New York: Free Press, 1992). I am not aware of the use of the term "deliberative democracy" prior to 1980.

3. Alexander Hamilton, James Madison, and John Jay, *The Federalist Papers*, ed. Clinton Rossiter (New York: New American Library, 1961), no. 63, p. 384. Unless otherwise noted, all references to *The Federalist Papers* are to the Rossiter edition.

4. *Federalist* no. 71, p. 432, and no. 63, p. 384.

5. *Federalist* no. 39, p. 240, and no. 22, p. 146.

6. *Federalist* no. 10, p. 82.

7. *Federalist* no. 42, p. 268.

8. For example, on the Constitutional Convention's next to last meeting day, with the Constitution in nearly final form, George Mason of Virginia rose to oppose the plan as one that "would end either in monarchy, or a tyrannical aristocracy." Mason was one of three delegates present at the end who refused to sign the Constitution. Max Farrand, ed., *The Records of the Federal Convention of 1787*, rev. ed., 4 vols. (New Haven: Yale University Press, 1966), vol. 2, p. 632 (September 15).

9. See, for example, Aristotle's *Politics*, 1281b30–1282b13, 1286a25–31, 1291a23–33, 1297b35–1301a15, 1329a1–16, and *Nicomachean Ethics*, 1112a17–1113a14. Deliberative rhetoric, as employed by speakers in democratic assemblies, is a principal topic of Aristotle's *Rhetoric*. For an Aristotelian analysis of the rhetoric of the *Federalist Papers*, see Larry Arnhart, "The Deliberative Rhetoric of *The Federalist*," *Political Science Reviewer* 19 (Spring 1990): 49–86.

Chapter Two

1. John Marshall, *The Life of George Washington*, 5 vols. (Philadelphia: C. P. Wayne, 1807), vol. 5, p. 87.

2. Alexander Hamilton, James Madison, and John Jay, *The Federalist Papers*, ed. Clinton Rossiter (New York: New American Library, 1961), no. 1, p. 33.

3. Quoted in Gordon S. Wood, *The Creation of the American Republic, 1776–1787* (New York: W. W. Norton and Company, 1969), p. 393. Historians emphasizing the critical nature of the 1780s include John Fiske in *The Critical Period of American History, 1783–1789* (Boston: Houghton Mifflin, 1888) and Andrew Cunningham McLaughlin in *The Confederation and the Constitution, 1783–1789*

(New York: Harper and Brothers, 1905). Among the more sanguine interpretations of the events of the 1780s, the leading example is Merrill Jensen in *The New Nation: A History of the United States during the Confederation, 1781–1789* (New York: Alfred A. Knopf, 1950).

4. Wood, *Creation of the American Republic*, p. 394.

5. Herbert J. Storing, *What the Anti-Federalists Were For: The Political Thought of the Opponents of the Constitution* (Chicago: University of Chicago Press, 1981), p. 26.

6. James Madison, *The Mind of the Founder: Sources of the Political Thought of James Madison,* ed. Marvin Meyers (Indianapolis: Bobbs-Merrill Company, 1973), pp. 83–92.

7. Ibid., p. 88.   8. Ibid.

9. Letter to Thomas Jefferson, October 24, 1787, in *Letters and Other Writings of James Madison,* 4 vols. (New York: R. Worthington, 1884), vol. 1, p. 350.

10. Allan Nevins, *The American States during and after the Revolution, 1775–1789* (New York: Macmillan, 1924), pp. 189–90.

11. Ibid., p. 380.

12. "Notes on the State of Virginia," in Thomas Jefferson, *The Portable Thomas Jefferson,* ed. Merrill D. Peterson (New York: Viking Press, 1975), pp. 164–65.

13. Nevins, *The American States,* pp. 263–66, 179–81.

14. Ibid., p. 365.

15. McLaughlin, *The Confederation and the Constitution,* p. 140.

16. Fiske, *The Critical Period,* p. 181.

17. Nevins, *The American States,* p. 524.

18. Fiske, *The Critical Period,* p. 178.

19. Letter to Thomas Jefferson, December 4, 1786, in *Letters,* vol. 1, p. 261.

20. Letter to George Washington, December 7, 1786, in *Letters,* vol. 1, p. 264.

21. Nevins, *The American States,* p. 317.

22. This episode is recounted in Nevins, *The American States,* pp. 228–33 and 539–41; Fiske, *The Critical Period,* pp. 185–90; Jensen, *The New Nation,* pp. 323–25; Frank Greene Bates, *Rhode Island and the Formation of the Union* (New York: AMS Press, 1967), pp. 107–48; and John P. Kaminski, "Rhode Island: Protecting State Interests" in *Ratifying the Constitution,* ed. Michael Allen Gillespie and Michael Lienesch (Lawrence, Kansas: University Press of Kansas, 1989), pp. 370–75.

23. Bates, *Rhode Island,* pp. 127, 130.

24. Nevins, *The American States,* p. 230.

25. For more detail on the case *Trevett v. Weeden,* see especially James Bradley Thayer, *Cases on Constitutional Law,* 2 vols. (Cambridge: Charles W. Sever, 1895), vol. 1, pp. 73–78, and Brinton Coxe, *An Essay on Judicial Power and Unconstitutional Legislation* (Philadelphia: Kay and Brother, 1893), pp. 234–48.

26. Jensen, *The New Nation,* p. 325, footnote 30.

27. *Federalist* no. 10, p. 80.

28. Ibid., p. 78.

29. This episode is recounted in Nevins, *The American States,* pp. 535–37; Fiske, *The Critical Period,* pp. 177–85; McLaughlin, *Confederation and the Constitution,* pp. 154–67; and Forrest McDonald, *E Pluribus Unum: The Formation of*

the American Republic, 1776–1790, 2d ed. (Indianapolis: Liberty Press, 1979), pp. 249–56.

30. Letter to Thomas Jefferson, April 23, 1787, in *Letters,* vol. 1, p. 319.

31. *Federalist* no. 10, p. 80.

32. Ibid.

33. *Federalist* no. 63, p. 387. This is one of the Federalist essays for which authorship is disputed between Madison and Hamilton. In such cases I have followed Jacob E. Cooke's scholarship in determining likely attribution. See his edition of *The Federalist* (Cleveland: World Publishing Company, 1961), pp. xx–xxx and 644.

34. *Federalist* no. 71, p. 433.

35. Letter to Edward Carrington, August 4, 1787, in *The Life and Selected Writings of Thomas Jefferson,* ed. Adrienne Koch and William Peden (New York: Modern Library, Random House, 1944), pp. 427–28.

36. Quoted in Louis Fisher, *President and Congress: Power and Policy* (New York: Free Press, 1972), p. 257.

37. *Federalist* no. 71, p. 433.

38. Nevins, *The American States,* p. 229.

39. Ibid., p. 363.   40. Ibid., p. 386.

41. *Federalist* no. 68, p. 414.

42. *Federalist* no. 11, p. 87.

43. *Federalist* no. 10, p. 82.

44. Max Farrand, ed., *The Records of the Federal Convention of 1787,* 4 vols. (New Haven: Yale University Press, 1966), vol. 1, p. 56. Quotations from the Convention debates have been modernized for spelling, capitalization, and abbreviations.

45. Ibid., p. 133. Emphasis in the original.

46. *Federalist* no. 10, pp. 82–83.

47. *The Mind of the Founder,* p. 508.

48. James Madison in Farrand, *Records,* vol. 1, p. 50.

49. *Federalist* no. 64, p. 391.

50. Ibid.

51. *Federalist* no. 35, p. 217.

52. *Federalist* no. 10, p. 80.

53. *Federalist* no. 68, p. 414.

54. *Federalist* no. 51, p. 322.

55. *Federalist* no. 57, p. 350. Authorship of no. 57 is disputed between Madison and Hamilton. See Cooke, *Federalist,* pp. 641–42.

56. *Federalist* no. 55, p. 342. Authorship of no. 55 is disputed between Madison and Hamilton. See Cooke, *Federalist,* pp. 636–37.

57. *Federalist* no. 58, p. 360. Authorship of no. 58 is disputed between Madison and Hamilton. See Cooke, *Federalist,* pp. 642–43.

58. "Letters from The Federal Farmer" in *The Complete Anti-Federalist,* ed. Herbert J. Storing, 7 vols. (Chicago: The University of Chicago Press, 1981), vol. 2, p. 230.

59. Ibid., pp. 268–69.

60. *Federalist* no. 55, p. 341.

61. Article I, section 2.
62. *Federalist* no. 55, p. 343.
63. Farrand, *Records*, vol. 2, p. 644.
64. Interestingly, both Madison and Hamilton argued in favor of beginning with a larger House of Representatives. Madison's concern was not so much that sixty-five was too few but that decisions might be made by a *"majority* of a *Quorum* of 65 members"* (perhaps as few as seventeen representatives?). This would be "too small a number to represent the whole inhabitants of the U. States." His motion to double the initial number of representatives was defeated on July 10, nine states to two. See Farrand, *Records*, vol. 1, pp. 568–70 (July 10) and vol. 2, pp. 553–54 (September 8).
65. Ibid., vol. 1, p. 51.   66. Ibid., 151.
67. In his personal notes taken during the Convention, Alexander Hamilton indicated substantial reservations with the views of other leading framers that elections in large districts would solve the problem of the election of demagogues and the dominance of popular passions in the legislature. See Farrand, *Records*, vol. 1, pp. 146–47.
68. *Federalist* no. 53, pp. 332 and 334.
69. Ibid., p. 333.   70. Ibid., p. 334.
71. *Federalist* no. 62, p. 379.
72. *Federalist* no. 64, pp. 391–92.
73. *Federalist* no. 53, p. 331.
74. Article V.
75. Whether abrupt shifts in public opinion remain a problem for American democracy is addressed in chapter 8.
76. *Federalist* no. 15, p. 111.
77. *Federalist* no. 37, p. 231.
78. *Federalist* no. 46, p. 296.
79. Ibid., pp. 296–97.
80. *Federalist* no. 10, p. 79.
81. Ibid., p. 80.
82. *Federalist* no. 51, p. 325.
83. *Federalist* no. 10, p. 78.
84. Ibid., p. 77.   87. Ibid., p. 83.
85. Ibid., p. 80.   88. Ibid.
86. Ibid., p. 82.
89. *Federalist* no. 46, p. 296.
90. Ibid., p. 297.   91. Ibid.
92. *Federalist* no. 57, p. 350.
93. *Federalist* no. 62, p. 379.
94. *Federalist* no. 64, p. 395.
95. "Address of the Senate to George Washington, President of the United States" in James D. Richardson, *A Compilation of the Messages and Papers of the Presidents, 1789–1897,* 10 vols. (Washington: U.S. Government Printing Office, 1896–1899), vol. 1, p. 55.
96. Ibid.
97. The framers' belief in a genuine "common good" or "public interest" not

merely reducible to the preferences of the states or of the individual citizens obviously distinguishes them from the modern pluralist, who denies that "there is an interest of the nation as a whole," and from the modern social choice theorist, who views collective decisions as the aggregation of individual tastes or preferences. See, for example, David Truman, *The Governmental Process: Political Interests and Public Opinion,* 2d ed. (New York: Alfred A. Knopf, 1971), p. 50, and Kenneth J. Arrow, *Social Choice and Individual Values,* 2d ed. (New Haven: Yale University Press, 1963), p. 2 and passim.

98. Article II, section 3.
99. *Federalist* no. 73, pp. 445–46.
100. *Federalist* no. 70, p. 423.
101. Ibid.
102. Ibid., p. 424.   103. Ibid., pp. 426–27.
104. *Federalist* no. 74, p. 449.
105. Ibid.
106. *Federalist* no. 63, p. 384.
107. *Federalist* no. 71, p. 432.
108. *Federalist* no. 78, p. 469.
109. *Federalist* no. 71, p. 432.
110. *Federalist* no. 49, p. 317.
111. *Federalist* no. 71, p. 432.
112. Ibid.
113. *Federalist* no. 10, p. 82.
114. Ibid.
115. *Federalist* no. 57, pp. 351–53.
116. *Federalist* no. 68, p. 412. Hamilton seems to have assumed that the state legislature would vest the selection of electors in the people directly, as six states did in whole or in part in the first presidential election.
117. Ibid.
118. See, for example, Wood, *Creation of the American Republic,* pp. 403–13, and Jackson Turner Main, *The Sovereign States, 1775–1783* (New York: Franklin Watts, 1973), pp. 200–206.
119. Patrick T. Conley and John P. Kaminski, eds., *The Constitution and the States: The Role of the Original Thirteen in the Framing and Adoption of the Federal Constitution* (Madison, Wis.: Madison House, 1988), pp. 241–46.

Chapter Three

1. Carl Friedrich, *Constitutional Government and Democracy,* 4th ed. (Waltham, Mass.: Blaisdell, 1968), p. 327.
2. *Burke's Politics: Selected Writings and Speeches of Edmund Burke on Reform, Revolution, and War,* ed Ross J. S. Hoffman and Paul Levack (New York: Alfred A. Knopf, 1949) pp. 115–16.
3. John Adams, *The Works of John Adams,* ed Charles Francis Adams (Boston: Charles C. Little and James Brown, 1851), vol. 5, p. 495. I am grateful to Thomas West for this reference.
4. *The Portable Thomas Jefferson,* ed. Merrill D. Peterson (New York: Viking Press, 1975), p. 328.

5. Ibid., pp. 559, 579, and 561.

6. Alexis de Tocqueville, *Democracy in America*, ed. J. P. Mayer (Garden City, N.Y.: Anchor Books, Doubleday and Company, 1969), p. 395.

7. John Stuart Mill, *Considerations on Representative Government* (New York: Henry Holt and Company, 1882), p. 102.

8. Ibid., p. 109.   9. Ibid., p. 116.

10. Woodrow Wilson, *Congressional Government* (Cleveland: World Publishing Co., Meridian Books, 1956, originally published in 1885), p. 62.

11. Ibid., p. 71.   12. Ibid., pp. 128–29.

13. Woodrow Wilson, *Constitutional Government in the United States* (New York: Columbia University Press, 1961, originally published in 1908), p. 109.

14. Ibid., p. 105.   15. Ibid., p. 134.

16. Ibid., p. 135. For another brief account of the origins of "deliberative government" see *The Power of Public Ideas*, ed. Robert B. Reich (Cambridge, Mass.: Ballinger Publishing Company, 1988), pp. 8–9.

17. Jane J. Mansbridge, *Beyond Adversary Democracy* (Chicago: University of Chicago Press, 1983), p. 3.

18. See, for example, Benjamin Barber, *Strong Democracy: Participatory Politics for a New Age* (Berkeley: University of California Press, 1984), esp. pp. 261–311. In a book that focuses on improving citizen deliberation in presidential elections, James S. Fishkin proposes the innovation of a "deliberative opinion poll," whereby a representative sample of citizens would be brought together for some days early in the presidential primary campaign to meet, listen to, and interrogate the candidates and then reason together about who would make the best president. The results of these citizen deliberations would be publicized and potentially influence the results in upcoming primaries and caucuses. See his *Democracy and Deliberation: New Directions for Democratic Reform* (New Haven: Yale University Press, 1991), esp. pp. 1–13 and 81–104. Other recent books that have focused attention on the prospects for citizen deliberation in the United States include Jane Mansbridge's *Beyond Adversary Democracy* and *Why We Lost the ERA* (Chicago, University of Chicago Press, 1986) and Benjamin I. Page and Robert Y. Shapiro's *The Rational Public: Fifty Years of Trends in Americans' Policy Preferences* (Chicago: University of Chicago Press, 1992).

19. Baron de Montesquieu, *The Spirit of the Laws* (New York: Hafner Publishing Company, 1949), p. 154.

20. Willmoore Kendall, "The Two Majorities" in *Congress and the President: Allies and Adversaries*, ed. Ronald C. Moe (Pacific Palisades, Cal.: Goodyear Publishing Company, 1971), p. 284. Originally published in *Midwest Journal of Political Science* (November 1960):317–45.

21. Ibid., p. 285.

22. Jane Mansbridge has argued that when interests are shared in a democracy—what she calls "unitary democracy"—then "goodwill, mutual understanding, and rational discussion can lead to the emergence of a common enlightened preference that is good for everyone." In an "adversary democracy," on the other hand, where interests conflict, bargaining is the natural means for reaching collective decisions. *Beyond Adversary Democracy*, pp. 6–7 and 25–28. See also Steven Kelman, *Making Public Policy: A Hopeful View of American Governmnet* (New York:

Basic Books, 1987), on the way institutions promote "public spirit" by requiring political arguments to be made "in terms broader than the self-interest of the individual or the group making the claim, because there is no reason for anyone to support a claim based simply on another's self-interest" (p. 22).

23. For a useful discussion of the difference between deliberation and the kinds of calculation presupposed in economic, or rational actor, theories of politics, see Bernard Manin, "On Legitimacy and Political Deliberation," *Political Theory* 15, no. 3 (August 1987): 348–51.

24. Bernard Asbell, *The Senate Nobody Knows* (Garden City, N.Y.: Doubleday and Company, 1978), p. 74.

25. David J. Vogler and Sidney R. Waldman, *Congress and Democracy* (Washington, D.C.: Congressional Quarterly Press, 1985), p. 101. See generally their chapter on "Informational Needs and Sources," pp. 101–21.

26. William K. Muir, Jr., *Legislature: California's School for Politics* (Chicago: University of Chicago Press, 1982), p. 19.

27. Asbell, *The Senate Nobody Knows*, pp. 370–71. See also Kelman, *Making Public Policy*, p. 35. For a broader discussion of the contribution of interest groups to deliberation in Congress, a topic beyond the scope of this book, see Jane J. Mansbridge, "Motivating Deliberation in Congress," in *E Pluribus Unum: Constitutional Principles and the Institutions of Government*, ed. Sarah Baumgartner Thurow (Lanham, Md.: University Press of America, 1988), pp. 59–86, and "A Deliberative Theory of Interest Representation," in *The Politics of Interests*, ed. Mark P. Petracca (Boulder, Colo.: Westview Press, 1992), pp. 32–57. See also James L. Payne, *The Culture of Spending: Why Congress Lives beyond Our Means* (San Francisco: ICS Press, 1991), pp. 132–33.

28. John Stuart Mill, *On Liberty* (London: Penguin Books, 1974), p. 80.

29. Angus McDonald, *The San Luis Reclamation Bill*, Eagleton Cases in Practical Politics No. 28 (New York: McGraw-Hill, 1962), p. 11.

30. Kelman, *Making Public Policy*, p. 34.

31. J. W. Anderson, *Eisenhower, Brownell, and the Congress*, Inter-University Case Program No. 80 (University, Ala.: University of Alabama Press, 1964), p. 76.

32. Randall B. Ripley, "Congress and Clean Air" in *Congress and Urban Problems*, ed. Frederic N. Cleaveland (Washington, D.C.: Brookings Institution, 1969), p. 251.

33. Ibid., p. 255. The actual quotation from Ralph Waldo Emerson is "A foolish consistency is the hobgoblin of little minds . . . ," *Familiar Quotations by John Bartlett*, 13th ed. (Boston: Little, Brown, 1955), p. 501.

34. Daniel P. Moynihan, *The Politics of a Guaranteed Income: The Nixon Administration and the Family Assistance Plan* (New York: Vintage Books, Random House, 1973), p. 428.

35. U.S. Congress, House, 91st Cong., 2d sess., 15 April 1970, *Congressional Record* 116:11879.

36. Richard F. Fenno, Jr., *The Making of a Senator: Dan Quayle* (Washington, D.C.: Congressional Quarterly Press, 1989), p. 37.

37. Asbell, *The Senate Nobody Knows*, p. 262.

38. The most extensive discussion of persuasion in Congress of which I am aware is James L. Payne's recent *The Culture of Spending*, esp. pp. 1–4, 7–11,

87–92, 132–33, 144–47, 163–74, and 181. In explaining the dramatic growth in domestic spending by Congress in recent decades, Payne argues that the members of Congress have been overwhelmed by arguments in favor of spending by administrators, lobbyists, and others—both in committee hearings and in informal contacts—and in the absence of substantial countervailing views have been persuaded by the merits of the pro-spending arguments: "The congressman, after all, is more than a simple vote-maximizing entrepreneur. He is a human being who meets people, and talks with them, *and is persuaded by them.* To a considerable extent, his views on spending issues are shaped by this persuasion" (p. 2, emphasis in the original).

39. Arthur Bentley, *The Process of Government* (Bloomington, Ind.: Principia Press, 1935, originally published in 1908), pp. 370–71.

40. Ibid., p. 372.

41. David Truman, *The Governmental Process*, 2d ed. (New York: Alfred A. Knopf, 1971, first edition published in 1951), p. 363.

42. Ibid., p. 368.

43. Theodore J. Lowi, *The End of Liberalism*, 2d ed. (New York: W. W. Norton and Company, 1979), p. 55, emphasis in the original.

44. John Manley, *The Politics of Finance* (Boston: Little, Brown, 1970), p. 131.

45. Leroy Rieselbach, *Congressional Reform in the Seventies* (Morristown, N.J.: General Learning Press, 1977), pp. 14–15.

46. Lewis Froman, *The Congressional Process* (Boston: Little, Brown, 1967), pp. 16–33; Walter Oleszek, *Congressional Procedures and the Policy Process* (Washington, D.C.: Congressional Quarterly Press, 1978), pp. 16–17, 216–17.

47. Roger Davidson, *The Role of the Congressman* (New York: Pegasus, 1969), p. 26.

48. Charles Jones, "Joseph G. Cannon and Howard W. Smith," *Journal of Politics* 30 (August 1968): 617.

49. Aaron Wildavsky, *The Politics of the Budgetary Process* (Boston: Little, Brown, 1964), p. 131.

50. Samuel Huntington, *The Common Defense* (New York: Columbia University Press, 1961), pp. 146–47.

51. Glenn R. Parker, *Characteristics of Congress: Patterns in Congressional Behavior* (Englewood Cliffs, N.J.: Prentice Hall, 1989), p. 117.

52. Davidson, *The Role of the Congressman*, p. 26.

53. See, for example, Froman, *The Congressional Process*, pp. 16–33 and Oleszek, *Congressional Procedures*, pp. 16–17.

54. Randall Ripley, "Legislative Bargaining and the Food Stamp Act, 1964," in Cleaveland, *Congress and Urban Problems*, p. 300.

55. Leon Billings, Chief of Staff of the Environmental Pollution Subcommittee, quoted in Asbell, *The Senate Nobody Knows*, pp. 432–33.

56. This distinction between bargaining and deliberation has occasionally been made in works outside of the congressional literature. For example, in *Organizations* (New York: John Wiley and Sons, 1958), James March and Herbert Simon delineate four major processes by which an organization reacts to conflict: (1) problem-solving, (2) persuasion, (3) bargaining, and (4) "politics" (pp. 129–31). The first two they term "analytic" (which may be taken as synonymous with

"deliberative") and the last two simply "bargaining." Analytical processes include efforts to identify or formulate ways of achieving shared objectives and the use of persuasion to settle disputes over subgoals by reference to common goals. The result is "private as well as public agreement to the decisions" (p. 130). Hence, the parties sincerely believe that the resolution is a proper or sound one. This is not the case in decisions arrived at through bargaining. Here the actors disagree over goals from the beginning and seek "agreement without persuasion" (p. 130). The struggle of conflicting views results in public agreements with which the individual participants are not wholly satisfied.

In *Political Argument* (Berkeley: University of California Press, 1990, originally published in 1965), Brian Barry similarly distinguishes bargaining from deliberation, which he calls "discussion on merits" (pp. 86–88). These are two of seven possible ways to resolve social conflict. The others are combat, voting, chance, contest, and authoritative determination. (Of the seven only bargaining, discussion on merits, and voting seem generally applicable to decisionmaking in a legislative assembly.) By bargaining Barry means "any discussion into which the merits of the question are not introduced" (p. 86). Discussion on merits, on the other hand, as "an 'ideal type' . . . involves the complete absence of threats and inducements; the parties to the dispute set out . . . to reach an agreement on what is the morally right division, what policy is in the interest of all of them or will promote the most want-satisfaction, and so on" (p. 87). Barry also argues that the difficulty of distinguishing bargaining from discussion on merits in practice does not undermine the principled difference: "Of course, many (perhaps nearly all) negotiations involve both bargaining *and* discussion on merits, but this does not dissolve the difference because (a) there are still clear-cut cases and (b) even in the combined cases one can often distinguish the respective contributions to the agreement of bargaining and discussion on merits" (p. 87). See also Mansbridge, *Beyond Adversary Democracy*, pp. 32–33, 260–61, and 264–69.

57. See also Barry's discussion, *Political Argument*, pp. 302–3, on how a compromise can involve both bargaining and "discussion on merits."

58. David Mayhew, *Congress: The Electoral Connection* (New Haven: Yale University Press, 1974), and Morris P. Fiorina, *Congress: Keystone of the Washington Establishment*, 2d ed. (New Haven: Yale University Press, 1989, first edition published in 1977).

59. Mayhew, *Congress: The Electoral Connection*, p. 122.

60. Ibid., p. 132.

61. Ibid.

62. Fiorina, *Congress: Keystone of the Washington Establishment*, 2d ed., p. 68.

63. Ibid., p. 47.

64. Mayhew, *Congress: The Electoral Connection*, p. 61.

65. Ibid., p. 62.

66. Fiorina, *Congress: Keystone of the Washington Establishment*, 2d ed., pp. 68–69.

Chapter Four

1. Morris P. Fiorina, *Congress: Keystone of the Washington Establishment*, 2d ed. (New Haven: Yale University Press, 1989, first edition published in 1977), p. 69.

2. This last criterion is the reason why, for example, a book like James L. Sundquist's very informative *Politics and Policy: The Eisenhower, Kennedy, and Johnson Years* (Washington, D.C.: Brookings Institution, 1968) is not included in the selection of case studies. It does not for the most part track the detailed legislative history of specific bills.

3. Although the Reciprocal Trade Act of 1955, the subject of *American Business and Public Policy,* is not technically an example of domestic policy, it is included here because domestic policy considerations—especially the impact of tariffs on domestic manufacturers—played a large role in its passage.

4. Although the law passed by Congress in the second of the Davidson studies falls just outside the arbitrary 1970 cutoff, the case study is included here because it tracks also the legislative history of the Employment and Manpower Act of 1970, which was the vetoed precursor of the 1971 Emergency Employment Act.

5. Roger H. Davidson, *Coalition Building for Depressed Area Bills, 1955–65,* Inter-University Case Program No. 103 (Indianapolis: Bobbs-Merrill, 1966), p. 6.

6. Roger H. Davidson, *The Politics of Comprehensive Manpower Legislation* (Baltimore: Johns Hopkins, 1972), p. 33.

7. Graham T. Allison, *Essence of Decision: Explaining the Cuban Missile Crisis* (Boston: Little, Brown and Company, 1971).

8. Theodore Marmor, *The Politics of Medicare* (Chicago: Aldine, 1970), p. 96.

9. Ibid., pp. 100–103.   11. Ibid., p. 72.

10. Ibid., p. 103.

12. For the sake of simplicity, this hypothetical example assumes that all votes but one were the result of judgments on the merits. In actuality, vote trading and deliberation are not the only possible explanations for the content of floor votes. Some legislators, for example, interested foremost in reelection may simply vote in accordance with dictates from powerful interest groups.

13. Marmor, *The Politics of Medicare,* p. 72.

14. Ibid., p. 64.   16. Ibid., pp. 68–69.

15. Ibid., p. 68.   17. Ibid., p. 105.

18. Randall B. Ripley, "Legislative Bargaining and the Food Stamp Act, 1964," in *Congress and Urban Problems,* ed. Frederic N. Cleaveland (Washington, D.C.: Brookings Institution, 1969), p. 299.

19. See, for example, U.S. Congress, House, 88th Cong., 2d sess., 7 April 1964, *Congressional Record* 110:7125.

20. Ibid., pp. 7140–41.

21. *Congressional Quarterly Almanac 1964,* vol. 20 (Washington, D.C.: Congressional Quarterly, 1965), p. 113.

22. Ripley, "Food Stamp Act," p. 292.

23. Ibid., p. 310.   26. Ibid.

24. Ibid., p. 302.   27. Ibid.

25. Ibid., p. 301.

28. U.S. Congress, House, Committee on Agriculture, *Food Stamp Plan, Hearings before the Committee on Agriculture on H.R. 5733,* 88th Cong., 1st sess., 1963, pp. 12–15. Hereafter cited as *House Hearings, Food Stamp Plan.*

29. Ibid., p. 12.   31. Ibid., pp. 46–47.

30. Ibid., p. 46.   32. Ibid., p. 48.

33. Ibid., p. 44.

34. Ibid., p. 67.

35. Ibid., p. 70.

36. U.S. Congress, House, 88th Cong., 2d sess., 7 April 1964, *Congressional Record* 110:7129.

37. *House Hearings, Food Stamp Plan*, p. 37.

38. U.S. Congress, House, Committee on Agriculture, *Food Stamp Act of 1964*, H. Rept. 1226 to Accompany H.R. 10222, 88th Cong., 2d sess., March 9, 1964, p. 2. Hereafter referred to as *House Report, Food Stamp Act*.

39. Ibid., p. 5.

40. Ibid., p. 8.

41. Ibid., p. 17.

42. Ibid., p. 18.

43. U.S. Congress, House, 88th Cong., 2d sess., 7 April 1964, *Congressional Record* 110:7129.

44. Ibid., 8 April 1964, p. 7289.

45. *House Hearings, Food Stamp Plan*, p. 17.

46. Ibid.

47. Ibid., p. 18.

48. Ibid., p. 21.

49. Ibid., p. 28.

50. Ibid., p. 20.

51. U.S. Congress, House, 88th Cong., 2d sess., 7 April 1964, *Congressional Record* 110:7154.

52. *House Report, Food Stamp Act*, p. 21.

53. Ibid., pp. 36–37.

54. U.S. Congress, House, 88th Cong., 2d sess., 7 April 1964, *Congressional Record* 110:7135–36.

55. Ibid., p. 7145.

56. *House Report, Food Stamp Act*, p. 19.

57. Ibid., p. 20.

58. Ibid., p. 51.

59. Ibid., p. 19.

60. *House Hearings, Food Stamp Plan*, p. 42.

61. Ibid.

62. Ibid., p. 98.

63. *House Report, Food Stamp Act*, p. 22.

64. Note that this interpretation is broadly consistent with the findings of Jon R. Bond and Richard Fleisher of the central importance of party and ideology (and thus policy preferences) in their study of presidential success in Congress from Eisenhower through Reagan: *The President in the Legislative Arena* (Chicago: University of Chicago Press, 1990).

65. Emmette Redford, *Congress Passes the Federal Aviation Act of 1958,* Inter-University Case Program No. 62 (University, Ala.: University of Alabama Press, 1961), p. 1.

66. Ibid., p. 34.

67. Alison Griffith, *The National Aeronautics and Space Act* (Washington, D.C.: Public Affairs Press, 1962) p. 4.

68. Ibid., p. 22.

69. Ibid., p. 100.

70. Ibid., p. 99.

71. Ibid.

72. Ibid., p. 102.

73. Ibid., p. 6.

74. Daniel P. Moynihan, *The Politics of a Guaranteed Income: The Nixon Administration and the Family Assistance Plan* (New York: Random House, Vintage Books, 1973), p. 400.

75. Ibid., p. 415.   76. Ibid., p. 427.

77. Ibid., pp. 429–30, emphasis in the original.

78. T. R. Reid, *Congressional Odyssey: The Saga of a Senate Bill* (San Francisco: W. H. Freeman and Company, 1980), p. 129.

79. Martha Derthick and Paul J. Quirk, *The Politics of Deregulation* (Washington, D.C.: Brookings Institution, 1985), p. 238.

80. Ibid., p. 244.   82. Ibid., p. 255.

81. Ibid., p. 246.

83. Jeffrey H. Birnbaum and Alan S. Murray, *Showdown at Gucci Gulch: Lawmakers, Lobbyists, and the Unlikely Triumph of Tax Reform* (New York: Vintage Books, Random House, 1987), p. 286.

84. Ibid., p. 289.   85. Ibid., p. xv.

86. Arthur Bentley, *The Process of Government* (Bloomington, Ind.: Principia Press, 1935, originally published in 1908), pp. 370–71.

87. David Truman, *The Governmental Process*, 2d ed. (New York: Alfred A. Knopf, 1971, first edition published in 1951), p. 368.

88. Glenn R. Parker, *Characteristics of Congress: Patterns in Congressional Behavior* (Englewood Cliffs, N.J.: Prentice Hall, 1989), p. 117.

89. Morris P. Fiorina, *Congress: Keystone of the Washington Establishment*, 2d ed. (New Haven: Yale University Press, 1989, first edition published in 1977), p. 69.

Chapter Five

1. Harry McPherson, *A Political Education: A Washington Memoir* (Boston: Houghton Mifflin Company, 1988), p. 128.

2. Elizabeth Drew, *Senator* (New York: Simon and Schuster, 1978), pp. 116–17.

3. Richard F. Fenno, Jr., *Congressmen in Committees* (Boston: Little, Brown and Company, 1973), p. 1, emphasis in the original.

4. Ibid., p. 9, emphasis in the original.

5. Ibid., p. 10.   7. Ibid., pp. 141, 142.

6. Ibid., p. 13.   8. Ibid., p. xvii.

9. See, for example, Charles S. Bullock III, "Motivations for U.S. Congressional Committee Preferences: Freshmen of the 92nd Congress" in *Legislative Studies Quarterly* 1 (May 1976): 201–212, and Steven S. Smith and Christopher J. Deering, *Committees in Congress*, 2d ed. (Washington, D.C.: Congressional Quarterly Press, 1990), pp. 85–110.

10. John F. Manley, *The Politics of Finance* (Boston: Little, Brown and Company, 1970), p. 111.

11. Ibid., pp. 122–24.   12. Ibid., pp. 124–25.

13. Daniel P. Moynihan, *The Politics of a Guaranteed Income: The Nixon Administration and the Family Assistance Plan* (New York: Vintage Books, Random House, 1973), p. 404.

14. Ibid., p. 415.   17. Ibid., p. 429.

15. Ibid., pp. 399, 401.   18. Ibid., p. 431.

16. Ibid., p. 427.   19. Ibid., p. 399.

20. Fenno, *Congressmen in Committees*, p. 239.

21. Ibid., pp. 260–61.   23. Ibid., p. 274.

22. Ibid., see especially p. 198.

24. Bernard Asbell, *The Senate Nobody Knows* (Garden City, N.Y.: Doubleday and Company, 1978), p. 50.

25. Ibid., pp. 76–77.
26. Ibid., pp. 29–30.
27. Ibid., p. 52.
28. Ibid., p. 203.
29. Ibid., p. 266.
30. Ibid., p. 30.

31. Ibid., p. 42.
32. Ibid., p. 376.
33. Ibid., p. 43.
34. Ibid., p. 267.
35. Ibid., pp. 113, 120.

36. Ibid., p. 210, emphasis in the original.
37. Ibid., pp. 192–93.
38. Ibid., p. 143.
39. Ibid., p. 152, emphasis in the original.
40. Ibid., p. 158, emphasis in the original.

41. Ibid., p. 277.
42. Ibid., p. 265.
43. Ibid., pp. 299–300.
44. Ibid., p. 300.

45. Ibid.
46. Ibid., p. 414.
47. Ibid., p. 452.
48. Ibid.

49. Richard F. Fenno, Jr., *The Emergence of a Senate Leader: Pete Domenici and the Reagan Budget* (Washington, D.C.: Congressional Quarterly Press, 1991).

50. Ibid., p. 3.
51. Ibid., p. 108.
52. Ibid., p. 172.
53. Ibid., p. 46.
54. Ibid., p. 47.
55. Ibid., p. 7.
56. Ibid., p. 93.
57. Ibid., p. 96.
58. Ibid., p. 16.
59. Ibid., p. 96.
60. Ibid., p. 72.
61. Ibid., p. 110.
62. Ibid., p. 15.
63. Ibid., p. 33.
64. Ibid., p. 10.
65. Ibid.
66. Ibid., p. 30.
67. Ibid., p. 8.
68. Ibid., p. 63.
69. Ibid., p. 106.

70. Ibid., p. 217.
71. Ibid., p. 27.
72. Ibid., p. 183.
73. Ibid., p. 180.
74. Ibid., p. 28.
75. Ibid., pp. 28, 30.
76. Ibid., p. 178.
77. Ibid., p. 189.
78. Ibid., p. 196.
79. Ibid., p. 119.
80. Ibid., pp. 210–11.
81. Ibid., p. 73.
82. Ibid., p. 74.
83. Ibid., p. 226.
84. Ibid., p. 228.
85. Ibid., p. 226.
86. Ibid., p. 227.
87. Ibid., p. 12.
88. Ibid., p. 228.

89. Jeffrey H. Birnbaum and Alan S. Murray, *Showdown at Gucci Gulch: Lawmakers, Lobbyists, and the Unlikely Triumph of Tax Reform* (New York: Vintage Books, Random House, 1987).

90. Ibid., p. 26.
91. Ibid., p. 27.
92. Ibid.

93. Ibid.
94. Ibid., p. 120.

95. Drew, *Senator,* p. 12.
96. Ibid., p. 13.
97. Ibid., p. 79.

98. Ibid., pp. 60–61.
99. Ibid., pp. 66–67.

100. Ibid., p. 49.
101. Ibid., p. 137.
102. Ibid., p. 145.
103. Ibid., p. 153.
104. Ibid., p. 56.

105. Ibid., p. 57.
106. Ibid., p. 88.
107. Ibid., p. 90.
108. Ibid., p. 98.
109. Ibid., p. 114.

110. Richard F. Fenno, Jr., *The Making of a Senator: Dan Quayle* (Washington, D.C.: Congressional Quarterly Press, 1989).

111. Ibid., p. 15.
112. Ibid., pp. 9–10.
113. Ibid., p. 17.
114. Ibid., p. 12.
115. Ibid., p. 23.
116. Ibid., p. 2.
117. Ibid., p. 18.
118. Ibid., p. 169.
119. Ibid., p. 30.

120. Ibid.
121. Ibid., p. 49.
122. Ibid., p. 120.
123. Ibid., pp. 37, 41–42.
124. Ibid., pp. 148, 149.
125. Ibid., p. 122.
126. Ibid., p. 151.
127. Ibid., p. 166.
128. Ibid., p. 165.

129. Leo Strauss, *Liberalism Ancient and Modern* (New York: Basic Books, 1968), p. 225.

130. Note that some of those who argue the dominance of the reelection incentive in Congress recognize that if all members of the institution were mere self-seekers, the institution would collapse. As David Mayhew puts it, "if all members did nothing but pursue their electoral goals, Congress would decay or collapse" (*Congress: The Electoral Connection* [New Haven: Yale University Press, 1974], p. 141).

131. McPherson, *A Political Education*, p. 29.

132. Ibid., p. 30.
133. Ibid., p. 34.
134. Ibid., pp. 38–39.
135. Ibid., pp. 39–40.
136. Ibid., p. 43.
137. Ibid., pp. 44–45.
138. Ibid., p. 46.
139. Ibid., pp. 46–47.

140. Ibid., p. 48.
141. Ibid., pp. 55–56.
142. Ibid., p. 57.
143. Ibid., p. 58.
144. Ibid., p. 79.
145. Ibid., p. 63.
146. Ibid., p. 64.
147. Ibid., p. 67.

148. Mayhew, *Congress: The Electoral Connection*, pp. 122, 132.

149. Martha Derthick and Paul J. Quirk, *The Politics of Deregulation* (Washington, D.C.: Brookings Institution, 1985), p. 239.

150. Ibid., p. 103.

151. It is interesting to ask whether the rapid rise of Democratic Congressman Tony Coelho from first-termer in 1979 to Majority Whip in 1987 indicates a movement in the conferring of power and prestige within the House of Representatives, away from serious legislators and toward those skilled in the money politics that so directly serves the electoral interests of the members. Upon first entering the House, Coelho had apparently decided that the surest route to power within the institution was not through "legislative expertise or command of facts and issues" but rather "from friendships built on small favors and courtesies" (Brooks Jackson, *Honest Graft: Big Money and the American Political Process*

[New York: Alfred A. Knopf, 19{], p. 46). Coelho's phenomenally successful chairmanship of the Democratic Congressional Campaign Committee, where he raised unprecedented sums for the reelection campaigns of his Democratic colleagues, gave him the opportunity to build many such friendships. He was rewarded with the third highest party position in the House, well situated to rise yet higher as vacancies occurred in the office of Speaker or Majority Leader. See also Burdett Loomis, *The New American Politician: Ambition, Entrepreneurship, and the Changing Face of Political Life* (New York: Basic Books, 1988), pp. 219–20.

152. Fenno, *The Making of a Senator*, p. 165.

153. Derthick and Quirk, *Politics of Deregulation*, p. 110.

154. Birnbaum and Murray, *Showdown at Gucci Gulch*, esp. pp. 189–91 and 234–35.

155. Richard F. Fenno, Jr., *Homestyle: House Members in Their Districts* (Boston: Little, Brown and Company, 1978), p. 215.

156. Ibid., p. 216.

157. Ibid., p. 221.

158. On the demise of the norm of committee deference see, for example, Steven S. Smith, *Call to Order: Floor Politics in the House and Senate* (Washington, D.C.: Brookings Institution, 1989), pp. 130–31 and 139–51.

159. Manley, *The Politics of Finance*, p. 51.

160. Mayhew, *Congress: The Electoral Connection*, p. 152. According to David J. Vogler and Sidney R. Waldman, *Congress and Democracy* (Washington, D.C.: Congressional Quarterly Press, 1985), the behavior of the House Appropriations Committee during the past decade or so has shifted under the influence of two rules changes: opening up markup sessions to the public, thereby decreasing the willingness of committee members to oppose spending requests, and ending the power of the full committee chairman to appoint subcommittee members. "Consequently, the previous practice of placing members on subcommittees in such a way as to minimize constituency pressures and free them to cut spending came to an end. Members now choose their subcommittee in order to be able to support the interests they favor, and the full committee, operating on the basis of reciprocity, tends to support the recommendations of its subcommittees" (p. 69).

161. On innovations in special rules in the House of Representatives in recent years, see Smith, *Call to Order*, pp. 69–83.

162. See, for example, ibid., pp. 25–28 and 36.

163. Manley, *The Politics of Finance*, p. 251.

164. Moynihan, *The Politics of a Guaranteed Income*, p. 440.

165. Ibid., p. 455.

166. Ibid., p. 482.

167. "House Leader Stalls Plan to Cap Credit-Card Rates," *Wall Street Journal*, November 19, 1991, p. A3.

168. For an insightful discussion of the relationship of private interest to deliberation, see Jane J. Mansbridge on the U.S. Congress in "Motivating Deliberation in Congress," in *E Pluribus Unum: Constitutional Principles and the Institutions of Government*, ed. Sarah Baumgartner Thurow (Lanham, Md.: University Press

of America, 1988), pp. 78–86, and William K. Muir, Jr., on the California state legislature in *Legislature: California's School for Politics* (Chicago: University of Chicago Press, 1982), esp. pp. 105–57 and 179–86. On the ways that the private ambition of legislators can undermine substantive policy accomplishment, see Loomis, *The New American Politician*, esp. pp. 209–232, 238–39, and 243–46.

Chapter Six

1. Debate in the House of Representatives, March 10, 1796, in *Annals of the Congress of the United States, Fourth Congress, First Session* (Washington, D.C.: Gales and Seaton, 1849), p. 493.

2. Representative Gary Franks (R., Connecticut), quoted in the *Washington Post,* July 31, 1991, p. B2.

3. James March and Herbert Simon, *Organizations* (New York: John Wiley and Sons, 1958), pp. 129ff.

4. Charles E. Lindblom, *The Policy-Making Process* (Englewood Cliffs, N.J.: Prentice-Hall, 1968), pp. 5, 28.

5. Edward C. Banfield, *Here the People Rule: Selected Essays*, 2d ed. (Washington, D.C.: AEI Press, 1991), pp. 374–76.

6. For example, when the House Republican Policy Committee refused in July of 1979 to endorse a proposed constitutional amendment to ban school busing, a reporter for the *Washington Post* concluded that "two factors are responsible for the Republican backoff, one of them political" (July 24, 1979). The "political" factor was the concern by Republican party leaders in the House that a formal endorsement of the amendment would hinder efforts to attract blacks to the party. The other factor dealt with the actual wording of the amendment: that it appeared to ban busing for nonracial reasons like overcrowding and to give Congress new authority over local schools. Presumably, this second factor was not "political" because it addressed the merits of the proposed amendment.

7. Hanna Pitkin, *The Concept of Representation* (Berkeley: University of California Press, 1972), p. 212.

8. Walter J. Oleszek, *Congressional Procedures and the Policy Process* (Washington, D.C.: Congressional Quarterly Press, 1978), p. 156.

9. Steven S. Smith, *Call to Order: Floor Politics in the House and Senate* (Washington, D.C.: Brookings Institution, 1989), pp. 239–40.

10. James L. Sundquist, *The Decline and Resurgence of Congress* (Washington, D.C.: Brookings Institution, 1981), pp. 135–36.

11. John Bibby and Roger Davidson, "The Executive as Legislator" in *On Capitol Hill* (New York: Holt, Rinehart and Winston, 1967), p. 220.

12. Emmette Redford, *Congress Passes the Federal Aviation Act of 1958*, Inter-University Case Program No. 62 (University, Alabama: University of Alabama Press, 1961), especially pp. 10–13.

13. Randall B. Ripley, "Congress and Clean Air," in *Congress and Urban Problems*, ed. Frederic N. Cleaveland (Washington, D.C.: Brookings Institution, 1969), p. 276.

14. Paul Dommel, *The Politics of Revenue Sharing* (Bloomington: Indiana University Press, 1974), p. 113.

15. Quoted in Bernard Asbell, *The Senate Nobody Knows* (Garden City, New York: Doubleday and Company, 1978), p. 267.

16. James A. Payne, *The Culture of Spending: Why Congress Lives beyond Our Means* (San Francisco: ICS Press, 1991), pp. 11–12.

17. Asbell, *The Senate Nobody Knows*, p. 42.

18. T. R. Reid, *Congressional Odyssey: The Saga of a Senate Bill* (San Francisco: W. H. Freeman and Company, 1980), p. 23.

19. Ibid., p. 26.

20. Asbell, *The Senate Nobody Knows*, p. 43.

21. Ibid., p. 16.

22. George Goodwin, Jr., *The Little Legislatures* (Amherst, Mass.: University of Massachusetts Press, 1970), p. 168.

23. See Randall Strahan, *New Ways and Means: Reform and Change in a Congressional Committee* (Chapel Hill: University of North Carolina Press, 1990), pp. 83–86, for a useful discussion of the relationship of the representativeness of the Ways and Means Committee in the House of Representatives to its deliberative responsibilities.

24. John W. Kingdon, *Congressmen's Voting Decisions*, 3d ed. (Ann Arbor: University of Michigan Press, 1989), p. 102.

25. Ibid., p. 212.

26. Oleszek, *Congressional Procedures*, p. 74.

27. U.S. Congress, House, 91st Cong., 2d sess., 16 April 1970, *Congressional Record* 116 : 12060.

28. Ibid., 15 April 1970, p. 11897. 29. Ibid., 16 April 1970, p. 12064.

30. Daniel Moynihan, *The Politics of a Guaranteed Income* (New York: Vintage Books, Random House, 1973), pp. 427, 429–30. Emphasis in the original.

31. Randall B. Ripley, *Congress: Process and Policy*, 2d ed. (New York: W. W. Norton and Company, 1978), pp. 190–91.

32. Donald R. Matthews and James A. Stimson, *Yeas and Nays: Normal Decision-Making in the U.S. House of Representatives* (New York: John Wiley and Sons, 1975), p. 45.

33. For a discussion of a kind of deliberative cue-taking in the California state legislature, see William K. Muir, Jr., *Legislature: California's School for Politics* (Chicago: University of Chicago Press, 1982), p. 95.

34. U.S. Congress, Senate, 86th Cong., 1st sess., 11 August 1959, *Congressional Record* 116 : 15488.

35. Ibid., p. 15489. 37. Ibid., 12 August 1959, p. 15649.

36. Ibid., p. 15491. 38. Ibid., 11 August 1959, p. 15488.

39. Ibid., pp. 15497, 15498, and 12 August 1959, p. 15649.

40. Stephen K. Bailey, *Congress Makes a Law* (New York: Columbia University Press, 1950), p. 56.

41. Ibid., p. 119.

42. Samuel Patterson, *Labor Lobbying and Labor Reform*, Inter-University Case Program No. 99 (Indianapolis: Bobbs-Merrill, 1966), p. 13.

43. Alan McAdams, *Power and Politics in Labor Legislation* (New York: Columbia University Press, 1964), p. 95.

44. Quoted in Oleszek, *Congressional Procedures*, p. 111.

45. Eugene Eidenberg and Roy Morey, *An Act of Congress* (New York: W. W. Norton, 1969), pp. 127–29.

46. Asbell, *The Senate Nobody Knows*, p. 262.

47. Kingdon, *Congressmen's Voting Decisions*, p. 99.

48. Reid, *Congressional Odyssey*, p. 65.

49. Kingdon, *Congressmen's Voting Decisions*, pp. 212.

50. U.S. Congress, Senate, 86th Cong., 1st sess., 12 May 1959, *Congressional Record* 105:8000. The legislative history of this bill is described in the account by the lobbyist for the National Farmers Union: Angus McDonald, *The San Luis Reclamation Bill*, Eagleton Cases in Practical Politics No. 28 (New York: McGraw-Hill, 1962).

51. U.S. Congress, Senate, 86th Cong., 1st sess., 7 May 1959, *Congressional Record* 105:7679.

52. Ibid., p. 7678.   56. Ibid., p. 7859.

53. Ibid., 11 May 1959, p. 7869.   57. Ibid., 7 May 1959, p. 7672.

54. Ibid., p. 7849.   58. Ibid., p. 7678.

55. Ibid.

59. Quoted in Reid, *Congressional Odyssey*, p. 56.

60. Ibid.

61. House Committee on Ways and Means, *Social Security and Welfare Proposals, Hearings*, 91st Cong., 1st sess. (1970), p. 2365.

62. See Burdett Loomis, *The New American Politician: Ambition, Entrepreneurship, and the Changing Face of Political Life* (New York: Basic Books, 1988), pp. 149–57, on the growing use of caucuses to serve the issue interests of legislators.

63. Asbell, *The Senate Nobody Knows*, pp. 94, 92, 96.

64. McDonald, "The San Luis Reclamation Bill," p. 8.

65. Ibid., pp. 13–14.

66. Senate Committee on Foreign Relations, *War Powers*, S. Rept. 250 to Accompany S. 440, 93rd Cong., 1st sess., 14 June 1973, p. 4.

67. James L. Sundquist, *Politics and Policy: The Eisenhower, Kennedy, and Johnson Years* (Washington, D.C., Brookings Institution, 1968).

68. Nelson W. Polsby, *Congress and the Presidency*, 3d ed. (Englewood Cliffs, N.J.: Prentice-Hall, 1976), pp. 99–100.

69. Paul J. Quirk, "In Defense of the Politics of Ideas," in *Journal of Politics* 50, no. 1 (February 1988): 40.

Chapter Seven

1. Woodrow Wilson, *Constitutional Government in the United States* (New York: Columbia University Press, paperback edition, 1961, originally published in 1908), p. 72.

2. Article II, section 3.

3. Leonard D. White, *The Federalists: A Study in Administrative History* (New York: Macmillan Company, 1956), pp. 54–55.

4. Quoted in ibid., p. 55.

5. The exceptions are recounted in ibid., p. 57.

6. Ibid., p. 56.

7. *The Life and Selected Writings of Thomas Jefferson,* ed. Adrienne Koch and William Peden (New York: Modern Library, Random House, 1944), "The Anas," p. 125.

8. Ibid., p. 123.   10. Ibid.

9. Ibid., p. 124.

11. Wilfred E. Binkley, *President and Congress,* 3d rev. ed. (New York: Vintage Books, Random House, 1962), p. 84.

12. E. James Ferguson, ed., *Selected Writings of Albert Gallatin* (Indianapolis: Bobbs-Merrill Company, 1967), "Introduction," p. xxii.

13. Leonard D. White, *The Jeffersonians: A Study in Administrative History* (New York: Macmillan Company, 1956), p. 50.

14. James D. Richardson, ed., *A Compilation of the Messages and Papers of the Presidents, 1789–1897,* 10 vols. (Washington: U.S. Government Printing Office, 1896–1899), "Protest," April 15, 1834, vol. 3, p. 90.

15. Ibid., "Veto Message," July 10, 1832, vol. 2, pp. 581, 590, 591.

16. Ibid., "Removal of the Public Deposits," Sept. 18, 1833, vol. 3, pp. 6–7.

17. "Veto Message," p. 589.

18. *Federalist* no. 63, p. 389.

19. David Donald, *Lincoln Reconsidered: Essays on the Civil War Era* (New York: Random House, 1956), pp. 191–93.

20. This account is from Jeffrey K. Tulis, *The Rhetorical Presidency* (Princeton, N.J.: Princeton University Press, 1987), pp. 97–116.

21. Ibid., p. 98.   24. Ibid.

22. Ibid., p. 107.   25. Ibid.

23. Ibid., p. 106.

26. Woodrow Wilson, *Congressional Government: A Study in American Politics* (Cleveland: The World Publishing Company, Meridian Books, 1956, first published in 1885), p. 144.

27. Woodrow Wilson, *Constitutional Government in the United States* (New York: Columbia University Press, 1961, originally published in 1908), p. 73.

28. Ibid., p. 68.   30. Ibid., p. 73.

29. Ibid., pp. 70–71.   31. Ibid.

32. Samuel Eliot Morison and Henry Steele Commager, *The Growth of the American Republic,* 2 vols. (New York: Oxford University Press, 1962), vol. 2, p. 596.

33. David Stockman, *The Triumph of Politics: Why the Reagan Revolution Failed* (New York: Harper and Row, 1986), p. 264.

34. Ibid., pp. 264–65.

35. The latter point derives from Richard Neustadt's well-known formulation: "The power to persuade is the power to bargain . . . . [P]ersuasion becomes give-and-take. . . . Power is persuasion, and persuasion becomes bargaining" (*Presidential Power and the Modern Presidents: The Politics of Leadership from Roosevelt to Reagan* [New York: Free Press, 1990], pp. 32–33). For a similar conjunction of persuasion with bargaining see Matthew Robert Kerbel, *Beyond Persuasion: Organizational Efficiency and Presidential Power* (Albany: State University of New York Press, 1991), esp. pp. 11–17, 35–41, and 43–75. The problem with using the word "persuasion" to denote bargaining is that it either obscures the fundamen-

tal difference between bargaining and deliberation or implies that no real persuasion through reasoning on the merits occurs within the executive branch or in relations between the executive and Congress.

36. Randall B. Ripley, "Congress Champions Aid to Airports, 1958–59," in *Congress and Urban Problems*, ed. Frederic N. Cleaveland (Washington, D.C.: Brookings Institution, 1969), p. 53.

37. John E. Moore, "Controlling Delinquency: Executive, Congressional and Juvenile, 1961–64," in Cleaveland, *Congress and Urban Problems*, p. 146.

38. Woodrow Wilson, *Constitutional Government*, p. 71.

39. Stockman, *The Triumph of Politics*, p. 170.

40. Ibid., p. 208.   45. Ibid., p. 268.

41. Ibid., p. 209.   46. Ibid., p. 251.

42. Ibid., p. 220.   47. Ibid., pp. 249–50.

43. Ibid., pp. 221–22.   48. Ibid., p. 222.

44. Ibid., p. 267.

49. See also the very useful discussions, "The Limits of Bargaining" and "Arm-Twisting," in George C. Edwards III, *Presidential Influence in Congress* (San Francisco: W. H. Freeman, 1980), pp. 131–34 and 139–44.

50. Stockman, *The Triumph of Politics*, p. 264.

51. Ibid., p. 263.

52. For a thoughtful discussion of the way the "rhetorical presidency" jeopardizes deliberation between the branches, see Tulis, *The Rhetorical Presidency*, esp. pp. 161–72.

53. See, for example, the critique of the White House decision process that resulted in the "Iran/contra" episode by the commission appointed by President Reagan (John Tower, Edmund Muskie, and Brent Scowcroft): *Report of the President's Special Review Board*, February 16, 1987 (Washington, D.C.: U.S. Government Printing Office, 1987).

54. Jeffrey H. Birnbaum and Alan S. Murray, *Showdown at Gucci Gulch: Lawmakers, Lobbyists, and the Unlikely Triumph of Tax Reform* (New York: Vintage Books, Random House, 1987), p. 43.

55. Ibid., p. 47.   59. Ibid., p. 80.

56. Ibid.   60. Ibid., p. 78.

57. Ibid.   61. Ibid., p. 89.

58. Ibid., p. 74.

62. The emphasis here on the deliberative, or analytical, nature of the Regan phase in the drafting of the tax reform proposal in no way denies that the members of the Regan group brought with them to the drafting process a host of ideas, preferences, or dispositions that may have been formed through experiences or mechanisms other than dispassionate analysis of the public good: for example, experiences in the corporate world, professional education, or the inculcation of values from partisan service. See the definition of deliberation in chapter 3.

63. Birnbaum and Murray, *Showdown at Gucci Gulch*, pp. 190, 192.

64. The principal exception to this generalization was James Baker's commitment to preserving tax breaks for the oil and gas industry.

65. Birnbaum and Murray, *Showdown at Gucci Gulch*, p. 286.

Chapter Eight

1. *Federalist* no. 49, in Alexander Hamilton, James Madison, and John Jay, *The Federalist Papers*, ed. Clinton Rossiter (New York: New American Library, 1961), p. 317.

2. *Federalist* no. 63, p. 384.

3. *Federalist* no. 10, p. 82.

4. See, for example, James S. Fishkin, *Democracy and Deliberation: New Directions for Democratic Reform* (New Haven: Yale University Press, 1991), pp. 82–83. Page and Shapiro note, however, that "by the time national polls are taken, public opinion has often been 'refined and enlarged' through public debate." See Benjamin I. Page and Robert Y. Shapiro, *The Rational Public: Fifty Years of Trends in Americans' Policy Preferences* (Chicago: University of Chicago Press, 1992), p. 391. Yet, as discussed below, there remain serious impediments to direct public deliberation about the details of public policies.

5. James Bryce, *The American Commonwealth*, 3d edition, 2 vols. (New York: Macmillan Company, 1909), vol. 2, p. 247.

6. Ibid., p. 248.	11. Ibid., p. 356.
7. Ibid., p. 249.	12. Ibid.
8. Ibid., p. 287.	13. Ibid., p. 250.
9. Ibid., p. 250.	14. Ibid., pp. 250–51.
10. Ibid., p. 331.	

15. Elihu Root, *Addresses on Government and Citizenship*, ed. Robert Bacon and James Brown Scott (Freeport, N.Y.: Books for Libraries Series, 1969, first published in 1916), pp. 94–95.

16. In the summer of 1992, when the first draft of this book was being completed, I was called for the first time to serve as a juror on both a criminal and a civil case in the Los Angeles County courts. These were fairly typical cases: a residential burglary and a personal injury claim from a traffic accident. Although there was little difference of opinion among the jurors about the guilt of the criminal defendant, opinion was sharply split in the civil case as to the appropriate amount of the monetary award (liability for the accident had previously been admitted). As a result, deliberations in the criminal case lasted only about an hour, while deliberations in the civil case stretched to seven hours. In both cases (no overlap of jury members but for me) I was struck by the seriousness and care with which the jurors approached their task. These were deliberative bodies doing their best to perform their civic duties in a responsible way.

17. For recent additions to the case for greater citizen deliberation, see especially the citations in note 18 of chapter 3. In *The Rational Public*, Page and Shapiro specifically contest the notion that public opinion is too tumultuous or capricious to serve as a reliable guide for policymaking. They argue that a wealth of public opinion data for the past fifty years refutes the framers' characterization of public opinion as subject to "popular fluctuations," "temporary errors and delusions," or "tumult and disorder." Although the framers may have been right about their own time, this problem, Page and Shapiro argue, seems not to afflict us now. Without entering into general discussion of Page and Shapiro's argument, I only note that my case here for a large institutional role in fashioning

the "cool and deliberate sense of the community" rests not on the problem of fluctuations of public opinion but, as noted above, on time constraints, competition for leisure time, and the number and complexity of public policy issues.

18. Michael J. Malbin, *Unelected Representatives: Congressional Staff and the Future of Representative Government* (New York: Basic Books, 1980), p. 246.

19. Ibid., pp. 247–48.

20. Ibid., p. 251. For Malbin's argument about staff and deliberation, see particularly *Unelected Representatives,* pp. 239–51, and "Delegation, Deliberation, and the New Role of Congressional Staff," in Thomas E. Mann and Norman J. Ornstein, eds., *The New Congress* (Washington, D.C.: American Enterprise Institute, 1981), pp. 134–77. See also Steven Kelman, *Making Public Policy: A Hopeful View of American Government* (New York: Basic Books, 1987), pp. 54–58 and 62.

21. David R. Mayhew, *Congress: The Electoral Connection* (New Haven: Yale University Press, 1974), pp. 61–62.

22. Bryce, *American Commonwealth,* vol. 2, p. 146.

23. Ibid.   25. Ibid., p. 119.

24. Ibid., p. 145.

26. David J. Vogler and Sidney R. Waldman, *Congress and Democracy* (Washington, D.C.: Congressional Quarterly Press, 1985), pp. 69 and 84. On the relationship between the budget deficit and open committee markups, see also James L. Payne, *The Culture of Spending: Why Congress Lives beyond Our Means* (San Francisco: ICS Press, 1991), p. 15.

27. Payne, *The Culture of Spending,* pp. 15 and 22.

28. R. Douglas Arnold, *The Logic of Congressional Action* (New Haven: Yale University Press, 1990), pp. 275 and 274.

29. Catherine E. Rudder, "Fiscal Responsibility, Fairness, and the Revenue Committees," in *Congress Reconsidered,* 4th ed. (Washington, D.C.: Congressional Quarterly Press, 1989), p. 229.

30. Randall Strahan, *New Ways and Means: Reform and Change in a Congressional Committee* (Chapel Hill: University of North Carolina Press, 1990), p. 144.

31. Ibid., pp. 143–45 and 173. See also p. 157. See also David R. Beam, Timothy J. Conlan, and Margaret T. Wrightson, "Solving the Riddle of Tax Reform: Party Competition and the Politics of Ideas," *Political Science Quarterly* 105, no. 2 (1990): 198, on the advantages of secrecy in the development of the Tax Reform Act of 1986 in both the executive branch and Congress.

32. Woodrow Wilson, *Congressional Government* (Cleveland: World Publishing Company, Meridian Books, 1956, originally published in 1885), p. 72.

33. Max Farrand, ed., *The Records of the Federal Convention of 1787,* 4 vols. (New Haven: Yale University Press, 1966), vol. 1, p. 10 (May 28).

34. Norman J. Ornstein, Thomas E. Mann, and Michael J. Malbin, *Vital Statistics on Congress, 1991–1992* (Washington, D.C.: Congressional Quarterly, 1992), p. 113.

35. Even the vice president, who is formally elected to office on the ballot with the president, achieves his position through a *de facto* appointment by the president.

36. Herbert J. Storing, "Political Parties and the Bureaucracy," in *Political Par-*

ties, U.S.A., ed. Robert A. Goldwin (Chicago: Rand McNally and Company, 1961, 1964), p. 155.

37. Ibid., p. 154.

38. Ibid., p. 146.

39. *Federalist* no. 71, p. 433.

40. Ibid., p. 433.

41. Ibid., p. 432.

42. "First Inaugural," in *A Compilation of the Messages and Papers of the Presidents, 1789–1897,* ed. James D. Richardson, 10 vols. (Washington, D.C.: U.S. Government Printing Office, 1896–1899), vol. 1, p. 324.

43. Lord Charnwood, *Abraham Lincoln,* 3d ed. (New York: Henry Holt and Company, 1917), esp. pp. 387–427.

44. Ibid., p. 426.

45. Ibid., p. 233.

46. Ibid., p. 424.

47. Elihu Root, *Addresses on Government and Citizenship*, ed. Robert Bacon and James Brown Scott (Freeport, N.Y.: Books for Libraries Series, 1969, first published in 1916), p. 17.

48. *Federalist* no. 63, p. 384.

49. *Federalist* no. 71, p. 434.

50. *Federalist* no. 49, p. 317, emphasis in the original.

51. *Federalist* no. 58, p. 360.

52. See James Ceaser's very useful discussion of the basic types of demagoguery, including the distinction between "hard" and "soft" demagoguery, in *Presidential Selection: Theory and Development* (Princeton, N.J.: Princeton University Press, 1979), pp. 317–27.

53. Of all the founders, few, if any, thought more deeply about the connection between politics and economics, between material interests and political views and behavior, than James Madison. It is interesting to note that as late as 1821 Madison believed that future population growth in the United States would eventually result in a propertyless majority, which would seriously threaten the security of property rights in the nation. See *The Mind of the Founder: Sources of the Political Thought of James Madison,* ed. Marvin Meyers (Indianapolis: Bobbs-Merrill Company, 1973), pp. 501–9.

54. Richard F. Fenno, Jr., *Home Style: House Members in Their Districts* (Boston: Little, Brown and Company, 1978), pp. 162–63.

55. Benjamin I. Page, *Choices and Echoes in Presidential Elections: Rational Man and Electoral Democracy* (Chicago: University of Chicago Press, 1978), pp. 152–53.

56. Jeffrey K. Tulis, *The Rhetorical Presidency* (Princeton, N.J.: Princeton University Press, 1987), p. 141.

57. Ibid., pp. 142–43.

58. "Farewell Address," in *Messages and Papers of the Presidents,* vol. 1, pp. 215–23.

59. Ibid., p. 223.

60. Jefferson, "First Inaugural Address," in ibid., pp. 323–24.

61. Lincoln, "First Inaugural Address," in ibid., vol. 6, p. 9.

62. For an account of the early history of the use of popular rhetoric by presidents see Tulis, *The Rhetorical Presidency,* pp. 67–93.

63. This account draws from Harry V. Jaffa's *Crisis of the House Divided: An*

Interpretation of the Lincoln-Douglas Debates (Seattle, Wash.: University of Washington Press, 1973, originally published in 1959).

64. The fifth Lincoln-Douglas debate, Galesburg, Illinois, October 7, 1858, in *The Collected Works of Abraham Lincoln,* ed. Roy P. Basler, 9 vols. (New Brunswick, N.J.: Rutgers University Press, 1953), vol. 3, p. 207.

65. The first Lincoln-Douglas debate, Ottawa, Illinois, August 21, 1858, in ibid., p. 16.

66. Ibid., p. 18.   67. Ibid., p. 27.

68. "Speech at a Republican Banquet, Chicago, Illinois," in ibid., vol. 2, p. 385.

INDEX